CATHOLICS
USA

BOOKS BY LINDA BRANDI CATEURA

Growing Up Italian
Oil Painting Secrets from a Master

CATHOLICS USA

Makers of a Modern Church

LINDA BRANDI CATEURA

WILLIAM MORROW AND COMPANY, INC.   NEW YORK

Library of Congress Cataloging-in-Publication Data

Cateura, Linda.
    Catholics USA : makers of a modern Church / Linda Brandi Cateura.
        p.   cm.
    Includes index.
    ISBN 0-688-07911-3
    1. Catholics—United States—Interviews. 2. Catholic Church—
United States—History—20th century. 3. United States—Church
history—20th century. I. Title.
BX1406.2.C35 1989
282′.73′09048—dc20
                                                                        89-35374
                                                                        CIP

Printed in the United States of America

First Edition

1 2 3 4 5 6 7 8 9 10

BOOK DESIGN BY HELENE BERINSKY

In an effort for wider understanding of present-day Catholics,
this book is dedicated to agnostics,
atheists and people of all religions
who live in this world together.

Author's Note

These narratives are based (with one exception) on personal interviews that took place between the subject and the author during the years 1987 and 1988. For ease in reading, most of the questions have been winnowed out. Two sections and part of a third appear in the question-and-answer form. In view of the unstoppable passage of time and the exigencies of deadlines, a few of the dates and circumstances mentioned here may need updating.

Acknowledgments

———·———

I wish to express my appreciation to all the Catholics in this book who received me into their inner lives for a brief moment and narrated their stories of the Catholic experience.

Because of limited space, not all the fine, exciting men and women who are helping to shape the Catholic Church are represented here, but I can, at least, mention them. Among these are the lawyers, doctors, nurses, other medical personnel and businessmen who are being guided by their beliefs in the practice of their professions; teachers in secular and religious schools who are trying, despite the odds, to give their charges a spiritual as well as a factual sense of things; and the many millions of American Catholics who are doing their best as Christians to live according to principle in a time of change and disruption within the Church.

Contents

Introduction

═══════ ▪ ═══════

FEW AMERICANS ARE aware of a religious upheaval that occurred in the 1960s, one of the most extraordinary events of the twentieth century. The consequences of it are being felt today more than ever and have still to reach their full impact. The upheaval was caused by Vatican Council II, an ecumenical (worldwide) meeting of Roman Catholic Bishops, which Pope John XXIII convened in October 1962 in Rome and which ended three years later in December 1965. It was the twenty-first ecumenical council of the Church, the first in this century, and the most widely attended and well prepared of them all. What further marked the Council off from all others was that it was *pastoral* in intent; that is, it related to the spiritual care and guidance of Catholics, rather than to promulgating dogma.

John's purpose was to update the Church. Under his guidance, the Council was to stimulate new development, loosen restrictions and rigid formulas, and provide a far-reaching charter for the future. As a result, the sixteen documents of the Council issued under his aegis have changed the coloration of Catholicism for all time. With rare insight, the documents called for revision in many areas, as well as new rules of thought and action. They touched on matters that for centuries the Church considered alien to her moral concepts. These included new attitudes toward peoples and other religions: the embracing of other Christian churches, the banishment of prejudice against Jews in the liturgy, and a welcoming of minorities, Blacks, American Indians and Hispanics. Concerning the practice of religion itself, the documents encouraged Biblical study, changes in the liturgy, which had been thought of as untouchable, and a full recognition of the apostolate of the laity—the participation by laypeople in the full life of the Church. The documents also comprised restatements of doctrine and of the

Church's role in society, including a rededication to missionary work and to helping the poor.

As best she could and not always wisely, the Church in America set about to put some of these new teachings into effect. In the process the foundations of Catholicism nationwide were badly shaken. On a basic level in the worship life of the Church, people became confused and disturbed. With the lessening of strictures and changes in rules, confessionals emptied and pews became half full. Altar boys disappeared from behind altar rails and the loss of their youthful presence is still felt. Nuns and priests who were having doubts about their calling found it easier to give up and leave. The guitar replaced the organ, and fish on Friday was a thing of the past. Latin again became a dead language. Bereft of their traditions, many left the Church and others stopped going to Mass.

But along with the struggle and disarray, Vatican II also gave birth to modernization and renewed vigor. In the twenty-four years since it ended, remarkable strength and vitality have risen within the Church. It is a strength that springs mainly from two sources. The first is a different breed of Catholics who, armed with the documents of Vatican II, are outspoken, argumentative and dedicated, who are bringing into the Church fresh ideas and new theologies. The second is the resurging conservative Catholics who have awakened from lethargy, renewed their faith in old traditions and are devoting their energies to maintaining an unbending Church. In positive ways these men and women are working for Catholicism either by emphasizing historical beliefs or by organizing new movements and presenting views of honest dissent. They comprise an exciting group of American Catholics and they come from every level—lay and clergy, young and old, from every part of the country. Their ranks have been joined by ethnic populations across the nation: Hispanics, American Indians and Blacks who are infusing new concepts and their own customs.

This book is a positive view of Catholicism in the United States. Based on personal interviews, it comprises more than two dozen of these voices: the makers and shakers, as well as the quiet performers. The interviewees are believers of every stripe. In their own words, they speak of their personal commitment and attempts to either mold, or maintain, the Church's thinking on today's vital issues. Some are well known; others are without renown. All show an individual approach to their religion that is both moving and remarkable. I interviewed them in their homes, at the conference table, in Indian territory, in a busy cathedral in San Antonio, in a monastery outside Birmingham. Aside from the subjects themselves, personalities from politics, other religions and the arts emerge briefly in these narratives: Pope John Paul II, Cardinal John O'Connor, President Reagan, President Nixon, Cardinal Joseph Ritter, Vatican officials, Eastern Orthodox bishops, Father Theodore Hesburgh, Madonna, Bruce Springsteen. They serve to add insights on the current scene.

In presenting these narratives, I have tried not to gloss over issues that are creating anguish, such as homosexuality within the Church, Catholic antagonism toward Jews, birth control, abortion, bad homilies, Church discrimination against American Indians, Blacks and Hispanics, and the hierarchical distaste for women. I have gone out of my way to interview people working in areas of controversy. These include Father Charles Curran, whose dissident views on sexual ethics have caused much concern; Father John McNeill, the homosexual priest who ministers only to homosexuals, and Father Andrew Greeley, author of "sexy" novels that have made millions.

Too often books on a Catholic theme are written by theologians and clergy and are understood only by other members of these groups. Such writings often serve merely to mystify the average reader. This book is another kind of effort. Its voices are clear and direct—in essence, they speak of the modern Catholic experience and represent the committed Catholic world. It is intended for *all* readers, be they Protestant, Catholic, Jewish, Muslim, atheist or agnostic since the spiritual concerns that any religion deals with are concerns that affect us all.

Senator Edward Kennedy of Massachusetts

DENNIS DE SILVA

Edward Kennedy

PERSONAL FAITH AND THE UNITED STATES GOVERNMENT

Our religion was a central part of our lives. We attended Mass and said the Rosary. . . . Each year that I attended a non-Catholic school, I always had weekly religious instruction and made a yearly retreat.

The only living male member of that generation of Kennedys who gave America its first Catholic president, Senator Kennedy of Massachusetts embodies a Christian-Catholic commitment in government. In Congress, as chairman of the Labor and Human Resources Committee and chairman of the Subcommittee on Immigration and Refugee Affairs, he has shown a dedication to his fellowmen—Blacks, the elderly, the poor—that extends from the small towns of his native state to the boundaries of Africa. In pursuing a decent quality of life for all citizens on this planet, he is bringing new strength to the Kennedy name. These activities constitute his witness to the Gospel.

Very much in tune with his times, Senator Kennedy is yet close, emotionally and spiritually, to the Catholic Church, where he still serves at Mass. When asked for this interview, he willingly agreed, with the request that it be in a written form, to which he could respond in leisure moments. As seen here, he typifies in many ways the religious longing of Americans over thirty. But his positions on abortion and other issues are not skirted: he makes them abundantly clear by sending along the text of a speech that deals with them.

> What emerges are two aspects of the Kennedy persona: the private citizen in relation to his faith and the Catholic senator at work in a religiously pluralistic society.

*W*ere you ever an altar boy? If you were, did you enjoy the experience? At what age did you make your First Communion, your Confirmation?

Yes, I was an altar boy, as were my brothers before me. My sons have also helped to serve Mass. In fact, I still serve Mass with them when we attend Mass with my mother at home in Hyannis Port. It has been an enjoyable and meaningful experience for us all. My First Communion was at the Vatican when I was six years old. I was twelve when I was confirmed.

It has been said that Mrs. Kennedy, your mother, believed that faith is the single most important source of strength for children. Was it so for you?

Faith has always been my mother's greatest strength and it has seen her through the times of crisis in her life. Her example of devotion was an inspiration to all the members of the family and it guided us well. My faith has likewise been a great source of strength for me during difficult times as well as a vital part of all of my endeavors. It is a source of inspiration.

Was your religious training different from that of other Catholic boys? How did you receive your Catholic education?

I really couldn't say. Our religion was a central part of our lives. We attended Mass and said the Rosary with regularity as well as observing saints' days. We also had family discussions and in my early youth I went to Catholic schools. Each year that I attended a non-Catholic school I always had weekly religious instruction and made a yearly retreat.

Mrs. Kennedy felt at one point that you might be a priest. Did you really entertain this possibility? Or was her feeling based on the fact that the priesthood was a choice of vocation urged on younger sons in Irish families?

Most young men entertain the thought, but after a considered judgment I felt public service was right for me, and I've found that to be an enormously satisfying career. My mother has always been supportive of that direction in my life.

Do you feel close to Catholicism today?

Yes, and I was reminded of that again during a recent trip to Rome where my family and I had the opportunity to have an audience with Pope John Paul II.

What aspects of it—ritual, holidays, beliefs—do you particularly enjoy?

The positive, hopeful sign—the Resurrection—the love and the hope that it brings.

What was your most moving and memorable experience connected with Catholicism?

The power that faith gave me to believe my son Teddy would live when he had cancer.

Do you prefer the Latin or English Mass?

I like the beauty and heritage of the Latin Mass, but I also like the English Mass for the fact that everyone can understand and perhaps better appreciate the meaning of it.

What American Catholic layperson, living or dead, have you most admired? Which Pope of recent times? Have you had great admiration for a priest?

I admire my brothers for their example of public service and for President Kennedy's achievement in becoming the first Catholic president. And although he is not an American, I have to say that I admire Lech Walesa for the great effort he has made, and continues to make, on behalf of human rights in Poland. Along with him I would include Father Jerzy Popieluszko who gave his life for his beliefs, and Mother Teresa who is a worldwide inspiration. I have also greatly admired Cardinal Richard Cushing, who was a great source of spiritual strength for members of my family. I think Pope John XXIII made an extraordinary contribution to the Church and to the world.

Many observers foresee a rift between the more liberal elements of the Catholic Church in America and the traditional Church in Rome. Do you find this possibility disturbing? If it did happen, do you think the Church could survive as still one Church?

I have always found open dialogue to be healthy and I have no doubt that the Church would survive.

What do you think are the biggest problems in the Church today?

I think they are the same problems that confront the world as a whole—poverty, hunger, homelessness, health care, and a decent quality of life for the citizens of this planet.

Has being a Catholic affected your actions as a politician? In what ways?

When I was elected to the Senate, I took an oath of office to uphold the Constitution. I expressed my thinking in answer to this question, and others you ask, in a speech I gave at Liberty Baptist College in Lynchburg, Virginia. To answer your questions in depth, I have attached my speech. [Excerpts from that speech follow this interview. They pertain to questions raised regarding Senator Kennedy's positions on abortion, the influence of religion in government, and religious tests for public office.]

Has there been any legislation that you have been instrumental in passing that is particularly beneficial to your Catholic constituency?

Although I know that Catholic Charities has availed itself of grants made possible by social legislation that I have sponsored, I like to think that my constituents, regardless of their religion, have benefited from my legislation on such things as job training, arms control, health care, meals-on-wheels, star schools, housing, civil rights, and so on.

Do you believe Catholics are in any way different from other Americans? Have you ever felt different?

Historically, like many groups, Catholics were singled out for repression. In my grandfather's day, and even to some extent in my father's day, there were signs in the windows that no Irish need apply for the work available. This was due not only to their nationality, but also to their Catholic religion. But these barriers and prejudices have come down and I think Catholics are very much part of mainstream America today. I don't think we feel different from other Americans, and I'm proud that the election of President Kennedy went a long way toward making that possible.

The lives of the Irish in America have centered around kinships, conviviality, politics and religion, with religion as the rock. Is religion a rock in your life?

My religion is a central part of my life and it has been a great source of solace and strength during times of tragedy and crisis.

Do you want to see Catholicism flourish in the Kennedy family future?

Catholicism is flourishing in the Kennedy family. Faith is a vital part of the lives of all of my children and nieces and nephews. I am happy for them that they feel this way for it has meant so much to their parents and to me. They can see that, and I think that it has influenced their feelings about the Church and its importance in their lives.

As the surrogate father of your brothers' children, have you involved yourself in their religious upbringing?

Yes, I have, whether it was general discussions, trying to be there for important events like First Communions, or rousting them out of bed in time for Mass up at the Cape.

Would you like to see your family continue the pattern of sending men to non-Catholic schools and women to Catholic schools?

That is a moot point. My nieces and nephews, as well as my own children, all chose their own schools and I support their decisions. Some chose to go to Catholic colleges and some did not. What concerned me was that they do their best at whatever college they attended, and that they have a good learning experience and an opportunity for growth. They were encouraged to study and to practice their religion.

As a famous American Catholic, do you feel a responsibility in the sense of setting an example to other Catholics in the nation?

The responsibility I feel is to my God, to my family, and the families of my brothers. If I fulfill those responsibilities, it is for others to judge whether that is setting an example.

[Excerpts from Senator Kennedy's speech "Tolerance and Truth in America," regarding religion and politics, delivered at the Liberty Baptist College in Lynchburg, Virginia, in 1983, appear below.]

*   *   *

I have come here to discuss my beliefs about faith and country, tolerance and truth in America. I know we begin with certain disagreements. . . . But I hope . . . we will always respect the right of others to differ—and that we will never lose sight of our own fallibility—that we will view ourselves with a sense of perspective and a sense of humor. After all, in the New Testament, even the disciples had to be taught to look first to the beam in their own eyes, and only then to the mote in their neighbor's eye.

I am mindful of that counsel. I am an American and a Catholic; I love my country and treasure my faith. But I do not assume that my conception of patriotism or policy is invariably correct—or that my convictions about religion should command any greater respect than any other faith in this pluralistic society. I believe there surely is such a thing as truth, but who among us can claim a monopoly on it? . . .

A deeper, more pressing question [is] whether and how religion should influence government. A generation ago, a presidential candidate had to prove his independence of undue religious influence in public life—and he had to do so partly at the insistence of Evangelical Protestants. John Kennedy said at that time: "I believe in an America where there is no [religious] bloc voting of any kind." . . .

This principle [the separation of Church and State], as vital as it is, is not a simplistic and rigid command. Separation of Church and State cannot mean an absolute separation between moral principles and political power. The challenge today is to recall the origin of the principle, define its purpose, and refine its application to the politics of the present. . . .

The separation of Church and State can sometimes be frustrating for women and men of deep religious faith. They may be tempted to misuse government in order to impose a value which they cannot persuade others to accept. But once we succumb to that temptation, we step onto a slippery slope where everyone's freedom is at risk. . . .

The real transgression occurs when religion wants government to tell citizens how to live uniquely personal parts of their lives. The failure of Prohibition proves the futility of such an attempt when a majority, or even a substantial minority, happens to disagree. Some questions may be inherently individual ones or people may be sharply divided about whether they are. In such cases—cases like Prohibition and abortion—the proper role of religion is to appeal to the conscience of the individual, not the coercive power of the State.

But there are other questions which are inherently public in nature, which we must decide together as a nation, and where religion and religious values can and should speak to our common conscience. The issue of nuclear war is a compelling example. It is a moral issue; it will be decided by government, not by each individual; and to give any effect to the moral values of their creed, people of faith must speak directly about public policy. The Catholic Bishops and the Reverend Billy Graham have every right to stand for the nuclear freeze—and Dr. [Jerry] Falwell has every right to stand against it.

There must be standards for the exercise of such leadership—so that the obligations of belief will not be debased into an opportunity for mere political advantage. But to take a stand at all when a question is both properly public and truly moral is to stand in a long and honored tradition. Many of the great evangelists of the 1800s were in the forefront of the abolitionist movement. In our own time, the Reverend William Sloane Coffin challenged the morality of the war in Vietnam. Pope John XXIII renewed the Gospel's call to social justice. And Dr. Martin Luther King, Jr., who was the greatest prophet of this century, awakened our national conscience to the evil of racial segregation.

Their words have blessed our world. And who now wishes they had all been silent? Who would bid Pope John Paul to quiet his voice about the oppression in Eastern Europe; the violence in Central America; or the crying needs of the landless, the hungry, and those who are tortured in so many of the dark political prisons of our time?

There are four tests which draw that line and define the difference.

First, we must respect the integrity of religion itself. People of conscience should be careful how they deal in the word of their Lord. In our own history, religion has been falsely invoked to sanction prejudice and even slavery, to condemn labor unions and public spending for the poor. . . .

Second, we must respect the independent judgments of conscience. Those who proclaim moral and religious values can offer counsel, but they should not casually treat a position on a public issue as a test of fealty to faith. Just as I disagree with the Catholic Bishops on tuition tax credits, which I oppose, so other Catholics can and do disagree with the hierarchy, on the basis of honest conviction, on the question of the nuclear freeze. . . .

Third, in applying religious values, we must respect the integrity of public debates. In that debate, faith is no substitute for facts. Critics may oppose the nuclear freeze for what they regard as moral reasons. They have every right to argue that any negotiation with the Soviets is wrong—or that any accommodation with them sanctions their crimes—or that no agreement can be good enough and therefore all agreements only increase the chance of war. I do not believe that, but it surely does not violate the standard of fair public debate to say it.

Mother Angelica interviewing Father Clarence Williams on her television show

Mother Angelica

CATHOLIC EVANGELISM IN THE SOUTH

We started this whole network without any money or skills. How much of a chance would you have given us? We didn't need wordly advice on how to build a network. The Lord said, "Build." We built.

Mother Angelica is the durable *grande dame* of television. In a medium that has seen evangelists come, build shaky empires and go, she has remained firmly rooted on the small screen, bringing to it an extraordinary dignity, humor, and humanity. In 1981, she started the Eternal Word Television Network in Irondale, Alabama. By 1984 she had eight million viewers; today the number far surpasses that. Her message is simple: to spread the Word of God.

The first cleric of contemporary Catholicism to see television as a method of reaching millions in a way no Apostle could have imagined, she has focused the attention of the Church on that medium. In the 1950s, when Bishop Fulton Sheen of Chicago pioneered the Church's entry into broadcasting, the Church awakened briefly to its possibilities, but then allowed the Bishop's audience to disperse after he died. Mother Angelica intends to keep her vision alive on the airwaves even after she dies. Her latest project is two new orders devoted to the contemplative life and to the television ministry she founded. One will comprise television priests and Brothers, and the other, television nuns. They will provide unique opportunities to young people of both sexes to enter both a contemplative religious vocation and the television world.

W hen people ask me how I did it, how I built this cable TV empire with a handful of unskilled nuns and $200 in the till, I respond by talking about the *theology of risk*. The world today is filled with the *theology of assurance*. This means that before you start any enterprise, you have to have everything you need. You have to have competent people, you have to have enough money, you have to have the assurance of success. But that's how you run a corporation! The theology of risk, on the other hand, is a total dependence on God's providence. That's how I operate. It is the theology of the Gospel. Look at the Apostles. When Jesus sent them out to preach, they had nothing in their pockets. *I send you out without scrip, or shoes or coppers in your purses*. God doesn't do things before the need is there.

Risk is the realization that God does it all. You're willing to step out, risk your neck with nothing for backing except God. And you put forth a tremendous amount of effort, but *the fruit, the fruit is the Lord's*. Another important aspect of the theology of risk is the question "Does God *want* me to do this?"—the answer to which requires much prayer. If the response is ascertained "Yes," then you begin. So what do you do? If you set up committees and go with feasibility studies, you get nowhere. I believe in benevolent dictatorship for the simple reason that *someone* has to make a decision and go with it. People have such committee-itis and board-itis, they spend so much time and money on these, that by the time they're ready to begin, they've lost their enthusiasm.

All this applies to the Church as well. We run things with corporate methods—our colleges, the Church itself. We no longer operate on a vision of something that *man feels God wants*. The vision is gone. My grandparents came from Italy and they couldn't read or write. To build a church in their little ghetto, they gathered people, neighbors who were skilled in bricklaying, *and they began*. They didn't wait for a committee to come along with $600,000 or $700,000. They began. You've got to put your hand to the plow and begin to sow your seed. We've lost all this in the Church, I think, because we run everything on corporate methods. And these don't work with God. We started this whole network without money or skills. How much of a chance would you have given us? We didn't need worldly advice on how to build a network. The Lord said, "Build."

We built.

We are closing our churches, closing our schools. I got a sad call yesterday from a nun who is president of a college. Her institution is closing. Why? Why are we closing our fine schools? Why are our motherhouses empty? We've gotten so corporate-minded. God doesn't work within a business structure. We need to examine ourselves and ask, "Lord, do we depend enough on You to bear fruit in our lives?" If we don't, that is the reason we don't bear fruit and our schools are closing.

When I first came to Alabama, television was far, far from my mind. We came as a cloistered community of nuns to do what we do best, that is, to pray and live a secluded life. But things evolved with no conscious plan on our part. At first I was asked by an Episcopalian group to give them a Scripture class during Lent. For four years I taught Scripture to Episcopalians and then Methodists and a mix of denominations. It was then I realized that the average person, the common man, has no concept of spirituality. My students knew a lot *about* Jesus, but they didn't *know* Jesus. All the beautiful things we learn in contemplative life are hidden from average people. And that's when the Lord began giving me the books [spiritual pamphlets] to write. I wrote fifty-seven of them and we printed them ourselves and started sending them to thousands of people in our effort to reveal the life of the Spirit. Well, naturally, when you start giving away so many books, people begin to ask you to speak. One time, I was asked to appear on a talk show on Channel 38 in Chicago. I walked toward the little television studio, and stopped in the doorway. It was very small, and I was amazed at how little it took to reach the masses. I remember saying, "Lord, I gotta have one of these."

If that wasn't the dumbest thing you could pray for! Nevertheless, I went home and made a videotape on a spiritual subject. It was a total disaster. Finally, we made one that was not half bad and sent it to the Christian Broadcasting Network (CBN). They called and asked if I would make sixty of them and I said yes. We rented time at a local TV station. At one point while making these tapes, I lost my temper with the local CBS affiliate because they were showing what I thought was an irreverent film on Jesus. I asked them not to show the film, they refused, and I walked out, determined to get my own television network. I did eventually. That's how I became a television evangelist.

The Church is on a new course in media. For six years our network, the Eternal Word Television Network (EWTN), has been broadcasting programs to enlarge the spiritual life of the average Catholic viewer throughout the country. Up until August 1987, we were on seven hours a day. Since then, after we acquired a full-time satellite transponder [channel], we've been on twenty-four hours. Our programs have a variety of subjects, such as Bible study, faith, love, Mariology, family and teens, the Rosary, suffering, pain, a hospital drama involving moral dilemmas and so on.

Outside of Bishop Fulton Sheen, myself and one or two others, the Church has had little or no exposure on television. Catholic speakers have not had the opportunity to appear and I'm hoping, now that we are on twenty-four hour programming, to go from diocese to diocese throughout the country encouraging people with the ability to speak to appear on our shows and to give an opportunity to everyone who wants it. We have plans for an exciting future in media, utilizing all its forms: TV and radio programming, VHS tapes, the publication of our little spiritual books, and a University in the Sky, which is education by cable satellite, a coast-to-coast enterprise that will comprise teaching programs.

Of course, all of these endeavors will require religious orders and commitment. Now we have a fine competent staff of laypeople—engineers, cameramen, and directors—and they will keep their jobs. In the future, qualified priests, Brothers and nuns, who will be schooled in the new media orders we are planning, will be the logical choices for replacements. Thus our University in the Sky will be conducted under the supervision of religious orders who will not only assure the orthodoxy of the programs, but will be skilled in television techniques as well. In the past, religious orders like the Jesuits and Dominicans, realizing that education was the need of the times, founded many schools. Today education is just as vital, and making the most of modern media, our new orders will supply education from the skies.

The new order for women will be called *Sister Servants of the Eternal Word* and the order for men, *Eternal Word for Priests and Brothers*. Both will be deeply prayerful and yet geared to media; the men's order will have seminarians. Mornings will be devoted to spiritual life, to prayer, study, reading, Scripture, Mass. In the afternoons, both orders will work in the television ministry as scriptwriters, directors, cameramen, engineers, secretaries, whatever is needed. In time we hope radio will be part of the ministry, with our Brother-engineers going into the dioceses and manning the radio stations. Thus, the Word of God will be spread not only in the United States but abroad, and we will have staff available for travel. The center, of course, will be here in Irondale.

Irondale will be like a wheel. The hub is the cloistered community, that is, my own community perpetually adoring the Lord in the Blessed Sacrament. All of the other orders—the two religious ones and a secular institute—will not only be geared toward adoration of the Holy Eucharist and devotion to Our Lady, but also to media in some form. Father Michael McDonagh, co-founder with me of the men's order, is handling the spiritual direction of the present staff and crew, including the laypeople. Mother Gabriel is co-foundress with me of the women's order. The Sisters, staff and employees all have to be spiritually oriented, so that whatever comes through the camera to your living room is done in the spirit of prayer.

Pope Pius XII was the first pope to recognize the possibilities of television for religion and felt it should be used to announce the Good News. Under his reign, Saint Clare and Saint Gabriel were chosen as patron saints of television: Clare because she had eyes that could penetrate the walls of her own room to see what was going on beyond them, and Gabriel because he was the first announcer of the Good News. One Christmas Eve, in the thirteenth century, Saint Clare was alone in her monastery cell, crippled with arthritis and not able to attend Midnight Mass. After the Sisters left, Clare was in tears and expressed her distress to the Lord. Suddenly, it was as if the walls opened wide and she saw the entire Mass, heard the music, the sermon, everything. When the Sisters returned, she told them what had happened and described the particulars of the Mass. That was the first indication in the Church of something so common today—television. It is significant, incidentally, that the Lord chose this Franciscan Poor Clare monastery in Irondale, Alabama, in which to build the first Catholic satellite network in the world. When the satellite dish was first installed [referring to the huge disklike antenna that towered at a slant above the shrubs and trees behind the monastery], we were fearful of what the neighbors would say. But most of them have been understanding—two are Catholic. However, when we were planning to get a rezoning to place another dish over there [pointing], they raised a ruckus about that and our request was denied. I don't know. There was a false concept about microwave systems that frightened the neighbors, but there's no more danger to that than sitting before your television or using your microwave oven. In fact, a microwave oven is more dangerous than that dish is. But I'm glad it turned out the way it did because that spot we had in mind for the second dish will now be used to build housing for the new order.

In the press the focus on the high-flying life-styles of a few TV evangelists has reflected badly on evangelism. Top names have been under fire and I feel sorry about this. On the other hand, I am not pleased when people call *me* "a saint." True, I draw no salary, have no personal funds or fancy cars, *but please don't call me a saint.* Let me tell you something, if I may. About three years ago [1985], an award was given to me in Toledo, Ohio, and for unknown reasons it took three people to introduce me. One person said very nice things about me, another followed suit, and so on. As I sat listening, a scene from childhood flashed before me from the days when my mother and I were living in a rat-infested apartment on the ground floor. The rats were so big they would eat through the floorboards. That night a rat ate his way up and I could hear him squeezing through the hole. I looked over and saw him scurrying across the floor. He stopped in the middle of the room and looked at me. He was a huge sewer rat with a long tail. I was petrified.

As the scene came to me, I realized where I would be without the Lord. I got up and said to the speakers, "Thank you for all the wonderful things you've said about me. The credit goes entirely to the Lord. Please let me share with you what I just saw as you were saying all these things and using the word 'saintly.'" I told them about the experience and said, "I realize what the Lord was saying as the scene came to me. 'Angelica, remember where you were and where you would be if it were not for Me.' If anyone sees any quality in me that is deemed to be saintly, I give glory to the Lord. The Lord has said, 'Without Me, you can do nothing.'"

Sanctity, incidentally, should *not* be the unusual. It's for everybody—children, teenagers, the elderly, the rich, the poor, the middle class. The trouble is that today we have become materialistic and we think of sanctity and religion in terms of how much money you give away, or of the physical help you can give. The more you give and the more pain you relieve, then the more religious or saintly you are. But that's putting the cart before the horse. Religion works *from within.* Jesus worked on the inside of a man, and then the man had compassion, the kind of compassion that is drawn to others with words like "I want to help you. I love you," whether he's a friend or enemy. Although sanctity today is something unusual, it can be common.

What was our life like before television? The Poor Clares and I came down here simply to start a cloistered community of prayer and adoration. While I was still in the monastery in Canton, Ohio, my leg was badly injured in an accident and before an operation, I was told it was unlikely that I would walk again. Praying to the Lord to be healed, I promised to start a new community of perpetual adoration to the Blessed Sacrament if He granted my plea. Further, I would start it in the Deep South where Catholics are few and far between and discriminated against. The Lord heard me. With the help of a brace, I was able to walk again.

Coming to Irondale, Alabama, an area that was practically all Protestant (only 2 percent Catholic), we did have problems, especially since we were a cloistered community. Although we did not begin with the intention of changing any of our rules, certain changes were made absolutely necessary because of our neighbors and the culture around us. It wasn't long before we realized that the cloister use of the grill—a metal partition of bars through which cloistered Sisters speak to outsiders—lost all spiritual meaning in this environment and created only fear and suspicion in the community. We were not making the impact that a praying community of the Catholic Church should. We asked permission of the Bishop to take down the grill and it was granted.

A change that was made for our own accommodation concerned family visits. The rules were *so* stiff. I never did think that parents should be penalized when their children enter monasteries. A certain separation is needed—you can't live two lives—but I felt mothers and fathers ought to visit their children in a home atmosphere. Before, our Sisters saw their parents for a few hours behind a grill. Now the family comes and stays for three or four days a year.

On a deeper level, there was another change of monastery rules. I've always felt that the danger in contemplative life in most convents is that everybody becomes a stereotype or clone of the founder, whether it's Saint Clare or Saint Francis or both [laughs]. Sisters and monks seem to adopt the style of the founder, and they look alike, sit alike, talk alike and all have their eyes cast down, in imitation of images of the founder. As we dealt with others in a non-Catholic environment, I did not want the Sisters to appear clonelike. What we needed, I felt, was a family spirit which would allow each Sister's personality to develop. The more individual you are, the more human and attractive you appear to others. So in the first ten years here as Mother Abbess, I tried to create an atmosphere whereby each Sister could express herself as the Spirit led her and not as a clone of Saint Clare.

Our order of the day—horarium—also was changed because our lives had changed. For one thing, our former work activities to make money did not fit the environment. Since there weren't many Catholic churches around, we could no longer bake altar breads to sell to churches. We had to get into other things. We started roasting peanuts and selling them. We made fishing lures. We did everything, all of which necessitated changes in our schedule.

Speaking of horariums, people often ask me how I divide the hours of the day since there are so many things perking here. About four hours are spent praying; if I didn't do that, the rest would be impossible. You know, you wouldn't have the wits. These hours provide a mental respite that supplies energy to work more intensely the rest of the day. The employees are competent and reliable and the Sisters get an awful lot of work done. Our hours of prayer are all the same. In addition, the Sisters are up all night on Saturday, Sunday, and Wednesday, in adoration of the Blessed Sacrament. They take turns relieving one another for one-and-one-half-hour vigils. The more you can pray, the more intense your life becomes. There is a tremendous lot of wasted time in the world. When we work, we work hard and with concentration. I get a little confused when people say, "How do you do all you do?" I'm not rushed, you know. My blood pressure is very low. It's God's work. I'm just His steward. He has to do it all.

[Following is the horarium of Mother and her nuns, which is subject to each day's exigencies.

HORARIUM

5:20 A.M.	Rise, dress. Mother often rises earlier for extra prayer alone in Chapel
6:10 A.M.	Morning prayer in Chapel
7:00 A.M.	Mass in Chapel
7:45 A.M.	Recital of Holy Rosary in Chapel
8:15 A.M.	Breakfast
9:00 A.M.	Lesson for the Sisters
10:00 to 11:00 A.M.	Work
11:00 to 11:15 A.M.	Daytime prayer in Chapel
11:30 A.M.	Lunch
1:00 P.M.	Free time
2:00 P.M.	Work
4:20 P.M.	Vespers in Chapel
5:00 P.M.	Dinner
6:00 P.M.	Free time. It may be used for work or extra prayer in Chapel
7:15 to 8:00 P.M.	Work at the monastery
9:30 P.M.	To bed

In addition, Mother and the Sisters each have one hour of Adoration of the Blessed Sacrament, in succession, throughout the day.]

What the Poor Clares and myself are trying to do with EWTN and our little spiritual books and our plans with the University in the Sky is to give God space in our lives again. Unless we're in a lot of trouble, we don't usually think of Him. In the days of Saint Teresa of Avila and John of the Cross and later, of Saint Dominic, Saint Francis and Saint Clare, He was *all* people thought about. That was why there were such tremendous Third Orders. Saint Francis started his Third Order because laypeople were seeking a deep spiritual life and wanted to follow him. [Today Third Orders are associations of the laity affiliated with different religious groups—Franciscans, Carmelites, Dominicans—whose members follow a daily practice of religion.] In early days, when family and friends got together in the evening, they talked about God and religion. Some indulged in fiery debates and feuds, as we know from the writings of Luther and others.

We here in Irondale are trying to revive what Francis and Clare, the founders of our order, did in those earlier centuries. Through the very medium that has lessened our spirituality, we seek to restore it and to do this within the Church's existing system of dogma, faith and morals. We seek to make manifest to the public how wonderful the Church is, what a vast reserve of untouched spirituality it has that can fulfill our daily lives and call us to holiness—all of us, doctors, lawyers, ditchdiggers and three-year-olds. It can give us the answer to the *why* of pain, suffering, and guilt. The labor that we at EWTN have appropriated for ourselves is to combine within the religious framework of every Catholic the doctrines, the dogma and the question of life's burdens, together with deep spirituality.

Because of attacks against Catholicism made by some TV evangelists, a good deal of prejudice was created. Our network, EWTN, has broken down a lot of that prejudice. And it has burst the bubble of myths that people have about the Catholic religious. People are accustomed to the schoolroom nun who teaches a kid the ABC's and two-plus-two-makes-four. Most people don't expect nuns to be human or tell it like it is. I've angered some who think I'm a little *too* earthy. The world needs to know that we are human beings under the habit, that we understand other human beings and have compassion and love for them. *But we've still got to tell it like it is* and to say to someone who strays, "Look, sweetheart, you've gone in the wrong direction."

What United States Catholics need today is to be loyal to our faith. They need to be faith-filled, to define and defend their faith. They need to know you can't live two lives at the same time: a faith-filled one, and one of accommodation. In other words, you can't bring the world into the faith to make it more comfortable. And there's something else: I have a real thing against the Positive Thinker. He attributes everything to himself, instead of emptying himself with the knowledge that God will replenish him because God does everything *in our weakness*. The power and ability to work come from God, and the more one attributes that ability to oneself, the less accomplished he or she becomes. God's power is at best in one's weakness.

"I can accomplish all things," says the Positive Thinker.

That's not true. Only God accomplishes all things.

The Lord is the greatest "public-relations man" in the world, so our work at EWTN is made somewhat easy. Our reception by the media has been wonderful. There's always someone writing something, somewhere. I've gotten phenomenal coverage and been on many shows and on a big book tour. We've been written about in the *National Geographic, USA Today, Time, Newsweek,* you name it. On our second anniversary, Peter Jennings, the newscaster, mentioned the occasion on his national show and said, "Good luck, Mother."

I think that's tremendous.

Father Charles Curran in the library at Cornell University

Father Charles Curran

THE MOST CONTROVERSIAL PRIEST
IN AMERICA

American Catholics disagree with the official teaching on many issues. I am articulating their experience and trying to incorporate it into the whole of Catholic understanding.

"The Curran Affair," as this story is spoken of, is not a romance between a man and a woman, but a torturous relationship between a man and his Church that has shaken the rafters of Catholicism in America. It is an emotional liaison between the Church, stern mistress who will not amend her laws on sexual ethics, and a priest/theologian who loves her, yet is trying to do just that to lessen the agony of fellow Catholics.

Father Curran began teaching moral theology at Catholic University in Washington in 1965 on one of its three ecclesiastical faculties that are accredited by Rome itself. It was here that he first set forth his dissident opinions on such issues as divorce, contraception, premarital sexuality and euthanasia. In 1986, for having promulgated these views, the Church found him not "suitable" to teach theology on an ecclesiastical faculty and stripped him of his teaching authority. The affair has developed into a crisis of authority versus authoritarianism and the legitimacy of theological dissent.

As a young priest, Father Curran was a traditional thinker. In this frank narrative, he describes his change from conservatism to the adoption of his present unorthodox ideas. In the process he presents some insider views of America's only Vatican-connected university, Catholic University, and some fascinating insights into Vatican practices.

Why did I change? What brought about this transformation from the older Catholic theology in which I was trained? When I was quite young and teaching moral theology in Rochester, New York, I was associated with a group of married couples. We used to get together every two weeks, praying, talking and discussing issues. I began to change very much from *their* experience. And from that of other people who came to talk with me. I was impressed by the difficulties that Catholic married couples were having with the Church's teaching. I knew these people were good, generous and very devoted. It was the hard realities they had to face in their daily lives that first raised questions in my mind about official teaching.

Another influence was my own reflection from the time that I began to realize that certain defects existed in the Church's teaching. Catholic teaching has always said that its moral positions are based not primarily on faith or Scripture or even Jesus Christ, but *primarily on human reason.* They are *reasonable.* A prominent defect to my mind was the Church ruling on artificial contraception and particularly the phrasing: *Every act of marital intercourse has to be open to procreation.* A few years before, for my doctoral dissertation, I had done historical research and realized how very dependent our theology was on what we know today to be an inadequate biological notion of things. Obviously, we're all conditioned by the time and circumstances in which we live.

The older Catholic teaching had grown up at a time when we knew nothing biologically about the whole female contribution to reproduction. We knew nothing of the ovum, we knew nothing of the graphian follicle, we knew nothing at all of modern biology. It was thought that the only active aspect of procreation was the male semen which is deposited in the woman. The word *semen* means seed, and the meaning here is based on the agricultural metaphor. What the woman supplied was simply the nest. After the semen was injected into the nest, life came forth. Nothing was known about the female contribution, the ovum, and so on. Thus, not only the Church but the biologists of the day thought that every single act of marital intercourse by its very nature was open to procreation. It was only much, much later in the twentieth century that we discovered that for a great part of the woman's cycle, she is *not* open to procreation.

I was also influenced by the contemporary shift in Catholic thinking to what has been called *personalism*. In the past the Church said, in effect, *One can never interfere with the sexual faculty or the sexual act.* On the other hand, personalism claims, *But one is not dealing with the sexual faculty or the sexual act. One is dealing primarily with persons. And for the good of the person, and for the good of the marital relationship of persons, one can at times and perhaps should interfere with the sexual faculty or the sexual act.*

Thus my understanding—in this instance with regard to the question of artificial contraception—began to change. That was the breakthrough.

My beginnings as a priest were in Rochester, New York. In the late forties I entered St. Andrew's Seminary, a high school and day seminary, and then finished my college work at St. Bernard's Seminary. I was then assigned to study theology at the North American College in Rome. While there, I studied at the Pontifical Gregorian University, where the theology was traditional and I was a dutiful and unquestioning seminarian. At the Gregorian, I received a licentiate in sacred theology (STL), an academic degree, and a doctorate in sacred theology (STD). While studying for my doctorate, I had come across the existence of the Academia Alfonsiana in Rome, run by the Redemptorist Fathers, whose founder was Alphonsus Liguori, the patron saint of moral theologians. The Alfonsiana provided a program for acquainting future teachers with the many different areas of moral theology—Biblical, historical, sacramental, philosophical, psychological, and so on. I enrolled and in 1961 received a doctorate with a specialization in moral theology. From 1961 to 1965, I was back in Rochester teaching at St. Bernard's Seminary, my alma mater. In September 1965, I started teaching at Catholic University.

It was during the period of postgraduate work in Rome (1959–1961) that things really began to open up for me, which resulted in the transformation of a submissive student into a priest with a questioning, contemporary state of mind. The themes on which I based my faithful dissent started to come through. At the Gregorian I ran into Father Joseph Fuchs from Germany, a teacher of moral theology who was preparing and developing somewhat new approaches. In keeping with the spirit of the times, I wrote and defended in 1961 a doctoral dissertation at the Gregorian, under Father Francis Furlong, on the prevention of conception after rape. At the Alfonsiana I studied with Father Bernard Häring, who, without a doubt, has done the most to change Catholic moral theology before and after Vatican II. The year before (1958), I had read the Italian translation of his groundbreaking three-volume work *The Law of Christ,* which proposed a new approach to moral theology and broke away from old formats. He pointed out that the danger of the past was that Catholics were presented with generic, legalistic rules that everybody had to follow. He argued that this kind of legalism was not sufficient for the Christian life, that you had to teach the *fullness* of the Gospel to assure the freedom of the children of God, a freedom that is both faithful and life-giving. Häring himself was an early critic of the Catholic official teaching on contraception and has spoken out against it, although actually I had changed my position on it before Häring publicly changed his.

In Rome one of my professors was Father Francis Hürth, a German Jesuit, who was a consultant for the Holy Office. It was an open secret that Hürth was the author of most of Pope Pius XII's addresses on morality. Occasionally Father Hürth and I had conversations in Latin about various moral questions. At about this time a Dr. Doyle from Boston had come up with an invention called the Doyle cervical spoon that was intended to help infertile couples. It was thought that by inserting this device into the vagina, the semen would be protected from the acids of the vagina and have a better chance of ultimately being fecundated.

An American Jesuit who was trying to gain approval for the spoon asked me to talk with Father Hürth to ascertain his thinking on this matter. I agreed and remember having an hourlong talk in Latin with Father Hürth about the spoon. He kept saying, "I have difficulty with this," and explained why he thought it was morally wrong. I argued the other side. He might have known that I was sent because in the end, he smiled and said in his precise Latin:

"Habeo difficultates. Tamen, est problema Americanum; non mihi pertinet." [Translation: *I have difficulty with this. But it's an American problem and doesn't pertain to me.*]

In other words, he was saying the Holy Office wasn't going to condemn it.

At Catholic University, I taught a variety of subjects in moral theology. But it was mainly my classes and teachings in sexual ethics that caused all the controversy and later led to my condemnation by Rome. (Oddly enough, I had not taught these classes in sexual ethics at the University for fifteen years.) My teachings differ *in varying degrees* from traditional Catholic doctrine; my positions are often nuanced. As I've indicated, they are based on my pastoral experience with conscientious married Catholics, on all I learned in Rome from contemporary-minded teacher/theologians, on the influences which nourished me as an adult student in Rome, and on subsequent developments in my thinking.

The issues involved were seven in number: contraception and sterilization, abortion, masturbation, homosexuality, premarital sexuality, the indissolubility of marriage, and euthanasia. So that the reader may know exactly what the teachings are, I suggest you use the brief summaries that appear in my book *Faithful Dissent*. I have written at length on many of these issues in other books as well. [The summaries from *Faithful Dissent* appear below. The book was published by Sheed & Ward in 1987.]

CONTRACEPTION and STERILIZATION: I have maintained that these actions are not intrinsically evil but can be good insofar as they are governed by the principles of responsible parenthood and stewardship. However, I have also pointed out the danger of abuse in connection with both contraceptions and sterilization.

ABORTION: My position can be succinctly stated: truly individual human life begins at the time of individuation, which occurs between the fourteenth and the twenty-first day after conception. One can be justified in taking this individual life only for the sake of the mother or for a value commensurate with life itself. In determining the time of individuation as the beginning of truly individual human life, I have rejected positions proposed by other Catholic theologians for a later time. My position on the solution of conflict cases in abortion is consonant with that proposed by all those theologians who accept a theory of proportionate reason.

MASTURBATION: Again, my position is quite nuanced. Masturbatory acts are ordinarily not very important or significant and usually do not involve grave matter. Such actions are generally symptomatic of other realities and should be treated as such. However, masturbation falls short of the full meaning of human sexuality and should not generally be seen as totally good or praiseworthy.

HOMOSEXUALITY: I have devoted a number of studies to homosexuality. On the basis of a theology of compromise, I propose that for an irreversible, constitutional or genuine homosexual, homosexual acts in the context of a loving relationship striving for permanency can, in a certain sense, be objectively, morally good. However, in accord with this theology of compromise, such acts are good for these persons because of their objective condition. In general, sexuality should be seen in terms of female-male relationships so that homosexual relationships fall short of the full meaning of human sexuality. This position obviously does not accept or condone homosexual acts without personal commitment.

I wish to emphasize that I am not for out-and-out homosexuality.

PREMARITAL SEXUALITY: I insist that the full meaning of human sexuality involves a permanent commitment of love between a woman and a man. Pastoral practice here requires prudence in dealing with people who do not accept such an understanding in practice. Only in very rare and comparatively few situations would I justify premarital sexuality on the basis of a theology of compromise.

THE INDISSOLUBILITY OF MARRIAGE: I have argued that the Catholic Church should change its teaching on indissolubility and allow divorce in certain circumstances. It should also be noted that many other Catholic theologians have taken a similar position about changing the teaching on indissolubility. One commentator has noted concerning my position that even while advocating the change, I urge that the real task is to "expend every effort possible to strengthen the loving marriage commitment of spouses."

EUTHANASIA: I have never done an in-depth study on euthanasia, but have occasionally referred to it as an illustration of other points. There I tentatively proposed that when the dying process begins, there seems to be no difference between the act of omission (not using extraordinary means) and the positive act of bringing about death. I point out that in practice this position would differ only slightly from the official hierarchical teaching and also recognize possible abuses which may be sufficient reason not to adopt this position in practice.

The danger in all these positions is that people can say I'm totally in favor of the issues involved. I am not. As you can see, my positions are nuanced and comprise varying degrees of dissent. I'm not in favor of abortion, I'm not in favor of euthanasia. I simply see a few more exceptions in those cases than the official Catholic teaching does at the present time.

On the other hand, probably my differences on questions like contraception, sterilization, divorce and even homosexuality are greater than my differences in other areas. But as a whole, the positions are nuanced. A colleague of mine at Catholic University who did some traveling around the United States was frequently questioned about me and said he was darned sick and tired of defending my *moderate* theology. Note the word *moderate*. Even within the Catholic community, my positions tend to be moderate. Remember, I was brought up in the old school, I was ordained way back in '58 before Vatican II, and I did my theology in the fifties. I changed my mind about the official Catholic condemnation of artificial contraception only in 1964.

I had taught at Catholic University for two years before my teaching was actively challenged. I was informed by the president, Bishop William McDonald, that the trustees had voted not to renew my contract. On hearing this, the theology faculty said they would not, and could not, function unless and until I was reinstated. They went on strike, and the rest of the faculty and the student body went on strike with them. The university was closed down for four days and then it announced that I would be retained and promoted. No reason was given for the original refusal to renew my contract, but we all knew that it was the question of artificial contraception in which I had been an active figure.

The following year Pope Paul VI issued his encyclical *Humanae Vitae* condemning artificial contraception. A group of theologians, with myself as spokesperson, composed a statement right after the encyclical was released, in which we concluded that Catholic couples in their own conscience *could disagree in theory and in practice* with the papal encyclical and still be loyal Roman Catholics. The Board of Trustees at the University, predominantly bishops at that time, instituted a faculty-committee hearing to see whether my colleagues and I, as spokesperson, had violated our responsibilities as Catholic theologians. Their conclusion was that we had acted responsibly and, therefore, we could continue to teach at the university.

Frankly, because of the tremendous support I received from my colleagues in those early years at Catholic University, I felt a commitment to do all I could to stay there and work for change both within the Church and the university. It was a congenial place, particularly in view of the encouragement. In the summer of 1979, I was informed by the Congregation for the Doctrine of the Faith in Rome that I was under investigation and was given a list of the issues and questions involved. For seven years we entered into a correspondence back and forth about these issues. In September 1985, I received a letter from Cardinal Joseph Ratzinger, then prefect of the Congregation, stating that they were giving me a chance to retract my position and that if I did not retract, I could not be looked upon as a Catholic theologian.

Cardinal Joseph Bernardin of Chicago, chairman of the Board of Trustees at Catholic University, Archbishop James Hickey, the chancellor, and myself had four or five meetings in the fall of 1985, during which I tried to work out some kind of compromise. I argued I would be willing to give up teaching in the area of sexual ethics (pointing out that I had not taught in this area for fifteen years) *if* everything else would be acceptable and I could continue to teach. Rome was unwilling to accept this compromise but offered to set up an informal meeting with me in March 1986. I accepted, but the meeting was unsatisfactory: we discussed everything, and Father Häring, who had arranged to be present, urged Cardinal Ratzinger to accept the compromise to no avail. In August 1986, I was informed by a letter from the Cardinal that I was no longer "suitable" or "eligible" to be a professor of Catholic theology.

Soon after, Archbishop James A. Hickey, as university chancellor, initiated the process to take away my canonical mission to teach on an ecclesiastical faculty. The three ecclesiastical faculties, or departments, at Catholic University are in canon law (the laws of the Church), theology and philosophy. They grant Rome-accredited degrees instead of the usual American or civil degrees accredited by state governments. [Since this interview, Catholic University has stripped Father Curran of his canonical mission to teach on an ecclesiastical faculty.]

May I stress a vital aspect of this entire affair? It is very important to distinguish issues that are core and central to the faith and issues which by their very nature are more removed and peripheral. Perhaps one of the great dangers in Roman Catholicism before Vatican II was the seeming acceptance of the fact that all Church teachings were of the *same order and had the same validity, same significance and same importance.* Even before Vatican II, there was a recognition from a theological viewpoint that a diversity existed and that some positions were more central than others. Catholic theology textbooks had a section of "Theological Notes" that tried to describe the differences. There were twenty categories detailing how close, or how remote, something could be in relation to the core of faith. Now I don't see how one can be a Catholic and disagree with what is core.

What are core and central beliefs? The divinity of Jesus, the Trinity embodying three persons, the role of the Holy Spirit, the forgiveness of sins, redemption, the future life, the role of the Pope and the Bishops, the seven Sacraments—these are all fundamental to Catholic belief and are based primarily on faith, or revelation, or Scripture, or Jesus Christ. What I am dealing with are moral issues and teachings that, in accordance with the Catholic approach, *are based on primarily human reason.* You see, this has given me the right to question them because in different historical circumstances, the solutions the Church has adopted for certain moral issues are no longer reasonable. Because of changing historical circumstances, one cannot claim a certitude on certain moral questions that excludes the possibility of error. In their pastoral letters on peace, war and the economy, the Catholic Bishops themselves have recognized that when you get down to specific complex questions, you cannot claim certitude that excludes the chance of error. The Bishops maintain, for example, that the first use of even the smallest nuclear weapon is wrong. I agree with them. But they also recognize that because this matter is so complex, other people within the Church might disagree with them and still consider themselves loyal Roman Catholics. Fundamentally, the Bishops are accepting the principle that I uphold, namely, that as you get more specific and complex, you cannot claim complete certitude. It is a fundamental law of the logic of human reason that when you're involved in a complex situation, you cannot be absolutely sure that this is the only one certain answer. And, therefore, you have to recognize the possibility of dissent in the Church.

I have always been careful to put my role in the Curran case in proper perspective and not to exaggerate it. Quite frankly, if I changed my position tomorrow, nobody else in the country would necessarily change his or hers. Most Catholic people have come to these judgments on their own. Public-opinion polls indicate that a great number of American Catholics disagree with the official teaching on many issues. In many ways, I am articulating their experience and trying to incorporate it into the whole of Catholic understanding. I have learned from, and been influenced by, the experience of lay Catholics. Yes, human experience can and does err so that one cannot absolutize human experience in an uncritical manner. In the light of this experience, I have critically reexamined past teachings.

People have said to me, "Why do you think that you were the one chastised by the Church rather than other theologians who have similar beliefs and sometimes more radical ones?" Probably I have been singled out for historical reasons and for the visibility that my past work has brought me: the controversy and strike at Catholic University in 1967, my role as spokesperson in 1968 for other scholars who disagreed with the official Church teaching on artificial contraception and the fact that I've written eighteen books.

I want very much to stay and teach at Catholic University. I just want to prove that an institution can be a true American university with academic freedom and *still* be Catholic. If I'm allowed to stay, given my positions, it would prove beyond a doubt that Catholic University can be both. In recent years there has been a great struggle on the meaning of a Catholic university. In the American sense of the term, "university" implies academic freedom; by dismissing me, Catholic University would show that it does not have it. I have written a great deal on the question and believe firmly that an institution can be both Catholic and a university with this necessary freedom. I fought for this in 1967 and 1968 and had a great deal of support from other people who have urged me to fight. So I am continuing the battle—I may have to go to civil court to defend my tenured contract at Catholic University. Tomorrow I'm going down to New York and talk to my lawyers, the firm of Cravath, Swaine, & Moore. I could teach elsewhere. I've had a number of invitations over the years, but have turned them all down because I wanted to stay on at the university to prove my point. [Shortly before this book went to press, Father Curran lost his breach-of-contract lawsuit against Catholic University, which pitted a professor's right to academic freedom against the Roman Catholic Church's authority to decide who can teach its theology.]

Right now I'm teaching temporarily at Cornell for one year [1987–1988] and am visiting professor of Catholic studies, the first person who has ever had the title of theologian at this university. I've taught two courses, "Renewal of Catholicism Since Vatican II" and "An Introduction to Catholic Moral Theology," and this semester I am teaching a course in "Catholic Social Teaching" and giving four public lectures. I've been performing my priestly function in different places. Last weekend I celebrated and preached at four Masses in little parishes along Cayuga Lake.

In conclusion, I'd like to say a word about the belief, held by Catholics and non-Catholics alike, that removal of all boundaries and limitations in man's life will only lead him to undisciplined pleasure and despair. To this I respond that one can never absolutize freedom. When you do so, that means that freedom is *the only thing,* and then it becomes license. Freedom *cannot* be set apart, or function alone. It always exists with other things, such as justice, truth, love. It must always be seen in conjunction with these other realities.

Historically, the Roman Catholic Church has not given enough emphasis to freedom. Yet we have always felt that God ultimately calls us in freedom, that He has given us freedom. You can say that the Cross that Jesus bore was payment for our freedom. Of course, we all have to recognize the danger of abusing it. On that score, we've all made mistakes. But the way of God *is to offer human beings freedom.* And so it seems to me that we have to give people that freedom and we have to urge them to use it properly, to use it to ultimately respond to God's gift.

I have tried to put all this together, especially in regard to the issue of dissent to the Church, with an old axiom of Christian thought, which says:

> *In necessary things, unity.*
> *In doubtful things, freedom.*
> *In all things, charity.*

If we in the Catholic Church can live up to that motto, we have done the best we can do.

J. Peter Grace, conducting business from his airborne office

J. Peter Grace

HELPING THE LEAST OF GOD'S BRETHREN

All I know is I'm a bottom-line businessman. When the profits go up, you're doing good, and vice versa. Since Vatican II the Church has deteriorated massively: nobody goes to Confession, few go to Mass. The bottom line is the Church is a helluva lot worse than it was.

J. Peter Grace is chairman, president and chief executive officer of W. R. Grace & Co., an American empire of enterprises in chemicals and selected interests in energy, manufacturing and service businesses that spread over forty-five countries. He is also adviser to presidents on government waste and economic problems. By parlaying his ties in these two worlds—with people at pinnacles of power in business and government—he has become the most active and dedicated private fund-raiser for the Catholic Church in the world. With the commitment of a crusader, he contacts the rich and the mighty, raising millions of dollars each year, and has become indispensable to popes and prelates alike.

Loath as he is to talk about his charitable activities, the result perhaps not so much of modesty but of spiritual reserve, he agreed to being interviewed. He calls things as he sees them and is not afraid to criticize, as he does here, bishop and archbishop, layman and acolyte, anyone he feels is undercutting what he considers the strength and holiness of Catholicism. The interview took place in the spacious conference room on the top floor of the sloping Grace Building in New York City. Also present were two aides, Fred Bona, a company vice-president, and Jack O'Connell, director of public affairs. Mr. Grace and the author sat opposite each other at one end of a U-shaped formation of tables. Responding with quick, pungent remarks, the subject gave constant evidence of the quintessential American tycoon. To preserve the immediacy of his answers, this interview is presented in the original question-and-answer form.

Mr. Grace: What do you want to talk about?

Author: I'm doing a book about Catholics: people who are making things happen in the contemporary Church, the activators in the Church, public figures and private citizens. . . .

Mr. Grace: What makes you think public figures who are Catholics will make average people think more of the Church?

Author: It will give them a new level of knowledge about the Church that is outside their experience. It may lead to better understanding. . . .

Mr. Grace: Maybe. After you read about Mother Teresa and then read about prominent Catholics, I'm not sure that you then have greater respect for the Church.

Author: I'd like to talk briefly about some of the awards you've been given. They are fascinating and not well known. For example, you were awarded the Laetare Medal by the University of Notre Dame. Can you tell us what that is and what in your background brought the award to you?

Mr. Grace: Well, I will answer this question carefully, but to be honest with you, I cannot give you a good answer. I do not take awards seriously at all and believe that anybody who gets a lot of awards in this world might get less in the next. So I'm not into awards and don't know very much about them. The medal is supposed to be for the prominent Catholic layman of the year. One of my best friends got it—George Meany, who was head of the labor movement. As for why I got it, Father Theodore Hesburgh was president of Notre Dame at the time and he knew my work in helping the poor in Latin America. He has always been interested in Latin America, as I have. In the late fifties and early sixties, I was visible in all the health programs for Latin America and was a member of the Point Four Board, and the International Development Advisory Board with Eisenhower, as well as a Kennedy appointee for the Alliance for Progress and the Freedom from Hunger programs. Was on the Peace Corps Board also. Probably got the medal for all this activity, plus the fact that I had been helpful at Notre Dame and done a lot of work. But I don't know.

Author: One award or gift you seem to be particularly fond of is something Mother Teresa gave you. Can you explain that?

Mr. O'Connell: The statue of Our Blessed Mother.

Mr. Grace: I don't call that an award—it's a gift. She gave me the statue she had been carrying around on her habit for years. She would put it up and recite the Rosary. And she said to me that if I would keep this always and say the Rosary before it, she would give it to me, and she did. A personal gift like that from Mother Teresa—yes, that's fabulous. It's a wonderful thing to be that much loved by Mother Teresa. And I still get little notes from her. I think she's the greatest, by far, of anybody in the world. Who's better? I think the Pope recognizes that.

Author: You are a member of the Cardinal's Committee of the Laity in New York City. Do you care to talk about that?
[This is a group organized by the Archdiocese and comprises business and community leaders who work on fund-raising and other public-service projects for the Church.]

Mr. Grace: We help the Cardinal with the different charities and with the hospitals. I'm also president of the CYO and have been for over forty years.
[The CYO, or Catholic Youth Organization of New York, runs a series of diocesan programs and conferences for young people, ministering to their spiritual, social and physical needs. As president, Mr. Grace is responsible for generating financial and community support for CYO activities, which involve nearly 200,000 youths annually.]

Author: You were national chairman of the Thirtieth National Bible Week. Can you describe your work as chairman?

Mr. Grace: I've been chairman once and associate chairman a number of times. We do nothing more than raise money to spread the use of the Bible. That's all that is involved—keeping the Bible before everybody. We get the Book into hotel rooms and different places. All the Marriott hotels have Bibles because the family are strict Mormons and very religious. But everybody isn't a Marriott, you know. It's a good thing to have the Bibles in the hotel rooms because businessmen would never see it otherwise. It takes a lot of PR work. People are getting away from the Bible, just as Catholics are getting away from Confession. Are you a Catholic? Do you see many people in Confession anymore?

Author: You belong to the Knights of Malta, or the Sovereign Military Order of Malta, and are president of the American Association of the Knights. Will you speak about this?

Mr. Grace: Yeah. You do everything you can to get the membership—the Association has fifteen hundred members—to help the sick and the poor all over the world. [To Jack O'Connell] You have the numbers—you can give the numbers of what we've done in the last five years. We've done more in this time than the whole Order has done in history . . .

Mr. O'Connell: In the past five years the American Association has done more in dollars than the entire Order, worldwide, has done in the same period.

Mr. Grace: Well, I make a broad statement. When you specify dollars like that, what else is there, besides dollars? What are you talking—shekels? [Everyone laughs]

Mr. O'Connell: If you measure it in dollars . . .

Mr. Grace: Well, what do you *want* to measure it in? You give me an alternative and I'll consider it.

[The Knights of Malta was begun before the Crusades by early Christians to tend to sick pilgrims who were visiting the Holy Land. These Christians formed the Order under the name of the Hospitallers of St. John of Jerusalem. Later, the Knights became a military order and fought off the invaders of the Holy Land. Today, the Knights, with headquarters in Rome, are a vibrant, worldwide order devoted to helping the poor and sick in many areas of the world. There are forty national associations in thirty-five countries, with three in the United States. The American

Association in New York with fifteen hundred members is the largest in this country and the second largest in the world. Peter Grace is president. In 1983, it formed an alliance with Ameri-Cares Foundation of New Canaan, Connecticut, the world's biggest provider of emergency hospital and medical supplies. Together, they arrange for the distribution of medicines for the needy in Latin America and Third World countries, with the Knights of each country managing the proper distribution.

Author: I have read about the investiture each January of new Knights and Dames in long black robes walking in procession in St. Patrick's Cathedral, and how fascinating and mysterious this is. Do you agree?

Mr. Grace: I think it is. But I'm interested basically in the substance of things and not in pomp and ceremony. Yeah. That ceremony is a big deal and the Cathedral is packed, and the Cardinal is up there and . . . But, I mean, *that's pomp,* it's ceremonial. I'm more interested in the substance.

Author: As supreme commander of W. R. Grace, as someone who travels constantly, as a husband, parent of nine children and grandparent of seventeen children, how do you cope with your day?

Mr. Grace: I get up about 6 A.M. and go to bed about midnight or one o'clock and work constantly in between.

Author: Among the many charities you are involved with, which are your favorites?

Mr. Grace: Mother Teresa. And the next one is Covenant House and Father Bruce Ritter who runs it. He's another big giant. The third is Father Peyton and the Family Rosary Crusade. *Any* devotions to Our Blessed Mother. These are my favorites.

Author: What draws you to a charity?

Mr. Grace: Our Blessed Mother, and the admonition that our Lord gave, *Whatsoever you do for the least of my brethren, you do for me.* That's what Father Ritter does. He takes in these kids who are in prostitution and drugs and alcohol, young kids who have run away from home and have a whole life ahead of them. They're probably the least of our brethren, right? In New York, anyway. I identify these children as the least of our brethren and then we go all out to help. Thus, to answer your question: the Blessed Mother and the least of our brethren. Those are the two criteria. And if anyone can tell me better ones, why I'm open-minded.

[About 50 percent of Mr. Grace's charitable activities are devoted to Catholic causes, the remaining to non-Catholic ones.]

Author: You have delivered many, many dollars in humanitarian aid to the Latin American poor. And it is these poor people who are involved in liberation theology and trying to shackle off their oppression. As an American industrialist and capitalist, what is your feeling about liberation theology?

Mr. Grace: I'm opposed to it. There are better ways of helping the poor. I don't agree with your comment that the poor are trying to unshackle themselves. Yes, some of them are, and some of them aren't. The poor aren't *able* to unshackle themselves or help themselves. Other people—leaders, politicians, economists, businessmen—have to help, and I'm saying liberation theology is not the way to go. Have you read Mike Novak?

[Michael Novak is a fellow at the American Enterprise Institute and publisher of the Catholic monthly *Crisis*.]

Author: No, I haven't.

Mr. Grace: Read his stuff about liberation theology—Jack can get it for you. He writes a helluva lot better than I can write. Keep in mind that Michael Novak is somebody who converted from socialism. There's nothing better than a converted socialist. He was active in the party, worked on all sorts of things, and suddenly said, "Hey, baby, this ain't the way to go." He has written one of the best articles on liberation theology, in or out of a magazine, from *whatever* source. I'll give it to you—he writes better than I do. And he's the guy that was there in the middle of all this liberation and liberal stuff. And he *left* it. He was convinced that was not the way to go. His is a better testimony than mine. He's one of the smartest people in America.

Author: You were a member of the Lay Commission that wrote a response to the Bishop's Pastoral Letter on the Economy. Would you comment on the Bishops' Letter and the Lay Commission response?

[The final draft of the Bishops' Pastoral Letter, called *Economic Justice for All: Catholic Social Teaching and the U.S. Economy*, appeared in November 1986. A controversial document, it presented suggestions toward a Christian way of handling certain economic problems. Among these were raising the minimum wage, vigorous action to remove barriers to full and equal employment for women and minorities, and a vision of economic life whereby no one should keep for his exclusive use what he does not need. In answer, and in defense of our economic system, a group of traditionally minded Catholics formed a Lay Commission under the aegis of the American Catholic Committee, including William Simon, Michael Novak, Alexander Haig, and Peter Grace. Their letter, entitled *Toward the Future: Catholic Social Thought and the U.S. Economy,* appeared in 1984, after the *first* draft of the Bishops' Letter was published.]

Mr. Grace: The whole thrust of the Bishops' Letter was that rich people have to do more for the poor people and you gotta have more social programs. Now we have 986 social programs that amount to $500 billion a year, which is about 70 percent more than the defense budget. And it's breaking us. When Kennedy was president, the social programs amounted to $38.5 billion or 5.8 percent of the gross national product. Now they are up to $500 billion or 13.5 percent of the gross national product, and they're not getting much progress. And the Bishops say, "Hey, step that up!" It's crazy. There are so many ways to help the poor. It's not the way they think.

Author: Were you happy with the response that the Lay Commission wrote?

Mr. Grace: I thought it was a good letter.

Author: Do you think it has had any effect on the Bishops?

Mr. Grace: Yes, on some of them. There are a lot of Bishops—about 350. They are organized in such a way under the banner of the National Conference of Catholic Bishops [NCCB] that about 10 or 15 run it. In other words, about 335 of the Bishops just go along, and I don't know how many of these really believe in the Letter on the Economy.

Author: One proposal in the Bishops' Letter is based on a quotation from Pope Paul VI's document *On Promoting the Development of Peoples,* published in March 1967, which says:

> *Private property does not constitute for anyone an absolute or uncon-*
> *ditioned right. No one is justified in keeping for his exclusive use what*
> *he does not need when others lack necessities.*

My husband and I have a small second house on Long Island, so according to the Bishops, we shouldn't keep it. I'm bothered by this.

Mr. Grace: [Pretending to be stern] No, you shouldn't keep it. I'm kidding. The idea is that there has always been the poor and there has always been the middle class, and so on. If you go way back in history, you'll find the poor. You can't get rid of the poor. I mean, no matter what you do for them, some people are either ill, or unmotivated, or mentally screwed up in one way or another, and you're never going to eliminate poverty.

What you do to help the poor is everything you can—within what you believe is your state in life—that is justifiable with God telling you, *Whatever you do for the least of my brethren, you do for me.* Whatever your conscience is clear with. If you have a second home on Long Island, you should not worry about that. I've talked with some wonderful holy priests on this subject. . . .

I have three or four homes. I got one on Long Island, I got one in Florida, one in Maine and one in Massachusetts. I have nine children and seventeen grandchildren. The only time we can get them together is at the Maine house. Everybody comes to Maine and it's wonderful for the family. In Massachusetts, I have a house next to a Trappist monastery. And then Florida—as people get older, they need Florida and the kids come down. I don't feel at all guilty about this. If I had a mansion with ten servants, I might feel different.

I was brought up in a huge household with sixty-eight servants and a yacht and twenty-eight crew members and a place in Scotland with eighty or one hundred people. In today's world, that might not be in keeping with what we're talking about, but I was brought up that way. I'm living at about one one-hundredth of the way I was raised as a child, and I don't think I'm overdoing it. We have a maid and a cook and a guy that helps clean around the house. Questions like *Why don't you have your wife do all the cooking? Why aren't you washing the dishes? Why aren't you mowing the lawn?* are all nonsense. It's not necessary at all. And if someone says to me *Why do you have a place in Florida? You don't have to go to Florida. Give it to the poor*—that's all baloney, too.

Furthermore, the Bishops don't realize that if I, or a thousand people like me, really felt that they could live only with what they needed, they probably wouldn't work very hard. You know, people are selfish: we're born that way, and we have to fight it within ourselves. But born selfish as we are, if everybody followed the Bishops' suggestions, no one would bother working. Let's take the head of General Motors, the head of Ford Motor Company: if they're not allowed to have any more than they need and have to give the rest away, I don't think they'd be working that hard to make the company prosper, do you? Therefore, the economy would be much weaker and everybody would be worse off. So it's crazy, that's really crazy. [To Jack O'Connell] You wouldn't work as hard as you do if you could only live in a small, tiny house and nothing else, no vacation trips?

Mr. O'Connell: That's right.

Mr. Grace: Just what you need . . . that's all you can keep. Would you work this hard?

Mr. O'Connell: You wouldn't, no.

Mr. Grace: Nobody would.

Mr. O'Connell: And who would create the jobs for other people? If people like you didn't work hard, there wouldn't be jobs. Or like the head of General Motors. You are the people who create jobs.

Mr. Grace: We've got a business now where we're creating a thousand new jobs. We wouldn't do that if we couldn't keep some of the rewards. You can't say to someone, "Hey, you have an apartment on Park Avenue. Move over to the West Side—a small apartment in the basement." The answer would be, "Fine. Bye-bye. I'm not going to work ninety hours a week on this project just to give everything I don't need away."

There's one last thing I want to say. The Bishops are assuming that everybody is a saint, and *they're* not even saints. Half of them are going around being uncharitable and high-hat and everything else. They're not coming *close* to being saints. Why do they think that other people should be saints and work their asses off morning, noon and night to give away everything they don't need? They would not do that; *they* wouldn't do it. They're not saints and it's silly for them to think other people are.

Now, you suggest this to Saint Augustine or Saint Francis. *They'd do that.* But how many saints are there? Mother Teresa does that; she might say, "Right now, everything, give it all away!" But people aren't going to do that. And as Jack said, there wouldn't be any jobs created because they wouldn't bother to work that hard. They'd hardly work at all, maybe just enough, maybe to give some away. But they wouldn't work morning, noon and night, wake up in the middle of the night worrying about bonds, making notes . . . falling out of bed in the morning after traveling from Japan for twelve hours, not slept the whole night, and go back to work. Yeah. Nobody'd do that, *and neither would the Bishops.*

Mr. Bona: He doesn't feel very strongly on this point. [Laughs]

Mr. Grace: I think it's crazy.

Author: Just a few more questions. I know that you're . . .

Mr. Bona: [To Mr. Grace] You've spoken for thirty-one minutes.

Mr. Grace: I have to go to this service. [To Mr. O'Connell] Are you going?

Mr. O'Connell: You mean to the Mass? No, I'm not.

Mr. Grace: Who is going?

Mr. O'Connell: The Doyles and Pat Ryan.

Mr. Grace: What time is the Mass?

Mr. O'Connell: At 5:30.

Author: Five more minutes?

Mr. Grace: Sure.

Author: Is it true that your father, Joseph, built and financed the Catholic church in Aiken, South Carolina, where he had a winter home, because his was the only Catholic family there and there was no church?

Mr. Grace: His brother was there, too. I don't know how they divided that up—I believe they both provided the funds, but I can't say for sure. My father didn't tell me what he was planning. I remember that the year my father was dying, Monsignor Smith, who was the pastor there, came up from South Carolina and lived in the house for eight days, praying every day over his body. So my father must have done a hell of a lot for him, but I can't tell you that he built the church.

Author: Is it still there?

Mr. Grace: Oh, yeah. St. Mary's Church in Aiken.

Author: What do you feel is your greatest contribution, as a philanthropist, businessman, to your fellow Catholics?

Mr. Grace: In the first place, I don't believe anybody should be proud of anything. Start with that. When you say, what is my greatest . . . that's not in keeping with the way I think and I don't believe it's right. If one said to Christ, *What was the best thing you did—get nailed to the Cross?*, what would he say?

Author: [Gasps, then laughs]

Mr. Grace: I don't believe in that kind of thinking.

Author: All right.

Mr. Grace: *Do the best.* The best thing to do is to do your best. Every tombstone should read, *He did his best.* That's about all you can do. Let God decide what was the best or worst. Yeah. I don't know the answer to that.

Author: Since Vatican II ended, do you believe the Church has gotten better or worse?

Mr. Grace: All I know is, I'm a bottom-line businessman. When the profits go up, you're doing good, and vice versa. Since Vatican II, the Church has deteriorated massively: nobody goes to Confession, few people go to Mass. The bottom line is, the Church is a helluva lot worse than it was. But some people think it's great—I don't know. One good thing is the Charismatic Movement that draws some very, very religious people in healing, the laying on of hands. There's much more dedication in small groups—maybe that came out of Vatican II.

If the Church were a private enterprise or government, and everything got this much worse, they'd say the whole program stinks. Vatican II hasn't improved anything that I can see. The bottom line is fewer people going to church, fewer people going to Confession. It is certainly a lot worse than when I was young.

I mean, *then* the churches were crowded. On Saturday nights, you couldn't get into a confessional. People had respect for priests, and Bishops stayed out of politics and concentrated on bringing the Word of God to the people. Now they're in every issue going on. Their job is to bring the Word of God, and they're *not* bringing the Word of God. And they're thinking, "Well, if we can't deliver the Word, if we can't do that well, let's get into economics, let's get into condoms."

But of course, the main thing—and this is *not* depressing—is that God's in his heaven and He knows what we're going through. He's very merciful and loving.

Author: One last question, and then you're free. Are you happy to have been born a Catholic?

Mr. Grace: Oh, yes. *The greatest thing that ever happened to me.* It would have been terrible not to have been born a Catholic.

Author: Why do you say that?

Mr. Grace: Because the faith is so comforting. Just like I said to you, it's not discouraging when you know that God's in his heaven, merciful and loving. And I have been able to say that sincerely because I'm a Catholic. I'm not saying that people who aren't Catholic can't say that either, but in my opinion, the surest way to get close to God is to be a Catholic.

Jacqueline Grennan Wexler

Jacqueline Grennan Wexler

A SPIRITUAL JOURNEY

I would hope, I would pray, I would press that the Church make a public confession of this most mortal sin of anti-Semitism in its institutional past life. I speak of an act of public contrition.

Over two decades ago Mrs. Wexler was perhaps the most talked-about nun of the era when she was Sister Jacqueline of the Sisters of Loretto in St. Louis, Missouri. An educational innovator, she transformed Webster College in St. Louis, a Catholic college for women, into a secular institution, thus changing the complexion of Catholic education for women throughout the nation. She was the implementer, as well, of other educational concepts that today are readily employed.

A deeply reflective woman with a fine intellect, she asked for permission to be dispensed from her vows after nineteen years of sisterhood. In the ensuing years she became president of Hunter College in New York City, and she married. Today she is president of the National Conference of Christians and Jews, a position she deems the most stimulating she has ever held.

If anyone is representative of a new Catholic woman, Mrs. Wexler might be that person. What her life illustrates more than anything is a sense of quest and questioning: quest for change and continuity, and questioning of Catholic doctrine that must withstand scrutiny. In all of this, she has been inextricably bound to, and a loyal member of, the Catholic

Church, which she deeply loves. Mrs. Wexler thought a long time before agreeing to this interview. Life is movement, but always preceded by careful reflection.

All my life I have been fascinated by, and committed to, continuity and change. I think that unless we keep our lifeline fundamentally continuous, we cease to be who we are. Continuity is part of our integrity. At the same time, continuity implies movement, forward movement, and growth, and that growth comes by our openness to what you and I were introduced to in the Baltimore Catechism as actual grace. Over and over I recall the Catechism's definition: *Actual grace is a person, or place, or thing (a book, a lecture) which becomes an occasion for our growth in the divine life.* I believe that important communications beyond cocktail-party chatter, certainly our espousals—our marriages, our lifelong friendships—but also sometimes brief encounters in which the exchange is beyond words, are such actual graces. We individually incorporate into ourselves the richness of what is shared with us by others.

Sometimes sharing is scary: it's discontinuous and it takes a great deal of time and contemplation and suffering and risk for us to find the *wholeness*, the *continuity* for ourselves. The best of my Catholic education—from the Sisters of Loretto who educated me from the first grade through college and then all of my nineteen years of religious life as a Sister of Loretto, as well as from my wonderful Irish Catholic parents, farmers in Illinois, and my family tribe there—the best of that education, I think, supported this idea of sharing of oneself, of always being open to the other person *all the while having faith in our faith.* That is the other concept that drives my life. Faith is *not* certainty, or why should we need faith? Faith in one's parents, faith in one's spouse, faith in one's friends, faith in the colleagues with whom one works, faith in one's country and in one's church, are deep espousals *but never absolute formulas.*

In dealing with sin, the Baltimore Catechism, which nurtured our most formative years, told us that mortal sin requires grievous matter, sufficient reflection and full consent of the will. Modern life confronts us with decisions of very grievous matter. Look at the turmoil in our Church today on questions of the dignity of life. Consider Cardinal Bernardin's thoughtful statement on the wholeness of the fabric of the issues involving the dignity of life—just war, the right to die, capital punishment, and abortion. There is no doubt that our Church says every one of these issues is a very grievous matter. I would expect her to remind all of us as Catholics that sufficient reflection on these issues is a heavy moral responsibility and that full consent of the will is a very, very decisive act. I am profoundly grateful for the role of my Church in making me a morally responsible person. It has allowed me, in what seems to some persons to have been a life of discontinuities, to see myself as a very continuous person and to see my espousal of my Church as an abiding faith commitment.

As a member of the Sisters of Loretto for nineteen years, I know something about sisterhood. I believe that the Catholic religious orders in the United States, at least a great number of them and certainly the Sisters of Loretto, were indeed the precursors of what the women's movement was to call "sisterhood." They provided for each other a marvelous supporting network, a footing that helped these women not only become their individual selves, but to share the critique and support of a network of people in a wonderful tribal family. This has been one of the greatest strengths of those of us who were part of Roman Catholic sisterhoods in the middle of this century.

In the initial years of my life with the Sisters of Loretto, from about 1948 until about 1960, we were untroubled by the direct intervention of the Church. We had very little encounter with the Church.

However, in that period around 1960, when the world of John XXIII, the world of John Kennedy, and the world of the Sister Formation Movement occurred almost simultaneously, things changed. The Sister Formation Movement of the late fifties was led by Sisters—today they would be considered quite conservative— who were determined that Roman Catholic Sisters get first-class educations in the best universities. They would have preferred them to go to Catholic universities, but they primarily wanted them to get very good undergraduate and graduate educations. Here was a group of women very committed to the Church, to the social service of the Church, who saw living the grace life as serving and nurturing others through teaching, nursing and social service. Now we were being very well educated, better educated than our opposite numbers who had chosen to marry and have families, for the simple reason that we had uninterrupted opportunity to lead fully professional lives. Many of us became managers of institutions, as I did on becoming president of Webster College in Missouri. We also were gaining experience that served us well as we took on corporate responsibilities. When you take on responsibility for institutions, for people in those institutions, you learn on the job that you can't simply throw off the consequences of your decisions.

The hierarchy was astounded at this transformation. They were in no way ready to understand or accept religious women as mature and independent decision-makers. Cardinals, Bishops, priests were incredulous. Cardinal Ritter [Cardinal Joseph Ritter of the St. Louis Archdiocese], who was a fairly liberal Cardinal, certainly on race relations, said to me in the mid-sixties when I was in the headlines a good deal, "No one in your degree of public life should be a Sister."

I remember asking him with the freshness of naïveté, "But, Your Eminence, what about Father Reinert of St. Louis University and Father Hesburgh of Notre Dame?" Both these priests were often in the news.

The Cardinal never responded.

There were many people in St. Louis at this point who told me that if I had been *Father* Jack Grennan, life would have been very different.

This attitude toward the educated Sisters on the part of the hierarchy became a real burden. But another problem was arising that was much more important and equally difficult. For a number of years before I was dispensed from my vows, I had been struggling with the question of whether or not I could take full responsibility as chief executive of Webster College and still be subject in my decision-making to the power of a church that had no legal fiduciary responsibility for the college. In speeches at that time, I asked:

> *Would you trust a university that was accountable to Standard Oil?*
> *Would you trust a university that was accountable to a political party?*

The comparison with the Catholic Church was implicit.

However, never did I say, and never would I say, that secularistic institutions are better than religious ones. I was addressing only *juridical* control of an institution by the Church. There is no question that the Roman Catholic faith continues to inform many of the colleges that have been secularized, and in many ways Webster College itself. The Church is deep in its memory genes, deep in its lifeline; it is part of the continuity that is not subject to juridical control.

The problem for me was that I was vowed not just to the Sisters of Loretto, but to the juridical Roman Catholic Church. And I simply made the decision that for me to remain a devout Roman Catholic, it was necessary to free myself of that special juridical control of canon law. [In 1967, Mrs. Wexler was dispensed from her vows.] The analogy that might be helpful was the position of millions of Americans during the Vietnam War. You could remain a very patriotic committed American and be against the Vietnam War. Had you been a military person and been pressed into the service to fight in Vietnam, I think that in order to remain a faithful American, you would have had to resign from the military. To remain a committed Catholic, I asked for a dispensation from my vows to free myself of the hierarchical military control of the Church.

The Lorettines had come to a major decision themselves in this period. Through a lot of shared pain and challenge, they had come to the conviction that the Church ought to travel light, without owning and operating a network of institutions. The Superior General of the order asked me to work out a transition of the control of Webster College from that order, which would, of course, remain under the juridical control of the Church, to a lay board of trustees. It became for me a double challenge: first, to find a way to remain a devout Roman Catholic and certainly a lifelong member of the tribal family of the Sisters of Loretto and, secondly, to find a way for the Lorettines to free themselves from being directly accountable for an institution under state law and yet answerable to a church for some of the decisions made in view of state law. We worked very hard to effect a solution. At times, it was torturous.

Essentially, this is how the secularization of Webster College came about. The Sisters of Loretto made a direct request to Cardinal Ritter to "alienate the property." That's a phrase in canon law that means that in order for a religious group to sell or trade property, permission is needed from the proper hierarchical level to yield that property. Wanting to do this legally, the Sisters asked for official permission to turn the property over to a lay board of trustees. The Cardinal sent the request to Rome. It was a very "iffy" situation. We had informal word that the request would not be granted. It was at that point that I made the decision to ask for a dispensation from my vows. But the Superiors weren't at all sure that the hierarchy would allow me to remain president as a lay-person. I wrote the Cardinal and told him about my request for a dispensation, explaining that I had come to agree with him that no woman in my degree of public view could be a Roman Catholic Sister at that time, but that I hoped to remain at Webster College to nurture a secular institution in which the power of the Christian presence remains a real and productive force. If this were not possible, I told him I would accept a position in some other institution of higher education or in government. In either case, I asked for his blessing. He never answered directly but he did tell a businessman-intermediary that he would accept my decision.

Four months later Rome gave approval for the property transfer. No one will ever know what the background actions were. Suddenly, there was enormous turmoil in our lives. We were the very first Catholic college to transfer its fiduciary responsibility to a lay board of trustees. That was part of the problem in some ways—the publicity it generated. We did not set out to do things for publicity, but because we were the first we couldn't avoid the publicity. The Cardinal asked that I take a sabbatical while people got used to the situation. But the Sisters felt that there was no way to go on with the development of plans without my presence and so they effected a compromise in which I did work at the State University of New York and literally commuted for a semester in alternate weeks between St. Louis and New York.

One of the wonderful, bemusing aspects of the transition is that the Sisters of Loretto went the *absolutely legal route* in canon law. They asked for alienation of property, which none of the men's institutions ever did when they transferred board control to lay-people. They simply changed their boards and, as far as I know, have never alienated the property. Perhaps because women, and particularly Sisters, are so much more straightforward about their commitment to the Church, we followed the prescribed regulation.

Since their beginnings, the Lorettines have been committed to the individual needs of those who are to be educated. They were a frontier order born in Kentucky in 1812, intent on taking education to the Southwest where no other women in the world would go to teach. They were part of the Westward Movement, nuns who slept on the open prairie as they traveled to the Southwest in covered wagons. An open approach to people and schooling finally led them, over a century later, to venture into transforming their own school, Webster College, into a secular one.

I have never become cynical about my Church; I simply say she has her limitations. All Catholics, clerical and lay, including me, have limitations. I hope and trust that most of them will be patient with my limitations, as I try to be patient with theirs. Approaching my sixty-second birthday this summer, I am much more free to love and cherish my Church, to disagree with her at times about personal and political matters, *but only after sufficient reflection,* because I take her teaching authority very seriously. She is my great teacher and not my manipulator. The Church more than any other institution—unless my mother could be thought of as an institution—has taught me that I have free will and am responsible for the use of that free will. I cherish that, am humbled by it, and empowered by it.

On some questions, such as sexuality, the Catholic Church can be rigid and even paranoid. I want my Church to be extraordinarily rigorous but *not* rigid. I think she errs by making the issue of abortion the quintessential litmus test for our political candidates. It hurts me precisely because if she could free herself from her rigidity and paranoia, she would liberate herself to be what I think she also is—the graceful teacher whose commitment to marriage and to children is the most dignified, worthy commitment. Rigor is of great value, but rigidity denies rigor. It is very hard to be understood on this question. The most rabid feminist and the most rabid right-to-lifer will both accuse me of selling out. In my opinion, neither believes in rigor; both believe in absolute *yes* or absolute *no.*

Yet I am certainly closer to my Church on the issue of abortion *as a citizen,* not just as a person, than I am to those groups who would say, "A woman has a right to her body any time, any place," and others who make abortion sound like a whimsical decision: "I'll do what I damn well please." So that as a citizen as well as a person, I feel the question of viable life inside the womb has great importance to me. I'm now talking as a citizen who may have some leverage on the decisions of others. If I were counseling anyone considering abortion, Catholic or non-Catholic, I would insist that this is one of the most important decisions anyone can ever make, that there is no decision more weighty than taking a life—whether it's taking a life in just war, or deciding on what steps to take for sustaining life, or applying capital punishment or taking life in the womb. In my judgment, there just are no more important decisions than those. In these cases, grievous matter is absolutely certain; it *is* grievous matter. Sufficient reflection on each one of them is weighted with complications, and what full consent of the will for any individual is I don't know.

On taking-of-human-life issues in general, the Church has a wonderfully good history. For example, she is the most flexible of institutions on certain aspects of death-with-dignity. She has always said, in effect: *You don't have to take extraordinary means to sustain life. You can't directly kill, but you do not have to use complicated means to sustain life that has no future.* Compared to the Church, the medical profession is a reactionary group on that one. I was fifteen when my only brother died of a brain tumor in 1941. The president—also a priest—of the small Catholic college in Iowa where my brother was a student, counseled my mother and father that they did not have to use all of the crazy machinery to keep him alive after there was no hope. The machinery was not as complicated in 1941 as it is today.

On the question of just war, the Church has taken a position almost all of her institutional life that there are just wars, and I do agree with that. I'm not a total pacifist. The reality of Nazi Germany would tell me that I could never be a total pacifist. I am very much at home in my Church on those positions.

Let me conclude this point by saying that I take the teaching authority of the magisterium in our Church very seriously. I take it certainly as seriously as I would take the teaching authority of the best medical professional. *But then, I still believe I have the right and the responsibility to be sufficiently reflective and to make my own decisions.* On most topics I would probably make that decision in consonance with the Church 99.999 percent of the time. I remain a reverent daughter who loves her Church with all her wonders and all her warts.

In 1969, I was offered the presidency of Hunter College in New

York City, which is part of a huge city-university system. I accepted. Being responsible for a small institution you could get your arms around was an important experience to have had before going to Hunter. There was no way I could touch everybody at Hunter in the way that was possible at Webster. But I did bring that kind of view of nurturing people to my responsibilities at Hunter. I tried to devise systems and strategies that would be more likely to have students treated as people. [In the 1970s, Mrs. Wexler guided Hunter College through the political and economic pressures of student demonstrations, open admissions, the severe fiscal problems of New York City, and the changing authority structures of the City University of New York.] I stayed at Hunter for ten years.

Since 1982, I've been president of the National Conference of Christians and Jews. [The National Conference, or NCCJ, is a nationwide human-relations organization with offices in seventy-five cities, whose aim is to serve as a kind of marriage broker to bring together people of all races, religions and ethnic groups. One of its guiding principles is the First Amendment of the Constitution: *Congress shall make no law respecting an establishment of religion, or prohibiting the free exercise thereof; or abridging the freedom of speech, or of the press; or the right of the people peaceably to assemble, and to petition the government for a redress of grievances.*] In this job, I have opportunities and responsibilities that are closer to my personal, professional and philosophical lifeline than anything else I've done.

The founders—Charles Evans Hughes, Jane Addams, William Sloane Coffin, and David DeSolo Poole—said in 1927: "The intergroup problem of the nation rises like a specter in the path of democracy and dares for it to come on." Had they been classical academics, they would have studied this problem for the next twenty years, but instead, they took the dare and formed the National Conference.

The founders declared that this institution would take *all* aspects of pluralism seriously. It would take race and sex and ethnicity and nationalism *and* religious commitment seriously. It would address itself to how individual citizens and groups of citizens in these United States would manage to make the trade-offs and continue to effect the compromises which had to be made to get a Constitution signed in the first place and which have to be made by every generation of Americans if we are to have an ever more workable pluralistic democracy.

I come back to the question *How does each fallible, finite human being make decisions, personal decisions and decisions about how we live together in towns, in states, in this country, and, I hope, sometime in the world community after this generation is gone?* How do we make those decisions, informed by our religious faith, informed by our ethnic tribal memory genes and consciences? How do we make those decisions with each other when those consciences have been, and remain, informed by somewhat different and sometimes very divergent convictions? Unless we can continue to resolve the paradox of commitment and openness rather than turn it into a cynical irony, America will not be a beacon to the world community.

On a personal religious level, the question is vital for me. I am convinced that if there is a person, a presence outside ourselves—and I obviously believe there is, be that person the Triune God of my own faith, or Yahweh, or Allah, or Emerson's transcendental being, or the concept of Buddhism or Hinduism or the Bahais or countless others—it seems to me that God has to have been the common parent of us all. Each of our faiths starts in this way: God is the creator and the sustainer of all human beings. Thus, He/She could never have meant His/Her words as testaments to divide us from one another, hate one another, perpetrate pogroms and religious wars and vicious heresy trials on one another. But rather, He/She must have meant those words as testaments to speak to the individual child or group of children *where they are, in their context, in the way they can learn.*

My two sisters and I live geographically far apart. When we get together, we spend a great deal of time sharing Mother's and Dad's testaments—words—precisely so that none of us misses anything. We want to be sure that in our adult lives we share the nuances each may have heard in different ways when we were young. My most fond hope and prophetic dream is that humankind out there in many, many, many generations after yours and mine will be able to see religious faith in that way.

I believe that Jewish-Christian relations in the United States of America today are profoundly better than they were when I was a child in a little town in Illinois. I was still blissfully unaware of Jewish-Christian problems. In parochial school then, children were still saying "perfidious Jews" in the Good Friday liturgy. I find it mind-blowing that those words could have come out of my mouth on my "highest of high holy days." But they were in the liturgy of the Church and they didn't get into the liturgy without sufficient reflection and full consent of the will of the institutional Church. Again my great love John XXIII personally and through Vatican II exorcised in a major way that devil of anti-Semitism from our institutional history. The decision on the part of Vatican II to recognize two distinct covenants is an incredibly important decision, a monumentally important decision. It says Christianity is a covenant with God but not the *only* covenant with God. It says it in respect to the Jews and may indeed begin to say it for others yet to come. That was a decision of such magnitude I'm not even sure our generation can recognize how important it was. Not just the Pope's decision, but Vatican II's decision.

That event, and living together in America, are two major, *positive,* aspects of Jewish-Christian history. Christians and Jews living together in this wonderfully pluralistic country, with its First Amendment guarantee of protection from state religion and protection of religious worship, has given us a marvelous learning-laboratory novitiate, if you will. It allows us to go on living and learning experientially, not simply going back over the past, but addressing common agendas which Americans have to do in dealing with one another, both in our mercantile life and in our civic life.

In a general sense, the trend line is significantly *up* in Jewish-Christian relations. Obviously, like all improving situations, expectancies go up and so whenever there is a *down* trend, whenever there is a setback, we are far more aware of it. In recent times, the Waldheim affair, for instance, was clearly that kind of setback. But it was a setback that would have surprised no one before Vatican II. It is precisely because of the monumental, macro change in Vatican II that people are scandalized that it happened. On the other hand, many Catholics don't yet understand *why* there was such a furor about Waldheim. They say, *Can't the Pope as head of the Vatican state have the right to receive anybody?* These Catholics don't yet recognize the wrong—the institutional anti-Semitism—that allowed you and me to say "perfidious Jews" in the thirties and forties in parochial school and in our Good Friday liturgy. The Pope as the symbol of authority in the lifeline of the Church is a critically important symbol and carries the burden of the sins of omission and commission in the anti-Semitic history of our Church. My biggest reason for hope for the future is that in the discussions that followed the Waldheim affair, the Pope and some of the Vatican officials committed themselves to a serious, long study of anti-Semitism in the Church. That's the most important thing our Church could do in this area.

I would hope, I would pray, I would press that the Church make a public confession of this most mortal sin of anti-Semitism in its institutional past life. I speak of an act of public contrition. She would be most loyal and faithful to herself if she could do that. She would be going to the very depths, to the profundity of her theological teaching on contrition. And if she could, then, forever exorcise that devil, free herself of that cancer, she would be much more free to be graceful and gracing within herself and to be credible to the Jewish people about what she says now. Such an action would also be a great challenge to the Jewish people. Suppose the person of Jesus could be freed of the menacing symbol of the Cross raised in pogroms. The Jewish people would thus be challenged to have as much respect for the significant other of Christianity, certainly of Jesus Christ, as we are challenged to have respect for the significant other of Judaism.

One big advantage the Catholic Church has in view of this problem is that she has institutionally dealt with it in Vatican II.

The National Conference of Christians and Jews will be, I think, my last executive responsibility. After that, there are some things I would like to write about if I can discipline myself to do this. It is important that a history of Roman Catholic Sisters from about 1950 moving toward the year 2000 be done. I used to think I was too close to write about it. I am often told that I may be one of the few people who now has enough aesthetic distance but also enough investment and continuing commitment to trace that history. That's long been in the back of my mind. Years ago, David Riesman, the Harvard sociologist, told me while I was still a Sister that the Sisters' Movement might be one of the most profound examples of *radical change with continuity* that he has perceived. I also believe that. That is the way I would like to try to understand and communicate it—both in itself and for what it means as a model for the way other institutions can go through profound change with continuity.

Looking back, I never feel that I "left" the sisterhood. Rather, I was dispensed from my vows. I no more left the Sisters of Loretto than I left my farm family. True, I left my farm home but not my farm family. I still go back to tribal gatherings, and see my sisters once a year. When my parents were alive, I returned every month to Sterling and Rock Falls in Illinois. I certainly went home every month while my mother was alone and living in a home. I reverenced her. She was wonderful.

For the past eighteen years, I have been married to a man of the Jewish faith, Paul Wexler, who was a widower. I had the blessing of inheriting two Jewish children—a son and a daughter—from his first marriage. Our marriage has not posed any particular problems for him or me. We married at a mature age when the possibility of our having children was very small. We have not had any. I think the real problem in a mixed marriage is what to do about children, and I obviously have not had to deal with that. Paul recognizes that a profoundly important quality of the woman he cherishes is her Roman Catholic faith and lineage. He loves my Sisters of Loretto and goes to the motherhouse to visit with me. If we're out of town or out of the country on Sunday, he often goes to Mass with me. He certainly doesn't when I go to my own parish. Like so many Jews, he is not a formal Temple Jew. He has enormous reverence for his mother, who is in her middle nineties and lives in a marvelous Jewish home. He cherishes her integrity as a devout Conservative Jew. She loves me; I've never been able to do any wrong in her eyes. For her, I think, my being a professor is more important than my being a *shiksa*. Looking back, it strikes me that from the first day Paul and I spent together, the thing we recognized about each other was our shared reverence and devotion for family—he to that Jewish mother, and I to my Roman Catholic farmer parents. That reverence may tell you more about the spiritual life of a person than anything else.

I have been on a continuing voyage or odyssey in which I have tried to have the courage to be large-minded and openhearted *and to have the faith to know that's risky.* I want to remain connected to, and invested in and by, all of the important persons and institutions that have nourished me. My great mentor and second mother, Sister Francetta Barberis, picked up the saying of a French poet: *"Life is a mystery to be lived, and not a problem to be solved."*

Francetta added to it by saying: *"Life is a mystery to be lived and loved, and not a problem to be solved."*

Indeed, we have to solve little problems every day and sometimes big ones. But in the end I do believe life is a mystery to be lived and loved, and not a problem to be solved. I take some degree of joy in not knowing where the future will go. If life is good enough to let Paul and me live to be very old together, I have a fair idea of where I'm going. If it doesn't work out that way, I'll have to think all over again. But rather than approach life as a series of options or a long-range plan, as in business, I would rather live it as a mystery, to be lived and loved, and apply the best that's in me to solve what problems come along the way.

Bill Reel at the lectern of a Brooklyn church

Bill Reel

ONE CHURCH, LOST AND FOUND

> *One of the unfortunate things about being a Catholic is that it's practically impossible to be a good one.*

Bill Reel has had a long, involved relationship with religion, a subject that keeps cropping up frequently in the things he says and writes. His triweekly column on big-city life for the New York *Daily News* is peopled not only with figures like Mayor Koch, Donald Trump, funny Irish guys, his sources Splash and Hoople (both denizens of a Brooklyn diner), but respected churchmen like Bishop Paul Moore, Reverend Jesse Jackson, Father Bruce Ritter and not-so-respected reverends like Jim Bakker, Al Sharpton and Jimmy Swaggart. A former religion writer on the *News* and a Catholic-of-sorts, Bill Reel is a quiet, lyric voice of religious urban culture.

His personal connection with the Catholic religion has shaped—and saved—his life. What follows is a moving account of exploration and discovery, including an addiction and cure that finally brought him release from a particular bondage.

I began to take Catholicism seriously in my late teens and early twenties. As a sophomore at Yale, I got involved with a group of guys who were Catholic. They went to Mass every morning and knew a lot about the Catholic Church and I knew nothing, even though I had been raised in a family where the grandparents—my mother's mother and my father's father—were practicing Catholics. They had lost their spouses and went to Mass regularly. My sister and I would go to Church with them; neither of my parents was a churchgoer. Despite my religious lapses in later life, my grandparents had a great influence on me, and to this day, the example they set—you know the old saying, *People would rather see a sermon than hear one*—still holds.

I grew up in Canaan, Connecticut, and went to a nearby Episcopal prep school, Salisbury School, where we went to chapel every morning. The people who ran the school were all just impeccable. Very good people. That was a WASPy scene and I didn't quite fit in; my father was a mailman and I was a day student, coming from very modest means. Most of these guys had money. My father was "trying to improve the breed"—that was his expression—so he sent me there.

At Yale, I rediscovered the Church. In my sophomore year, I had a kind of emotional crisis and didn't know what to do. One night I went to St. Thomas More Chapel and met a fellow there named Frank Arricale who today is an official in the New York City school system. Frank wasn't a student, but he was friendly with the Yale chaplain, who asked him to come up to Yale occasionally and talk to the students. Frank was from the Bronx and had gone all through the seminary but wasn't ordained. I walked over to see him and remember being depressed. I had been drinking too much.

"I really don't know why I'm here. I feel kind of down. . . ."

"It was the grace of God that brought you here."

At that time the phrase, *the grace of God,* meant nothing to me. I had never heard it. It isn't a country expression; it's a city line. You don't usually hear people say *the grace of God* in rural Connecticut or in prep schools or at Yale. In the late fifties and sixties Catholics were a real minority group at Yale, not embattled or anything, but a minority.

Frank kind of got me. He talked to me and said, "Well, you should go to Church."

But I didn't really have an understanding or any knowledge of the Church. I'd never read the New Testament and barely knew what the Sacraments were. I had that sort of vague cultural sense that you have as a kid: *You go to Mass on Sunday, and it's a sin if you miss, and you can't eat meat on Friday and anything to do with sex is wrong.* And perhaps a sense of God being vengeful. In later years I've come to appreciate that line in the hymn "Amazing Grace"—

" 'Twas Grace that taught my heart to fear/And Grace my fear relieved." There's a wonderful paradox here in the sense that you have to be afraid of the consequences of defying God before you can open yourself up to receive the grace of God and achieve peace.

That Yale period, the late fifties and early sixties, was the fear-of-God period of my life and I didn't get much relief from it. I was mainly just afraid. Anxious. Insecure. Alcohol was my escape, as I was very much preoccupied with self-gratification. But in any event, I became aware of these religious realities and began to develop a conscience and to realize that materialism—as much as I was always chasing pleasure—results in emptiness.

As a result of this meeting with Arricale, I came to know a group of guys at Yale who were daily communicants. The leader was John Guarnaschelli, a graduate student in history, who had gone to Holy Cross. He was an extremely lovable guy, brilliant, who had you laughing all the time. He dazzled me with his wit—I had never met anyone like this. Then there was a guy named Al Lavalle, another Holy Cross graduate, who was studying English literature. There was Steve Clark, who was one of the architects of the whole Pentecostal movement in the Church in the 1970s. He's part of an Ann Arbor–Notre Dame crowd who were the first people involved in both the Charismatic and Pentecostal movements of the Church. Paul Robinson, now a professor at Stanford University, was in the group. Another member was Chris Lydon, who is the anchorman on the public-television news up in Boston. On the phone Chris was telling me the other night that he left the Church right after Yale. So many of these guys have left. I think the only ones still in it are Steve Clark and myself. And I didn't stay with it right from there.

I tagged along with this set, but on the fringe. They were very intellectual and well read and knew a lot more about Catholicism than I did. Underneath I was a guy who was a typical college boy. None of them was a sports buff, but I was always playing basketball and going to games, and doing plenty of drinking and no studying. But along with that was a sense of the spiritual dimension of things.

Being in the process of flunking out of Yale, I decided to quit before they threw me out. I went to Frank Arricale for advice. When he learned what was happening, he got me a job at a Catholic orphanage on Staten Island, where I stayed for a year and a half, 1960–1962. It was a home for dependent children, called St. Michael's; it's out of business now. It was my first real taste of

Catholic culture; there were nuns, priests, everybody living by strict rules. All the counselors came from Catholic backgrounds. It was then that I began to appreciate the Catholic culture that figures so much in my columns today—the funny Irish guys. This was around 1960–1961, a time when the Catholic Church was at its peak.

In 1962, I went back to Yale. By that time my drinking was out of hand. Drinking and studying didn't mix and after six months, I flunked out. I came to New York, got a job as a copyboy on the *Daily News* and carried on for the next several years. One day, I telephoned my old girlfriend from Albertus Magnus, Suellen Norkin, whom I dated while at Yale. She was working in Washington. We started seeing each other and wound up getting married in 1964. And, of course, we were married in church. In New Haven, she went through St. Mary's High School as well as Albertus Magnus College, both run by the Dominican Sisters. Her parents owned the Sea Cliff Inn in East Haven, which is now Amaranti's. Even after marriage, my drinking was pretty heavy—I remember complaining about having to drive my wife to New Haven to visit her family. I didn't want to be bothered—I wanted to drink. In New York, my wife got a job as a programmer with UNIVAC and she was great at it. It's a shame I couldn't bear children and have her continue working. We'd be rich today.

While I was employed at St. Michael's on Staten Island, I met a man who became very important in my life, probably the most important person, Father Joseph Riordan, who was then an assistant pastor. We became friendly. After I started working at the *Daily News,* I called him up one day to say hello. It was during the 114-day strike at the paper in 1962–1963.

"Let's have dinner," he said.

He took me out to dinner and, as he dropped me off, handed me a $100 bill. Now, in 1963, a $100 bill—that thing looked like the size of a football field. By the way, it took me years to pay him back.

"When your mother was in trouble with me, she called a priest," I've often told my kids. After my drinking got completely out of hand and my wife was really worried, she called Father Riordan. It's an interesting thing to me how important a priest is. A priest is someone you reach out to in desperate circumstances. He came over and told me what I ought to do about my drinking. When I was dying of a fatal disease, alcoholism, he's the guy that directed me to help.

"Okay. You go see these people," he said.

And he pointed me in the direction of recovered alcoholics—other men and women who had come to terms with their disease and were applying spiritual principles in their lives to recover. I did the same and that was in 1968. I stopped drinking, and my life changed. I saw spiritual principles in a different light and began to understand that God is merciful, that if you turn your life and will over to the care of God, He will relieve you of obsessions like the one I had with alcohol. And that God works through other people who have had problems at one time or another.

As a result of coming to understand these truths, I got interested in the Church more and more and began to listen to the New Testament when it was read at Mass. I also began to appreciate the wisdom of a book like Thomas Merton's *Life and Holiness*. A little book about this size [uses hands] which talks about spiritual principles, things like the power of prayer, the way prayer works in your life, the way to be less conscious of your own problems and try to identify with other people's. You know, Saint Francis's idea that you should *Seek not so much to be consoled as to console, to be loved as to love, to be understood as to understand.* That type of spirituality is very, very important in my life today. One of the ways I continue to be conscious of my religion is to do spiritual reading, go to church on Sunday, and read the New Testament.

The Pope would not consider me a good Catholic, though, because of the birth-control situation. It's one of the unfortunate things about being a Catholic; it's practically impossible to be a good one. There are some things that are true *and* impossible, and the birth-control thing may be one of them. At least, impossible for me, and that's not a copout. But I'm not criticizing the Pope. I love the Pope; I wouldn't knock a word he says. He seems to be a highly intelligent guy. As difficult as the teachings are that he upholds, I appreciate the fact that there is at least one guy out there who is saying sex isn't for recreation. And thank God the Pope is anti-abortion. There ought to be at least one such person left. If the Pope ever came out for free love and abortion, then we might as well write everything off. He stands for something. He stands for civilization. He stands for holiness. He stands for devout practices.

Generally, I don't quarrel with the teachings of the Church. It is the most fascinating institution in the world; it's one of those inexhaustible outfits. There are a certain few things on earth that are so interesting that whatever you say about them, the opposite is also true. Brooklyn is one of those things. Anything you say about Brooklyn, the opposite is also true. In some places Brooklyn is going to hell. Absolutely true. But it's renewing itself someplace else. What's true of Brooklyn is true of the Catholic Church. You can say it's disintegrating, but it's always regenerating. While church attendance will be falling off in some areas, the parish renewal movement and work with the homeless will be growing in others. Like Father Bruce Ritter who started up Covenant House in Times Square with five or ten street kids and next thing you know, he's got six or seven places all over the country to help street kids.

In my column, Catholicism is a subject I like to bring up since I'm familiar with it. The editors find the column a little too heavy on Catholic matters sometimes. They're not opposed for ideological reasons, but they'd like to get me off that kick. Colleagues and readers have said I'm too churchy. But I don't feel *compelled* to write about Catholicism, or religion. You see, I consider myself more of a spiritual person than a religious one. A lot of the Catholic stuff in the column results from years of covering the Church as a religion editor, and I have a residue of thoughts and ideas on the subject.

In today's Church, when you consider what liberal attitudes have wrought, you almost crave for aged monsignors to come back and tell you that you'll go blind if you play with yourself. It's almost gotten to the point when you wish they were back talking that nonsense again because the reaction *against* that nonsense has been worse than the nonsense. We've got practically every high-school girl in Brooklyn running around pregnant and we have AIDS and herpes problems. A general decadence has set in. I don't know whether you can blame the Church in any sense, but it's interesting that the liberalization in the Church's teachings has been accompanied by this terrible decadence we see all around us.

As I look back at all the things that were supposed to be so bad about the old Church, I'm not sure how bad they actually were. The priests and nuns whacked a few people around. But I can argue both sides on this because I know a million guys who complain about the nuns and Brothers beating them up, but they'd be the first to tell you that they were bad guys who *deserved* a beating. I heard a guy say once, "Well, at least they cared enough about me to hit me."

Joe Paterno, the football coach at Penn State, spoke at a luncheon

I was at recently, which was given in his honor by some antipornography group. Cardinal John O'Connor was there and a lot of Evangelical Christians (one place where the Evangelicals and the Catholics meet happily is on the antipornography and the antiabortion fronts). Joe is a Brooklyn boy and certainly the outstanding college football coach of this era, a guy who has turned down chances to go pro. In fact, Wellington Mara once offered him the Giants job and he refused it, saying, "I like to work with the kids. I think I can do something for them."

At the luncheon, Joe got up to speak.

"It was a wonderful thing to grow up when I did in an era when the Church told you what was right and wrong. It's not like the kids today who have to find out for themselves. When I was in the first grade at St. Edmond's in Brooklyn, my cousin Frankie and I were throwing chalk at the blackboard. This big Irish Dominican nun came in, called me up in front of the room, made me put my arm out and she hit me a shot, BOOM!"

Joe is at the podium telling this, and there's Cardinal O'Connor sitting up there, probably saying to himself, "Geez, I gotta listen to another one of these . . ."

"BOOM!" Joe Paterno is a real Brooklyn Italian. He's got the hands and he's got the gestures.

"BOOM! I went home," Joe continued, "and my mother said, 'Joey, what's the matter?' She saw I was upset. 'Aw, Sister hit me.' "

"BOOM! My mother knocked me right across the kitchen."

"Wha-a-a-a . . . ?"

"That's for getting Sister mad at you."

How bad was that? I mean, look at Joe Paterno today, an outstanding role model, a guy who makes a tremendous impression on people. There's no end to the guys that I could find who would say that the interest the nuns and priests took in them was important. What about me and Monsignor Riordan? I could have died drunk if he didn't take an interest. Soon as my wife called, he came right over.

The problem today is that there's not enough priests for them to come right over. They're stretched too thin. Sunday night, I had a priest in my house for dinner. Great guy, Father Tom Bergin. He's the principal of Monsignor Farrell High School on Staten Island, which is probably the finest Catholic high school in New York City, excellent school, all boys, an old-fashioned type of place. He was telling me that on that Sunday, he said five Masses—two in one church and three in another—because they're stretched so thin. This guy's a full-time principal, and he's got to preach. By the time he'd finished preaching at the fifth Mass, he was pretty tired. He's fifty-three years old. How long can he keep that up?

Was Vatican II successful? Let's put it this way and talk numbers. Suppose you were running a club and in 1962, you said, *All right, now we've got a group here with one hundred members but it's a little stodgy and we've got a lot of old-fashioned practices. We've got to renew ourselves. We'll loosen our ties, not get dressed up for every meeting and be more informal.* You call all your members and you have sit-downs every week. *We're going to draft a new constitution and get away from this old idea of discipline, discipline, discipline. We're going to be more free and easy, open ourselves up to other people, be more accepting of outsiders. We're not going to be quite as exclusive as we used to be.* And you did all that, and everybody said, "This is terrific."

Twenty-five years later you have thirty members instead of one hundred.

How successful were you? Could you really say, "Wasn't this a tremendous breakthrough?" You had one hundred members, then you renewed yourselves and now you've got thirty. Look at the Sisters of Charity. They're going to be out of business by the year 2000. There were thousands of them all over the place teaching school. All these parochial schools are going to go under. It's got to happen. Father Bergin was telling me that his tuition at Farrell has gone from $15 a month, or $135 a year, in 1963 to $1,750 a year, and he has to get $450 a year for each kid from other sources. There is such a shortage of priests and brothers that he has to hire lay teachers to staff the school, and that shoots up the expenses. This is a very inexact analysis of post-Vatican II, but do I have any regrets for not having grown up then while all this was going on? No, none whatsoever.

I'm the world's most unorthodox Catholic. Let's hope the other people you interview are not as off-the-wall as me. Just as an example: I got in a terrible snit one day back in the early seventies with someone in the Chancery Office of the Archdiocese of New York who wasn't leveling with me on something I was writing. I was covering the Church a lot in those days. So I said, "All right. I quit."

I became an Episcopalian and spent five or six years in the Episcopal Church. Took the family right with me. Went right over to the Episcopal Church.

But what happened was, simply: It's very difficult to be a Catholic and to become *something else*. Culturally, it's impossible. My wife used to say, "God, I hope we don't ever have to get invited to another covered-dish supper." My wife is a Polish girl from New Haven and it was very tough for her to start hanging out with Episcopalians. They asked her to join the Altar Society, which she did, and she used to wash the altar cloth. But after a while, she thought it was silly to be decorating the altar all the time. My wife is strictly a Sunday-morning Catholic. She's not interested in the little niceties of tending Church. She goes on Sunday, and that's it. I think she thinks I'm a little silly to be so interested in the Church. She's an old-fashioned Catholic: you go on Sunday and then keep quiet about it. Let's not hear a lot of talk about it.

The Episcopalians are the nicest people in the world. I would never knock them. In fact, there's no nicer guy in the world than Goldie Sherrill [the Reverend Franklin Goldthwaite Sherrill] over at Grace Church in Brooklyn Heights. And the people of the church we attended on Staten Island were just as nice as could be. But if you're raised a Catholic, there's just something about them. . . . We joined the Episcopal Church in 1974. We went up to the Cathedral of St. John the Divine and went through a ceremony and were received into the church. Afterward, we had iced tea on the lawn with the other Episcopalians. We were both beginning to say, "Gee, you know, we're Catholics after all. . . ."

I noticed from a writer's standpoint there's nothing to say about the Episcopalians. They're too boring, you know what I mean? You can't *write* anything about them. They don't *say* anything. They don't *do* anything. They make speeches about . . . they're effete, is what they are, and moribund. Nothing personal, but that's just the way it is.

We were in the Episcopal Church for about five years when we went to the 1978 Holiday Festival Basketball Tournament here in New York. Duke was playing St. John's. Duke had a great team and was a big favorite. They were up 17 points at the half. They scored off the tap and they were up 19 when St. John's started to come back. Frankie Gilroy made a steal and a layup; Gilroy started diving on the floor and doing this and that, making steals, scoring, dunking to finish a fast break. He was a tough Irish Catholic and watching Frankie out there bringing St. John's back, the Garden just went crazy; it was a nuthouse. The place was full because Duke was rated tops in the country. People were screaming and hollering. Gilroy had one of the greatest games I've ever seen a college player have, and St. John's won the game at the buzzer. It was an exhilarating experience.

As we were walking out of the Garden, my wife turned to me—I'll never forget this—and said, "The Episcopalians could never produce a Gilroy."

The next day we went back to the Catholic Church.

It's true. The Episcopalians don't know how to get up off the floor. They don't know how to scrap. *That's* the New York Catholic. You know yourself as an Italian. That ethnic Catholic—you just can't beat them. They're funnier than anybody else. They got more on the ball. They're quicker-minded. They've got more vitality. They've got more heart, you know.

We have three children: Joe, John and Ursula, young adults, still unmarried. As they were growing up, I didn't talk so much about the Church as about God—about the way God works in people's lives. When they were little, I'd buy these wonderful books of Bible stories with pictures, put out by a Lutheran outfit in St. Louis. The kids loved these stories, and after reading them we would always start a discussion. We had a lot of conversations. My favorite bit of advice was: when you're depressed and things don't go right, always say a prayer and turn the problem over to the care of God. I never told them anything I didn't believe in myself. Once I had a wonderful talk with Ursula, who was about three, and I wrote a column about it. She was riding in the backseat of the car—you know how kids stand there talking—and somehow or other, we got started talking about religion. I said, "God can do anything. God is omnipotent."

Ursula said, "Can God stand on His head?"

How do you answer a question like that? After a lot of mumbo jumbo and equivocation, I said, "Yes. God can stand on His head if He wants to."

"Without no hands?"

The thing got deeper. The more I tried to explain, the more she would ask questions. The talk became ludicrous, but it was typical.

We always had discussions. To this day we say grace before we eat. They know the old man takes religion very seriously.

When people say the Church is dying—there are so few vocations to the priesthood and sisterhood, church attendance is way off—I suggest they go to St. Teresa's on Staten Island. That church is pretty busy with hundreds of people going to Mass there every Sunday. And that's only one of thirty-five Catholic churches on Staten Island, and only one of four hundred in the Archdiocese of New York, and only one of twenty thousand in the United States of America. If you have one hundred people in each parish in this country who are interested in the Church, that's twenty thousand times one hundred—an awful lot of people. Despite all the problems, I don't see that as dying off.

Some changes are inevitable. They're going to have to make some kind of accommodation about ordaining married men. It has to be. From what I understand, studies show that the problems of getting young fellows into the priesthood are too severe, and there doesn't seem to be any indication that any turnaround will happen. There aren't enough guys to fill the needs and I can't find any good reason anymore to require celibacy. The argument that Cardinal O'Connor and Bishop Mugavero might make is that a single man or a celibate man can give his whole life to the Church because he has no other obligations. There's truth to that, but married men could make some kind of contribution.

Another problem with the priesthood is that the type of guy they're getting is not the same type you used to have. You don't have the sports-minded person anymore. In many cases, the priest today is not the man's man that you've got to have. It's a delicate question, but one that has to be faced. A kind of feminization has taken place. For instance, the emptiest place in the world, they tell me, is the gym at Dunwoodie Seminary. No problem if you want to go up to play squash or basketball—it's always empty. Nobody plays. Sports used to be a big thing at Dunwoodie. Now you have a very passive type of guy, and you can't run a church with one type. You need more of a cross-section.

But still this outfit isn't going out of business. Although the future seems uncertain, the Church will survive. I have no doubt about that. John Tracy Ellis, the Catholic historian, once gave a speech and quoted something from Saint Justin who wrote in the year 150 or so. It was about how Christians celebrate: they get together, hear Scripture and a sermon, eat the bread and wine, and have an offering for poor people. As I read the speech, I kept thinking, *My God, this was going on in the second century and it's what we're doing now in almost the twenty-first century!* I was so struck by this. If all this has been going on all this time, as long as there is any kind of a civilization at all, people will go on celebrating Mass, having Communion and Christian fellowship.

But the *form* the Church will take is going to change radically. In 1964, there were 5.6 million students in Catholic grammar and high schools. Today there are around 2.6 million. In twenty-three years there are 4 million fewer Catholic students. I don't say that's necessarily a bad thing, but it certainly points to a tremendous change in institutional Catholicism. What are we going to have in the year 2000? Will we lose all Catholic education in this country?

Then again, as I said earlier, one thing may be true about the Catholic Church, but the opposite is also true. At Notre Dame there's a tremendous religious commitment. Recently, Father Joe O'Hare, president of Fordham University, said he was very impressed by the religious commitment of the students at Fordham. The other day, I was talking with Frankie McLaughlin, Fordham's athletic director, who used to be basketball coach at Harvard, and asked, "What's the difference in the kids?"

Frankie said, "The Catholic Church was very strong at Harvard. Maybe because there were so few Catholics and that strengthened them. It tested their faith and their faith was stronger." My son Joe, who went to the Massachusetts Institute of Technology, told me that the Masses there were pretty well attended. When you have a strong Catholic community at Harvard and MIT, that's a pretty good indication to me that this outfit isn't going out of business.

I hope my kids will always be a big part of the Church, and myself as well. What part I'll have somewhere down the road is still to be seen. My wife teases me about a lot of things.

"If I should die first," she says, "try to figure out a way that you can get from the cemetery into a monastery someplace. Get there for supper because you won't be able to do your own cooking." She always kids me that I'll be moving right in with the monks.

"If I should drop dead at noon," she says, "get to the monastery in time for dinner so you don't starve to death!"

Archbishop Roger Mahony of Los Angeles

Archbishop Roger Mahony

CATHOLICISM IN CALIFORNIA: IS THERE A DIFFERENCE?

Whichever way people travel [in Los Angeles], they would move over . . . some five hundred miles of freeways, ribbons of concrete that no city in the world equals. But there would remain something they would never see. They would not see the poor.

In California, where life-styles are found of every variation, as well as short-lived religions to suit them, Catholicism under the leadership of Archbishop Mahony remains rocklike and unchanging. But under that same aegis, the religion in California is marked by a humanity and concern for many different colors of Catholics and varying backgrounds.

At the age of fifty-three, Archbishop Mahony is head of the Archdiocese of Los Angeles, the largest in the nation with some three million Catholics. His flock comprises immigrants from Asia, Europe and Africa, out-of-state and in-state migrating Americans, and Hispanics (60 percent), the people he grew up with and cherishes. His pastoral activities embrace them all, as he seeks in different areas to achieve their moral and economic well-being. Although he is a defender of traditional teaching (he recently debated Father Charles Curran, the dissident theologian), it is impossible to apply a label to his views but more appropriate to say, *He is a follower of Christ.*

So that the reader may have a more rounded view of the

Archbishop's thought than the interview presents, excerpts
from his homilies and statements are included, with his permission.

I don't find labels particularly useful. I prefer to take a look at
Jesus Christ in the Gospels and see how Christ Himself proclaimed
the Good News of His Father and the kingdom and how He
balanced in His own life all of these elements. I think that's what
we're really talking about—how we balance all aspects of our life in
ministry. Now, for example, Christ was very involved in many
controversial issues. He wasn't crucified because He didn't pay the
rent, you know. He was crucified because He was talking about a
new way, about the quality of people in God's eyes, about forgiveness, about the breaking down of barriers, and so on. So I think we
need to be very conscious that we, as disciples of Christ, need to do
the same. I see myself as pursuing the same direction as Our Holy
Father, Pope John Paul II, that is, being very faithful to God's
revelation, particularly with respect to human conduct and behavior, so that the faith, belief and practices of our tradition as Catholics are maintained. We don't have the authority to change those
beliefs and practices because of some Gallup poll. It is not a question of popular attitude; rather it is what God has told us, and what
He expects of us. In the whole area of beliefs and practices, I believe
we really are called to remain faithful to the traditions that God has
given us.

With some people, what is conservative theologically and liberal
on social issues gets translated into something like this: *I agree with
your position on social issues; therefore I see those as liberal. I don't agree
with your position on Church teachings and therefore I call you conservative.* That's what the bottom line often ends up at. And that's
why I don't find those particular labels helpful. Rather, what I try
to seek in my own life is fidelity, being faithful to the *totality* of God's
revelation, the totality of Jesus' message and His witness in the
Gospel. Now the totality of His message has three parts: prayer,
theology and social issues. The area that no one seems concerned

with is prayer, His own prayer life. What is mainly discussed is theology and social issues—questions like "Where does a bishop stand theologically?" "Where does he stand on social issues?" I would add the other dimension, prayer, which is very important in Jesus' life. He very, very consistently balances His time in the mountains and in the desert with the Father at prayer. How often did Luke, in particular, remark about Jesus' getting away for prayer? The second part of Jesus' message, theology, is the proclamation of the truth as He has brought it from the Father. For example, Jesus speaks about divorce very, very plainly and says that divorce is not of God's origin. Therefore, it is wrong. The third part, social issues, is a concern for people whom we could call victims, that is, people who are ill, who suffer discrimination, who don't share in the economic resources equitably. All of those issues which we can lump together as social issues are ones which Jesus Himself dealt with. In summary, then, I try to be faithful to the prayer life of Jesus, faithful to teaching God's revelation, and aware and concerned for the economically disadvantaged. I see faithfulness to all three as the measure.

I was born in Hollywood, California, and the reason I was born in that city is that in 1936 there was no hospital in North Hollywood where my parents lived. Hollywood was where the hospital was. However, I was brought up in North Hollywood, which is quite different. Our family name comes from County Cork in Ireland. It's O'Mahony over there; the *O'* was knocked off at some point. But it has no *e*, and this is the way it's spelled in all the coats of arms or heraldry from Ireland. From my understanding, the British added the *e*, and that's the way it is spelled in England and in this country. As another example, there is *Sweeny*, which is spelled without an *e* in Ireland; in England and the United States, it's *Sweeney*. My spelling is one that you would find authentically in Ireland.

When I got my master's degree in social work, I had already been ordained a diocesan priest for the diocese of Fresno in California. Priests with social-work degrees usually become directors of Catholic Charities or social services. I became director of Catholic Charities for the diocese of Fresno, and much of my work has been devoted to the Hispanic population. Where I grew up in North Hollywood, there were Hispanics—quite a few Mexican-Americans—living there. A lot of my growing up was with them and so I became very interested in their lives and language. I loved them and learned to speak Spanish. You've got to remember that California used to belong to Mexico and only became part of the United States in 1848. All the principal cities in California have Mexican-Spanish names, like Los Angeles, San Francisco, San Diego, Santa Monica. The whole state is filled with Hispanic influence. I worked heavily with the migrant workers, that is, the agricultural workers in the dioceses of Fresno and Stockton. Actually, I have two areas of focus with the Hispanic people of California, one being the pastoral—the whole spectrum of pastoral activity providing Mass and religious services—and the second focus being social issues, involving farm workers, Cesar Chavez and related matters.

Our Spanish ministry was deeply involved in the *Encuentro* of 1985. [Three *Encuentros*, or national meetings of Hispanic Catholics, have taken place—in 1972, 1977 and 1985—with pastoral ministry as their first and central concern. Following their recommendations, five areas have been focused on: evangelization, education, leadership development, youth ministry and social justice.] We have developed our own pastoral plan for Hispanics here in Los Angeles. In June 1986 we filled Dodger Stadium with 55,000 Hispanics for a special celebration to promulgate our diocesan commitment to Spanish-speaking peoples. Our latest endeavor has been the legalization amnesty program of the immigration law. That is a large area in which the Archdiocese has been very active. We actually signed up and submitted applications for residence for more people in the Archdiocese than anywhere else in the country.

Since becoming a Bishop in 1975, I have been deeply involved with the National Conference of Catholic Bishops (NCCB) and its operational secretariat and service agency, the United States Catholic Conference (USCC). The NCCB was mandated by Vatican II—it's not that Bishops in this country dreamed this up and established it. Vatican II gave us a lot of new structures and vehicles for action in the life of the Church, not just here, but throughout the world. [Archbishop Mahony has been chairman of the NCCB's Committee on Arbitration, Committee on Conciliation and Arbitration, Committee on Farm Labor, as well as a member of the Committee on Evangelization, Committee on Conference Priorities and USCC's Oversight Committee on Migration and Refugees.]

*   *   *

The Holy Father, and the documents of the Church, have increasingly and clearly spoken of the role of women in the Church. In my diocese, we've been trying to find as many opportunities for the participation of women as we can in the life of the Church on the parish level, the diocesan level and the national level. This is nothing necessarily new or a turning point, but it is an emphasis that Vatican Council II gave us and one which we in this country are attempting to fulfill. [The first draft of the National Conference of Catholic Bishops' Letter on the Role of Women in the Church was published six months after this interview.]

My immediate predecessor, Cardinal Timothy Manning, had a whole series of hearings and listening sessions on the subject throughout the Archdiocese. After studying the results, I issued a pastoral letter in August 1987 called "The Role of Women in the Church," responding to those issues and concerns and encouraging as much participation as possible by all members of the Church at all levels. It urged the support of women in new ministries, such as chancellors, editors of diocesan newspapers, members of seminary faculties, diocesan directors of family life or religion-education offices, pastoral ministers, and so on. Now as I go around the Archdiocese for parish visitations, I see increasingly that there are very large numbers of women in important leadership roles as full-time and part-time ministry people, employees, volunteers, and so on. Whenever leadership roles open up, we've attempted to bring as many women into those as possible, and in the published edition of my pastoral letter, you'll find pictures of women whom I've brought personally into leadership in the Archdiocese.

Concerning sexist language in the liturgy, I have two points to make. The first is that I do not think using the pronoun *He* in speaking and writing about God is intended to be, or is, sexist. Obviously, we all realize that God is neither male nor female. But our limited human experience and vocabulary don't give us a whole lot of other examples since we don't have any pure spirits whom we address on a regular basis. We use language that is somewhat traditional. To be honest with you, in this Archdiocese, I don't find many women who see this as a major issue—whether we call God *He* or *It* or *She*. In my experience, that is not a big problem. The second point—the greater issue—is using *men, he, him* when you're talking about people in general. That kind of exclusive language is much more problematic. I have suggested that we use inclusive words and names as specifically as possible those to whom we speak, and say what we mean: *brothers and sisters* instead of *brethren, all of us* instead of *all men,* and so on.

The gist in the Curran case [see interview with Father Charles Curran, the dissident theologian] really is *Who does the teaching in the Church in the area of pastoral behavior?* or *What is the role of theologians and what is the role of Bishops?* My problem with Father Curran is that he has blurred the two. The role of theologian is to explore and investigate theologically the various teachings of the Church, *but as a theologian* not as one who then tells the people this is how you live your life. A very, very big difference and an important distinction. In the history of the Church, the Bishops are the shepherds of the people and the use of theologians is *part* of the whole structure. *It is the Bishops, with the Holy Father, the Pope, who decide what the application of theology is to daily living.* To my mind, Father Curran not only did theological speculation but then said, "And, by the way, you individual Catholics can live your life according to my speculation." Well, that's not *his* role, and that's not the role of theologians. Theologians are very important, and in this country they are given high visibility by the media. So it's much more difficult to keep a balance—much of what a theologian says is in print very quickly.

[The following remarks are a response to certain comments from the J. Peter Grace interview that were quoted to the Archbishop. In the comments, Mr. Grace attacks the Bishops' Pastoral Letter on the Economy, especially its views on capitalism. In particular, Archbishop Mahony refutes Mr. Grace's claim that out of the some 350 bishops who comprise the National Conference of Catholic Bishops, only 10 or 15 run it and the others follow their lead.]

First of all, the Pastoral Letter on the Economy was not an attack on capitalism. It attempted to show the pluses, the good points, and where we still had room to develop. For example, the document points out that as good as capitalism is and as helpful as it has been for our country, we still must face the fact that 35 million Americans live below the poverty line. We have not reached the fulfillment of all the goals and dreams of capitalism. I don't find that an attack on capitalism. We reminded the nation that there is still some unfinished work and that we have an agenda that we can't just ignore as pastors of the people. I think reactions depend on the point of view. And certainly all the Bishops in the country were involved in every stage of developing that Pastoral Letter. We all received a copy of every draft, we were encouraged to have meetings with top corporate business people in our dioceses and to urge them to send in recommendations and offer amendments. The Pastoral went through several major drafts. To say that ten or fifteen bishops impose their views on the rest of us is just simply not true. I think there was a very open and very healthy process that resulted in this document.

[Appearing below are two excerpts from the Archbishop's public statements that reveal further aspects of a leader who follows Christ.]

METROPOLIS IN THE TWENTY-FIRST CENTURY

From "The Mission of the Church in Los Angeles," a homily delivered on his installation as Archbishop, September 1985

How often we have heard—whether by way of hope or by way of boast— that Los Angeles is the city of the twenty-first century. There is so much that gives foundation to that claim. The city stands massive before us in its energy! If, for example, you travel from Santa Monica Bay, from the John Paul Getty Museum, to the county art museum in Hancock Park, to the Norton Simon and the Huntington Galleries in Pasadena, you would see a city emerging to become one of the greatest centers of art in the Western world. Or take the opposite route and pass by the Claremont cluster of colleges, then drive to the California Institute of Technology, to Occidental, then over to the University of Southern California, Mount St. Mary's and the University of California at Los Angeles and finally to Loyola- Marymount, and you will get some fleeting glimpse of the intellectual and academic talent. . . . Emerging on the horizon are towering new structures which house major business and financial ventures and now identify our community as the great economic center for the entire Pacific Basin. Prominent on our skyline as well are several large, modern medical centers where some of the most brilliant medical minds in the world are gathered to foster and sustain human life. . . . Whichever way you travel, you would move over the gigantic freeway system that connects one section of this city and county with another, some five hundred miles of freeways, ribbons of concrete that no city in the world equals. . . .

But for those who move through our city this way, there would remain something they would never see in this brilliant mixture of art, intelligence, business and medical advancements, concrete structures and the vast, conquered space.

They would not see the poor.

You can drive from the center of our city to Long Beach and never see Watts or our Black brothers and sisters still struggling to be accorded basic human dignity and opportunity. You can move downtown toward Riverside and Santa Ana and miss the hundreds of thousands of Hispanics, with some 40 percent unemployment, in East Los Angeles. . . . You would overlook them quite literally because the very freeway system that joins the worlds of culture and opportunity with the worlds of the great hotels and restaurants allows those who use it to drive over the poor. The poor are unseen beneath. . . .

To all this ambiguity of riches and poverty, of discrimination and opportunity, of greatness and serious sin, the Church is sent. . . . The Church, its ministers and its Gospel, are fundamentally here for one and only one reason. We are here because we have been sent, because through the centuries we have read and reread this Gospel in our churches and have found in it the mandate of our lives, the final self-understanding of Christ, and the final charge to His disciples: "All authority in heaven and earth has been given to me. Go, therefore . . ." (Matthew 28:18–19). Jesus is Lord, and out of His sovereignty comes command, and that command is our mission. . . . "Teach them to carry out everything I have commanded" (Matthew 28:20). I shall take seriously my charge as your new Archbishop to renew continually God's call to our community and Jesus' teachings as they touch upon contemporary society.

ON CATHOLICS IN PUBLIC OFFICE

From "Moral Teaching and Public Office," a statement issued to the Catholics of his diocese, September 1984. The statement appears in its entirety. For an opposing point of view, see Governor Mario Cuomo's remarks: "Religious Belief and Public Morality: A Catholic Governor's Perspective."

In today's society and in the current political debates taking place around the country, a critical question has arisen: When a Catholic becomes a public official, does Catholic moral teaching have any relevance in his or her exercise of public authority?

As your Bishop, I feel that you need to understand the Church's response to this important question.

There are those who deny there is a connection between religious moral teaching and public office. Let us examine their positions in the light of Catholic moral teaching.

One position holds that the state is supreme in its own sphere. Our Lord said, "Render to Caesar the things that are Caesar's" (Mark 12:17). Our Constitution teaches that Church and State are separate. Therefore, it is said that the officeholder who lets religion tell him what to do has mixed up the two spheres.

A second position claims that in a pluralistic democracy, an officeholder does wrong by imposing his or her religious beliefs on those who do not hold them. If the conscience of others is to be respected, then each person should be allowed to hold views without interference by a public authority acting under the influence of the religious convictions of officeholders.

A third stance assumes that officeholders can be split into a "private person" and a "public person." As private individuals, they have one set of beliefs and values. As public men and women, they may have another. This suggests a following of private conscience for private actions and a public conscience in public actions.

Each of these theories must be considered as seriously flawed and wrong.

Let us take the first—that the state is supreme in its sphere. History is a vivid refutation of this. In recent times we have had the judgment of Nuremberg on personal responsibility for crimes committed in the exercise of state authority. War criminals could not shelter themselves behind the state. Closer to home was the judgment on the My Lai massacres in Vietnam. The officers responsible could not claim they were only obeying orders from above. Caesar's sphere could not be shut off from the moral order—when it touched the lives of human beings, it was also God's sphere.

As to the second, respect for pluralism, no conscientious officeholder wants to impose on others of different beliefs his or her rituals or theological views. For example, the Catholic law of abstinence from meat, liturgical norms and the Catholic belief in the Pope as the Vicar of Christ are remote and removed from the public sphere. Other teachings, religious in origin, bear directly on the moral life and our responsibilities to our fellow human beings.

"Thou shalt not kill" is among them. How could a legislator fulfill his or

her legislative role in indifference to this commandment? If a group of persons had formed consciences which told them it was morally acceptable to harass, harm and even destroy other members of society and acted on this belief, it would be a legislator's duty to oppose them. He or she would have to seek remedial legislative action. The excuse that the persecutors believed they were right would be intolerable.

Respect for conscience—even the erring conscience of others—must be safeguarded. But we cannot accept actions dictated by an erring conscience when those actions involve the deprivation of the human rights of others and serious harm to the common good.

As for the third theory on the "private" and "public" person, it conflicts with a fundamental human need—that of integrity. Integrity means wholeness: wholeness of mind and body, wholeness of heart, wholeness as a person. Psychologically, it is no doubt possible to pigeonhole one's life, to compartmentalize one's beliefs, to set up areas of amorality. Spiritually, though, it is fatal. We are one flesh and spirit, one conscience, one person. As men and women, we seek integrity. We want it for ourselves. We must demand it in our officeholders.

These observations bear directly on an issue much debated today—the stand a Catholic officeholder should take on abortion. It is an evil, which in America has become an epidemic, a plague, annually taking the lives of 1.4 million unborn human persons. The evil is not an accident of Catholic ritual or peculiarly Catholic theology. Rather, it is condemned because of the essential command of God, "Thou shalt not kill."

Catholics in public office cannot shrug and shelter themselves behind the Supreme Court's approval of abortion. They must attempt to change the law and work to cut off the funds that finance the taking of the life of the unborn. Otherwise, such Catholics render to Caesar what is God's.

It should be noted that the Catholic principles enunciated here apply equally to the many other areas of moral concern: the treatment of the poor, the sick, the aged, the handicapped, the unemployed and the alienated; the elimination of racism and discrimination from our midst; the halting of the sinful arms race and the nuclear madness. These concerns all involve basic rights which center on the divine dignity and eternal destiny of every human person.

Furthermore, the issue is not confined to one particular political party or one particular group of Catholic officeholders. The problem is one for all the major parties, the officeholders belonging to them and the candidates standing for office in the forthcoming elections. Neither the diocese nor the parishes of Stockton endorse any political party or any political candidate.

We simply ask all to work for the essential respect for human life in all its manifestations.

It is a grave moral error to accept or uphold the action of those who deny the basic right of every human person to life from the moment of conception to natural death. It is to lack the wholeness, the integrity that is sought by the rightly formed conscience. It is to walk in darkness when we are called to live in the light of Christ that has come into the world.

Bishop Pelotte in Gallup, wearing Indian headdress

Bishop Donald Pelotte

"HOUSE MADE OF DAWN, HOUSE MADE OF EVENING LIGHT."

House made of dawn,
House made of evening light.
House made of grasshoppers.
Happily may we walk.
May it be beautiful below us,
May it be beautiful above us,
For in beauty it is finished.

Lines from "We must build a house together"
Old Navajo chant

Beneath towers of rock, at Donald Pelotte's ordination as Bishop in Red Rock State Park, New Mexico, Zuni and White Mountain Apache Indians in ceremonial dress performed "Turkey," "White Buffalo," and "Eagle" dances, while Navajos chanted songs in Navajo. In procession, Indians from various tribes throughout the southwest diocese presented him with pottery, Indian headdress, beaded necklace, stoles, sash, and pectoral turquoise crosses handcrafted by the Zuni. It was a historic moment in May 1986, as the first Native American was ordained to the Catholic hierarchy.

This country's 400,000 Indian Catholics, some of whom had crossed the country to be present, rejoiced. Although the Church had established the Catholic Mission among the Colored People and Indians and the Bureau of Catholic Indian Missions in the Southwest, Indian Catholics felt these agencies had treated them as a subservient group. "Before, this was a mission 'to' the American Indians," one Indian priest said, "but now we can build our own church."

An Algonquin Indian from Maine on his father's side, Bishop Pelotte is one of the nation's youngest Bishops. He comes to Gallup after eight years as Provincial, or leader, of the Blessed Sacrament Fathers and Brothers in Cleveland. As a youth he attended Eymard Seminary in Hyde Park, New York. His goal as Bishop is to help the Gallup Diocese "build a house together" in the Church.

I am the Coadjutor Bishop of the diocese of Gallup, New Mexico. That title simply means a co-bishop who will assume leadership when the current Bishop retires. There are only four Coadjutor Bishops in the United States.

Our diocese has 55,000 square miles and it's the only one that covers two states—the northwestern part of New Mexico and the northeastern part of Arizona. [Opens a map of the Southwest and points.] We are here in Gallup. The diocese begins right as you leave Albuquerque and goes all the way to Page, to the rim of the Grand Canyon. This whole area has about 50,000 Catholics, the majority of whom are Native Americans and Hispanics. The remainder comprise thirty-one different ethnic groups. [Although "Native Americans" and "Native People" are terms generally accepted in place of the older phrases "American Indians" or "Indians," many Americans including Bishop Pelotte use both the old and new terms.]

We have seven tribes of Indians in the diocese. Let me name them. The largest is the Navajo Nation. They live on a huge reservation that covers the northern part of New Mexico and Arizona, this large brown area here [pointing at the map]. There are 200,000 Navajos, but only 5 percent are Catholic. The Hopi Reservation in Arizona is right in the middle of the Navajo. Right here, down the road from Gallup on Route 32, are the Zunis. We have two tribes of Apache: the Jicarilla [pronounced *hick-a-rí-ya*] in northern New Mexico and the White River Apache in Arizona.

They are two very different people. As you move closer to Albuquerque, you have the Acoma Indians whose reservation, "Sky City," is on a mesa. Here are the Laguna nearby. That's it: the Navajo, the Hopi, the Zuni, the Jicarilla, the White River Apache, the Acoma and the Laguna. These Indians are very different from those in the Northeast or in other parts of the country, and they even differ among themselves. There's a misconception that all Indians are alike. That is completely untrue—some are industrious and successful, some maintain their culture, others are deprived of it, thousands are jobless. The Algonquins of Maine—my father was an Abenaki Algonquin—have lost much of their cultural heritage, and their language is a thing of the past. The Hopis of Arizona, on the other hand, are an industrious people who maintain a fine Pueblo Indian culture and rank among the world's best dry-land farmers. The Navajo are impoverished, yet many of them speak the Navajo language. All these tribes are individualistic. There are approximately three hundred tribes in the United States with distinct customs and rituals.

Since 1986, when I became Bishop, I've visited as many places of the diocese as possible, particularly the reservations. Remember, the area covers 55,000 square miles. The first trip took ten days. I just got in the car and drove. Starting in Holbrook, Arizona, I would spend the day at each stop, say Mass for the Indians, take pot luck and move on. From Holbrook to Winslow, then from Winslow up to the northern part of the diocese to Page in Arizona. If you look at the map, you'll find Page just north of the Grand Canyon. I came down through the Navajo reservation to Kayenta and then went over to Tuba City, and then headed back east to Keams Canyon where there are mostly Hopi. After ten days, I came home. In the last two weeks I've visited Ft. Defiance and the Navajos in Tohatchi. Last summer I covered the fiestas at Acoma in Sky City and in Laguna and confirmations with White River Apache Indians and with the Jicarilla Apaches. I also visit the Spanish and Anglo parishes, and so it has become obvious to me that it's impossible to cover all the territory regularly by car.

Flying on the wings of hope, shortly after I arrived, I applied for a plane to help me travel around the diocese more quickly. There's a nonprofit organization in St. Louis that gets planes from various businesses which they repair and give to missionary dioceses. I got a six-passenger Cessna 337. The next step was *What do you call it?*

The Catholic schools of the diocese stepped in by holding a plane-naming contest for the children. The prize, of course, was a free flight. We got over one hundred responses and some pretty snazzy names, like "Christ Craft," "Holy Roller I," "Airangel," "The Flying Bishop," and "Pelotte Skywalker." "Faithful Eagle" got first prize and it was won by Jamesita Ahasteen, a twelve-year-old girl at St. Michael's School in Window Rock, Arizona. The next question was *Who's going to fly it?* I knew that Jim Pomeroy, a member of the parish and a convert, had flown in Vietnam. He used to fly for Northwest Airlines and later for the Gallup Flying Company that goes to the reservations to pick up sick Indians. Right now he's piloting for the chairman of the Navajo Nation. On his days off he agreed to pilot for me.

The Southwest has the largest concentration of Native People in the nation. That's why they call Gallup the Indian Capital of the World—it is the gathering spot, with the Navajo reservation surrounding it. Highway 66 runs right through Gallup and is the main street, with the railroad station, the airport, restaurants, diners, motels, turquoise jewelry emporiums, gasoline stations strung along this patch of the highway, lining both sides for several miles. There are a few residential streets off from it. And that's about the extent of Gallup. It has a population of twenty thousand but not all Indians. We have Hispanics, Croatians, Irish, Slovaks, Filipinos, Japanese, and Italians.

In general, the Pueblo Indians—people who do not exist isolated among themselves but live a community life, such as the Zuni, the Acoma, the Laguna, the Hopi—are doing fairly well. The poorest Indians we have in this area are the Navajo. Of the 200,000 Navajos in this territory, about 65 percent of them are unemployed. If you go from here and drive ten minutes out of Gallup, you'll see their hogans scattered on the reservation along the highway—they have no running water, no electricity, and no work. They're the ones you see roaming the streets, especially along Route 66. They tell me the population of Gallup doubles every weekend. Navajo men come off the reservation to spend the weekend here in town and obviously they spend their money on liquor. The alcoholic problem is a tragedy, a total tragedy, for *all* Indians, but particularly for our Navajos.

The Church is working very hard at least to try to keep them fed. We have a soup kitchen down the road where we serve over four hundred Navajos each morning from 9:30 to 11:30—they're being served right now [glancing at his watch]. They come here to get a meal, which means that the women and the children are on the reservation. I assume *they* eat, otherwise, they would die. Mother Teresa's community is staffing the soup kitchen right now, but there are volunteers from all over the country who also come and help. The winters are especially bad because it gets very cold here; with the storms from the Rocky Mountains, we get really bad winters. It's not as bad as Maine where I was born and raised, but it's bad. Indians die right there on Highway 66 because they get inebriated and then fall asleep on the side of the road and freeze to death.

The Navajos are the ones who are suffering the most in terms of unemployment. In their defense I have to say that the Navajo Nation just had an economic summit meeting in Gallup at the Holiday Inn about two weeks ago. Now that the mines are no longer being mined, what they are trying to do is bring in industry to the reservation so the Indians can work, or bring it close enough to supply jobs. Industry doesn't seem too interested—we don't have water and you know how important water is for any factory that needs power.

The Navajos live scattered throughout the 25,000 square miles— a vast desert—that comprises their reservation. It is difficult for me, or any priest, to minister to them—the space is so immense. They often live in extended families. It's not uncommon for them to have the grandmother and great-grandmother and the uncle and the aunt live along with them in a little spot or area in this vast territory.

Compared to other Native People, like the Pueblo Indians and the Indians of Maine, who are the opposite, the Navajo Nation is matriarchal. Women really have an important role, at least in the family. Bishop Hastrich said to me, "The Navajos are going to be very difficult to reach because they have been hurt badly for years. They are cautious, and it takes them a year or two to trust anyone."

And he added, "If you're going to reach them, you've got to reach the women first. From them, you'll get to the children, and only then to the men. Unless you reach the women . . ."

Yet the odd thing is that you see the women in subservient situations. There are unique exceptions, like Dr. Annie Wauneka, the famous Navajo woman doctor who was responsible virtually single-handedly for clearing up the old problem of tuberculosis on the reservation. But the thing that strikes me—and I'm sure you saw this while driving around town—is that when the men are driving in their pickup trucks, the women and children sit in the back *in the open, in all weather.* And the men sit in the cab up front. This perplexes me. I have a lot of unanswered questions. It's a whole new ball game for me because it's so different from the East. Why are women put in the back, particularly in the winter when it's freezing, and there are five or six men sitting up front? It's a strange inconsistency because the women have such an important role in the society.

As I've indicated, the biggest problem among *all* the Native People is alcoholism. It started when America was discovered and liquor was introduced. I'm convinced it has become our number-one Indian problem nationally, and internationally when you consider the Indians of Canada and Central America. To be honest with you, I think it's genetic. The doctors are saying that, and I stand by it. But we're not only dealing with a disease—I want to stress it's disease probably genetically inherited—we're also dealing with people who have no work, have been put down for years, are demoralized. For me, one of the worst things is to pick up *The Gallup Independent,* a local paper, and read *almost every day* about some young people who have died, with the names of the deceased, circumstances of death, time and so on. They may have been run over on Highway 66, or killed in a car accident, or committed suicide—the suicide rate here is unbelievable. The point is that these deaths are all *alcohol-related,* although drunkenness is not often mentioned. Let me read you this from yesterday's paper:

SHIPROCK: CROWNPOINT PAIR KILLED

A Navajo man and woman are dead as the result of a traffic accident on Navajo Route 36 West of Shiprock, officers said.

The victims were identified as Bernice M. Shorthair, 24, Shiprock, and Jefferson Jones, 22, Crownpoint.

Navajo police said Jones died in the one-vehicle accident about 5:45 P.M. Saturday and Ms. Shorthair died at Shiprock Indian Health Service Hospital shortly afterward.

The vehicle Jones was driving left Navajo Route 36 and rolled over, throwing both occupants out, Navajo police said.

It's obvious to every local reader that behind these simple lines is the tragedy of two young people driving while drinking, and terminating their lives. The disease of alcoholism is not discriminatory. It's across the board—women drink, and young girls, too.

My father was an alcoholic. The whole family has dealt with it, a serious tragedy for us. The disease triggers off something internally in our people and once it has started, it doesn't stop. It's endless; they just keep drinking. We talk about social drinkers, people who can have a drink and then put the bottle away. But for those who are genetically inclined to be alcoholics, like Native Americans, they just keep drinking. If the father is an alcoholic, the chances of the sons and daughters being alcoholic are like 95 percent. 'Course, it's even worse if both parents are alcoholic. In this county, we have the highest death rate related to alcoholism of any county in the nation.

Our Church and the local community both do a lot of work trying to deal with it. We have a fine rehabilitation center in town called Friendship Services, where we try to bring the Native People in to dry them out and rehabilitate them. What we need, in addition, is a good aftercare program. But for a program like that to work, it means that the patient has to come back for constant counseling and treatment and it's not easy to get them back from the reservations. They have to walk, or they don't come back. As Bishop, I hope to get the whole professional community in the area—the medical people, the civil and church groups as well as the politicians—to work together at a problem that appears unchangeable.

Our people are just dying—we have to do something.

The mayor has tried to get a law passed that would prohibit the sale of alcohol before 11 A.M. and to close down the drive-in liquor stores. These places sell bottles to drivers who never even leave their cars. It's like McDonald's when you drive up for a hamburger—you don't even have to go into the place. You order what you want and take off. But despite the mayor's efforts, the drive-ins are still open. What it demands is that all of us put our heads together and say, *How are we going to address this tragic problem that is killing so many people?* I'm not sure whether we can do it, but we are trying more than we have in the past. The Church has established a couple of places on the reservation called Talbot House and One Day at a Time, where we treat alcoholics. But it's a day-to-day temptation, a disease that is fatal and endless, and unless you can keep at it and get them to come in constantly, it won't work.

*   *   *

On my father's side, I'm descended from the Abenaki Indians of Maine. They originally came down from Quebec and Montreal and moved into Maine and other parts of New England. They are also called the Algonquin Nation because their language was Algonquin. These Indians have different names—the Penobscot, the Passamaquoddy, the Micmac—but they're basically all Abenaki Algonquin. We still have three reservations in Maine. The Algonquins were known for making canoes, their chief means of transportation since they lived in little villages along the Kennebec River and the lakes of Maine.

My grandparents were born on a reservation in Abenaki, Canada. In order to find work, my grandfather walked from Montreal to Maine and got a job with the lumber people. Northern Maine was where all the lumberjacks were. He walked to a place called Jackman, right on the border. After he moved his whole family down— he had twenty-two children— it became known as Pelotte's Valley. Jackman is also known as Moose River Plantation; nearby is a lake called Moose River where you find plenty of moose. My dad was born in Maine. The family lived very, very poorly and after my grandfather died, my grandmother moved closer to the center of Maine, to Sidney. My father was a mechanic, a good one. He met my mother, who was from a French-Canadian background, in Waterville. We lived with my grandmother on her farm. I had a twin and when we were three months old, my parents were divorced. We were five children by then and my mother raised us by herself.

Since my mother was from a French-Canadian family, the influences in my childhood, especially after my father left, were more French-Canadian. We spoke only French at home. My mother had no sense of Indian culture—she simply told us, "Your father was a Canadian Indian," whenever we asked about his family. She didn't talk much about him, particularly since he was a very abusive alcoholic. You have to have the experience of coming from an alcoholic family to know how painful it is for people to talk about it, even among themselves. Thus, my Indian heritage was largely unspoken, except that there was a sense—and I stress this though I don't know how it developed, obviously not from my dad since he wasn't around—but there was a strong sense of respect for the earth and for water, for *all* of nature.

The Indians I come from have lost their language completely and many of their traditions, and there are other tribes like them. Certain ones in Oklahoma have a language but can't speak it. Even here in the Southwest, where traditions are still lively, we just started having Mass celebrated in Navajo. Most of the Navajo, certainly the leaders, can speak Navajo, though they can't read it. The most that I can see happening right now with the Algonquin language of my ancestors is that some Jesuit priests and missionaries of Maine, along with one of the prominent Abenaki Indians, Joseph McNicholas at Peter Dana Point Reservation, are trying to put together an Algonquin dictionary. They also recite the Our Father and sing a few songs in Algonquin, but most people wouldn't know the language. For many years the Abenaki Indians of Maine and Canada didn't speak Algonquin; they spoke French.

It is vital to the question of Indian/non-Indian relations to remind Americans of the Pope's talk to the Native People in September [1987] because it is a recognition on the part of the Church of some of the past offenses it dealt them. First of all, he apologized and asked for forgiveness for what he called the terrible injustices inflicted on them. Secondly, he highlighted the importance of Native Americans as indigenous people. And, most importantly, he *challenged* them and, in effect, said: *It is better for you to create your own future. You have all the potential. Assume leadership in the Church for your own people.* And referring to the first Native American Bishop, he appealed to their self-esteem and tried to give them pride. His visit was profound because he recognized our lack of pride, and voiced it forcibly. But I'm not sure the Native People heard what he was saying. They were so stunned and thrilled at his presence, incredulous that he was there with them. You could see it in their eyes. They were crying.

The finest aspect of the Pope's visit was his strong affirmation before fifteen thousand Native People in Phoenix that there is *nothing wrong with being Catholic and being Native American at the same time.* In other words, to be Catholic today one doesn't need to adopt the complete ritual and symbols of Western European Catholicism, but can keep one's own ethnic and cultural traditions. He stressed respect for these and the necessity of using them, without fear, in prayer and liturgy. He himself was the recipient of an Indian blessing when a man from the Pima tribe, who was both a medicine man and a Catholic, waved an eagle feather before him. Because the Pope was in Phoenix, which is Pima territory, a Piman had been chosen to give the blessing. Later the Pope told me how moved he had been, finding it a prayerful experience.

As a result of Vatican II, this acceptance of a people's culture is the most beautiful thing that has happened in our Church in the last twenty-five years. Imposing Western European ways and Catholicism on those we are evangelizing can no longer be done, particularly on indigenous peoples. Thus, you see, it was possible to smoke a peace pipe at Mass celebrated with the Pope, and for a Pima Indian to wave an eagle feather to bless the Pope, and for the Pope to walk on shawls that the Pueblo Indians had taken from their shoulders and placed at his feet as a gesture of welcome. The first time this happened to me, being of Eastern Indian stock, I was taken aback. I felt uncomfortable walking on these beautiful shawls. The custom goes way back and it's a very important gesture for these Indians.

When the Pope spoke in Phoenix, I remember seeing a group of small, elderly Pueblo Indians from Laguna dressed in shawls, hunchbacked and just dragging themselves around. They probably didn't understand much of what he said, but the fact that he was there, that he went and kissed them and the children and held their hands and allowed them to lay their shawls on the floor so he could walk over them, meant so much to them. By his presence and by his touching, they understood deep down, even without his words, that he was personally welcoming them and their traditions into the Church.

But more than anything else, the Pope's visit to Phoenix threw into grand relief the question of abuse and forgiveness— forgiveness on the part of the Indians for all the disgrace they had suffered at the hands of Church missionaries. It was perhaps the underlying theme of his visit. At Mass, a few days earlier, I gave a sermon urging Indians to forgive those who have harmed them and quoted Peter who said, in effect, "Do we forgive seven times?" And the Lord answered, *"We have to forgive seventy times seven times."* But I also urged that the past be remembered, for to forget would risk the danger of the tragic story being repeated.

The Pope's visit was so rewarding not only for us, but I daresay, for the Pope as well. It seemed to be a time of learning for him, and expanding horizons. He was full of questions. After he had finished his ninety-minute visit with the Native People, I had the opportunity to ride with him, along with Bishop Thomas O'Brien of Phoenix and the Pope's secretary. The four of us sat in the limousine for the twenty-five-minute drive from the Coliseum to the stadium where the big Mass was being celebrated. The Pope asked me, "What is the biggest tribe in your diocese?"

"The Navajo."

"Are they predominantly Catholic?"

"No."

"What religion do they practice?"

"From what I can see, some of them still practice what they call the 'traditional way.' And many have been converted to Fundamentalism by the Pentecostals and the Mormons who are very strong here, particularly in the Arizona part of the diocese. My sense is that, although the Navajos may not be predominantly Catholic, those that are are strongly rooted."

The Pope found time to visit the Tekakwitha Conference, which was being held in Phoenix. The Conference is an annual gathering of Catholic Native People and the clergy, religious and laypeople who minister to them. The main focus of Tekakwitha is evangelization, with particular emphasis on the development of Native ministry and leadership. But the Conference is also involved in family life, social justice, drinking, drugs, Catholic teaching and the liturgy. The group is named after a Mohawk Indian maiden, Kateri Tekakwitha, who was born in 1656 in Auriesville, New York. At the age of twenty she was converted by a Jesuit missionary and lived a life devoted to prayer, penitence, the sick and the aged. She was beatified in 1980 and when she is sanctified, she will be the first Native American saint.

Under the present political administration in Washington, the Native People have not benefited. President Reagan is certainly not helping them very much. I heard again this morning how corrupt the Bureau of Indian Affairs is. The money is not going where it should. I'm willing to go before any congressional committee and testify in favor of Native Americans. But I don't usually get into the political thing and I don't want to go on record in *The New York Times* as saying that Bishop Pelotte condemns the Navajo chairman for corruption. But charges of corruption are in the paper every day. It's terrible. The Navajos are supposed to be a very wealthy Indian

Ruth McDonough Fitzpatrick

Ruth McDonough Fitzpatrick

WOMEN PRIESTS NOW!

A speaker announced, "Will the women who have a call to ordination please stand up?" Two hundred and eighty women stood up, and it knocked the socks off everyone.

In an attractive suburban home in Fairfax, Virginia, lives Ruth McDonough Fitzpatrick, mother of three, married to a retired army colonel and steady practitioner of the Catholic faith of her forebears. Her life appears to be that of a contented woman in her middle years, but it is not. As national coordinator of the Women's Ordination Conference (WOC), she is fighting for the ordination of women as priests in the Catholic Church. In her dining room and basement-turned-office, she manages a huge outflow of mail that circulates throughout the country in pursuit of WOC's goals to inform and activate all women who have a call to priesthood. She travels to conventions, edits and writes a bimonthly newspaper and gives talks whenever she is called. [Since this interview, she has moved into a suite of offices at a nearby shopping center and has a part-time administrative assistant, Sister Theresa Anderson, a Benedictine nun.]

From the time she was in high school, Ms. Fitzpatrick has wanted to be a priest. Statistics show that many Catholic women have a similar vocation. This newly awakened group is devoting enormous energy to bringing to the attention of the Church hierarchy the appropriateness and dire need for women to be priests.

The Women's Ordination Conference (WOC) is a grass-roots, international organization of people who are working for the acceptance of women as priests in what we are calling a *renewed* priesthood. It's important to say a *renewed* priestly ministry, because we do not want women to plug in to the clerical caste system as it exists now where the old-fashioned concept of "Father Knows Best" that came with the immigrant Church still exists. Catholics are now getting a very strong sense of themselves in this country.

I say international because we have members in Latin America, Canada, Europe and the Far East; our base is the United States. In 1973, an American laywoman named Mary Lynch wrote to friends on her Christmas card list, saying, "With the International Year of Women coming up in 1975, isn't it time to raise the question, *Should women be priests?*" This started the ball rolling and in 1975, a group of interested women held the first conference in Detroit, not knowing who would come, or how many. It was basically put on, and attended by, nuns because they were the ones who took Vatican II very seriously, and they were asked by Pope John XXIII to go back to their roots and renew themselves. They took this to heart. In some convents, nuns had a practice known as "reading at table," which usually took place at mealtime. At lunch, for example, while you and I might read a copy of *Time* magazine, the nuns were *having read to them* by another nun the documents of Vatican II as they were issued. With a much better understanding of what Vatican II was all about, they became the prophets of that Council. Although the people at that first meeting in Detroit were mostly nuns, there was a good number of laywomen, priests and some Brothers. At first, they planned to have the conference in a small place, but as the registration reached eighteen hundred, they got larger accommodations. They turned away five hundred more people. At the end of the three-day conference, a speaker announced, *Will the women who have a call to ordination please stand up?* Two hundred and eighty women stood up, and it knocked the socks off everyone. At the most, the leaders expected about fifty to respond. Now they were mandated to start an organization and a national office that would help coordinate activities. Their first step was to form a core commission, or board, of the organizers of the conference, nuns and laywomen both. In 1977, they hired me to open the WOC office and get things started, like incorporation proceedings, the newsletter, and so on.

Our hopes were high. At that time we honestly thought women would be ordained within five years. A number of them were starting to go to seminaries and go through training. Yes, seminaries *do* accept women, and as a matter of fact, women keep the seminaries in business. When you have a call, you have a call. And so they went. In 1974, the first woman Episcopal priest was ordained, and this gave our movement an impetus as people thought Catholic women would be next. In 1976, Pope Paul VI established a pontifical biblical commission to study the question of ordination of women through Scripture, that is, to see whether there was something in Scripture that indicated women could not be ordained. From Catholic history, we know that women have not been ordained priests, but there have been deaconesses. We also know from Scripture that Lydia, Saint Paul's first European convert, had a house church. In the catacombs, there are pictures of women presiding at the altar. Actually, Jesus didn't ordain men, either. In the early days, there was a discipleship of equals. But the major tradition in the Church is that women have not been ordained.

After a careful search the biblical commission, the Pope's own men appointed by him, found there was nothing in Scripture that said women could *not* be ordained, and the majority of them favored the ordination of women.

But the Pope went against his commission's recommendation. In 1977, he issued a declaration that said, in effect, women cannot be ordained as priests because first, it has never been done, and secondly, women do not "image" Jesus, meaning that they don't have the body that Jesus had and, therefore, cannot image Him. This was an affront to women, so much so that we wrote about it repeatedly in our bimonthly newspaper, *New Women, New Church,* saying that we either image Jesus throughout life as a member of the Body of Christ, or we're not full participants in the Church. We even had buttons printed up saying ORDAIN WOMEN, OR STOP BAPTIZING THEM.

Since Pope Paul VI's declaration not to ordain women, the WOC has moved on, in some ways thankful that women were not ordained right away. We began to realize that we had a lot of analysis to do, analysis of the Church, of hierarchical structure, and of patriarchal structures and attitudes. In our studies we came to the realization that women do not want to plug in to this system *as it exists* because it is a system built on structural sexism. In other words, women are not included in any level of decision-making and they are actually looked upon as incomplete males. The entire system has to change.

One thing that has influenced us greatly is the change in the Church in Latin America, and this has extended our Christian commitment as well. In the sixties, the Latin American Bishops called a meeting of all the Bishops that convened in Medellin, Colombia, in South America, to survey Vatican II and see how they could implement its teachings. Out of Medellin came a whole Church renewal in Latin America, with the Bishops taking a path they called "an option for the poor." This was to identify with the poor and oppressed, rather than with the triumphal Church of the past. From its very first days in Latin America, the Christian hierarchy sided with the conquerors, with dictators, with powers that oppressed the people, causing tremendous suffering. Go back and look at how Jesus related to people. He came to heal suffering and liberate captives.

From this renewal came the concept of Liberation Theology, when the poor began looking at the systemic structures, their own experience, their lives and reflecting on what the Scriptures say about them. Now, they are realizing that they, too, have rights to basic human dignity, food, housing, health care, jobs and education, and that certain structures are preventing that: systemic structures in the economy, in politics, and even at times in the Church.

All those influences that originated in Latin America have made their mark on us. After Vatican II, Pope John XXIII asked the American religious to go down to Latin America to help. Going down with the idea that they could solve some of the problems, they learned instead from the people they sought to help. Being greatly influenced by the ideas of Liberation Theology in Latin America, they brought them back to the States where the ideas have been widely discussed and disseminated. Many of the women who are called to ordination today have been missionaries in Latin America. In a sense, they too have been inspired to liberate themselves from a certain bondage within the Church and they have certainly been involved with helping the poor. At the start, most of the women missionaries were nuns; later laywomen also got involved.

Today, the Women's Ordination Conference has a membership of about three thousand. Ten percent of this membership are priests, the remaining members are divided about equally into nuns and laywomen, with a small number of supportive men. About three hundred of the women members have declared that they feel called to the priestly ministry in one way or another. They speak of things like a "priesthood of the people" and of a renewed priesthood among the priests themselves. All of this stresses the fact that they see priesthood in many different ways, which, I believe, are concepts that need to be reflected upon. The actual priesthood of men itself is changing—and needs changing. Priests who are WOC members say, in effect, "Yes, although I am already ordained, I'm called to a renewed priestly ministry." They have been very supportive of us; in fact, many women first hear about WOC through them. The majority of members see WOC as an important effort not only on behalf of renewal within the Church but also on behalf of the ecumenical movement among Christian churches, whereby the Catholic Church can demonstrate to other Christians that it *does* believe in equality among sisters and brothers in Christ. Seeing no reason why women cannot be priests, our members actually see a benefit in women as priests.

What is happening is that ordained women in other denominations are joining in and supporting our struggle. One woman wrote, "I am an ordained Methodist pastor. But my ordination isn't complete until yours is." They see women as part of the whole Body of Christ and if one member limps, they feel the need to restore health to that member so that the whole body flourishes.

So far we have had three conferences or national meetings: the first in 1975 in Detroit; the second in 1978 in Baltimore, where people from other faiths came and talked about the connections between racism, classism and sexism; and the third in 1985 in St. Louis, where only women who felt themselves called to priesthood were asked to attend. In the past, we had three tracks at the meetings and women could join whichever grouping they wished: strategy, theology or a general assembly. At the St. Louis conference, two hundred women who felt a call to ordination came, and that number does not, naturally, include *all* women who feel the call. We went through a process of envisioning the

Church in the year 2000, voicing concepts such as ecumenical participation, base communities or house churches. There was a clear vision that in the year 2000, the Church is going to have much more of an ecumenical involvement. Barriers between Christians have been lowered because people are working ecumenically in shelters for battered women, peace offices and parishes, and on social-justice issues.

I'm an army brat and went to Catholic school in New Rochelle, New York. Just before World War II, I received my First Communion and Confirmation from Cardinal Spellman. My father was in the New York National Guard, the Fighting 69th, and he was called to active duty. With the war on, we moved around and I went to public schools. After World War II, while I was still in grade school, we went to join my father in Korea. There I met some Maryknoll priests, and I was very impressed with how they related to people. The few clerics I had known, nuns mostly, kept themselves apart—they wore veils and taught in schools. But these priests were out there associating with the Korean people and working closely with them. After my father was assigned to the Drexel Institute in Philadelphia, I decided to go to Catholic schools. Philadelphia has a large Catholic-school system and I went to West Philadelphia Catholic Girls High School. At one point I remember writing to Monsignor Byrne, who was a Maryknoller, saying I wanted to join the Maryknollers, but not as a nun. The order had both priests and nuns. Although not specifying that I wanted to be a priest, I was saying just that. Now I knew there weren't women priests, *but I had a call.*

My call to the priesthood probably originates with my mother, who was not, by the way, a suffragette or anything like that. She came from a family of five sisters. The firstborn had been a son who died when he was six weeks old. Always wanting a boy, her father raised the girls to be companions to him, teaching them to ride, hunt and shoot. There were no male-female stereotypes in that family. Basically, though, my mother was just a typical wife, but she was a courageous woman. Even as her sisters were telling her she was crazy to uproot her family, she shifted all of us to Korea to be near our dad. That was a turning point in our lives—it made a big impression on us to go to a country that had been devastated by war. Although we were with the army of occupation, I was able to look at the underside and identify more with the Korean people, who had always been under domination of some kind.

I married John Fitzpatrick, an army officer, who came from a good Catholic family. I myself was strictly brought up, being a pre–Vatican II person. Our children, of course, were all raised as Catholics. In our marriage, John and I tried to follow Church rules, using the rhythm method and all that. The death of my brother-in-law, Ed, in Vietnam was a turning point in my life. It was then that the urgent, insistent questions began. Ed's body arrived home the day he was due on leave. My sister, his wife, was preparing to go live in the Philippines so she could be nearby and he could visit. I was very close to Ed; he was like a big brother. His death made a terrific impact. I suddenly had to look and know *why he died. What was it all about?* The peace movement had been going on at that time, but I had been terrified of peace people who threatened my whole existence and reality. After all, I was an army child and an army wife, and that was all I knew. But after Ed's death, I started looking into it and became convinced that the Vietnam War was wrong. One thing, in particular, convinced me and that was something I heard from some demonstrators in Frederick, Maryland, who said that Fort Dietrick produced germ warfare. Afterward, I attended a coffee of officers' wives and a colonel's wife told me that three high-ranking colonels from Fort Dietrick had been placed in Walter Reed Hospital and that one of them had died of the plague brought about by germ warfare techniques developed at Fort Dietrick. I was completely shaken and began to realize that sometimes people on the inside *don't know,* and that protesters do a lot of homework and know the facts and what's going on. Inherited knowledge isn't always accurate.

A short time later, John and I were in Naples, Italy, with the NATO forces—this was also a period that contributed to my growth. In Naples I became involved in the Military Council of Catholic Women and ran tours up to the Vatican. We had a tour every three months during which a small group of people would be presented to the Pope—officers, enlisted men, their wives. It was a wonderful opportunity to mix with people other than officers and their families. I had been a real snob and now was meeting people from all ranks. I also became more aware of poor people in Naples, the first time, really, and rather than react with, "Oh, isn't that a shame?" at the sight of terrible poverty, I got involved with the

Neapolitan destitute, the *scugnizzi*, the ragged children with no homes. I got to know an Italian priest, Mario Borelli, a social worker and sociologist, through whose skill and brilliance Americans were able to relate *directly* with the people of Naples. Morris West wrote the book *Children of the Sun* about him. His abilities of analyzing a political or economic situation opened up new worlds of understanding whereby one no longer accused the poor by blaming the victims, but instead challenged the whole system that is causing poverty.

While we were in Naples, John was on orders for his second tour in Vietnam. I told him I couldn't support him if he went back, although I supported him the first time around. It was 1972, the year of the downside of Vietnam. His orders were changed three times because we kept losing the ground he was assigned to. It was a bad period for John, and my feelings didn't help. Finally, we made a pilgrimage to the Holy Land, and there he decided to retire, which meant that he didn't know *what* he was going to do. He had always thought he would stay with the army as long as he could, but actually he was of an age where he could retire and had reached the maximum amount of retirement pay. After a period of indecision, he decided to go to law school, and as a good wife I helped him all I could.

With John going to Catholic University to study law and my daughter entering the same university, I thought, "Yet *I'm* the one who always felt incomplete because I hadn't finished college." So I went to Georgetown University and studied history. Our family life changed radically; we became more cooperative, with everyone pitching in to do the housework, shopping and so on. At Georgetown, I studied under Monica Hellwig, who had a big influence on me. She is a theologian and former nun, who participated in Vatican II. A single woman, she has adopted three children— altogether an interesting, wonderful person. I decided to switch from a history major to theology and got my degree in theology.

It was while I was at Georgetown that I became involved in the Women's Ordination Conference. Two good friends went to the first meeting in Detroit and helped organize it. When they returned, they began holding meetings locally to inform people about the new group, and I became active in organizing these meetings.

After graduating from Georgetown, my husband and I separated. We were not divorced, but we were apart for three and a half years. In 1979 we got back together and I always say that we wouldn't be together today if we hadn't lived apart. In that time, we redeemed our individuality and integrity and now we're able to live and work in a marriage of mutuality—this is so important. John graduated from law school and works with refugees. But I came to realize that being a separated person in this Church means being marginated. John and I had both become members of the Parish Council and the moment we separated, the Council didn't know how to relate to that. We no longer fit the stereotype of *happily married couple*. One time he dropped off a report at the house for me to deliver and when I got down to the Council and said, "I have John's report today because he couldn't make the meeting," they nearly fell off their chairs. It's an important experience for me to have gone through because it creates a feeling of identifying with the oppressed. There was no divorce, no nothing, but you're still a marked person, an incomplete person, a separated person.

I took a job at Georgetown doing the summer continuing-education programs on Scripture study, social-justice issues and religious education, bringing to this work perceptions and social interests that were beginning to develop in my consciousness. The whole world had opened up to me. Nuns, priests and laypeople from all over the country came to these summer workshops. The programs were outstanding and considered the best of their kind in the country. I brought in nuns from NETWORK, the social-justice lobby on Capitol Hill, who did a program on lobbying for social justice, and I brought in Jim Young, a Paulist priest who started an organization for separated and divorced Catholics.

But because of the distress that my social-justice programs were causing, I lost my job at Georgetown. It was too threatening to my Bishop, the president of Georgetown, and the status quo. Having become involved in a small base community that was concerned with Latin American issues, I worked for a time at the Quixote Center, a social-justice group that takes on difficult issues. I made several trips to Central America, and took a month-long trip to Brazil to study basic Christian communities. Then, in 1985, WOC asked me to take over WOC management, saying they needed someone with a lot of experience and background.

The Women's Ordination Conference is a movement that has come up from the grass roots all over America. Women who join hear about it from others or come across literature on it. I believe that by the year 2000, there will be women priests. There are two things working toward this. First, the Church moves pragmatically and out of basic necessity. They are going to be ordaining women and married men and calling back the priests who left to get married. Remember, there is going to be an incredible shortage of priests; it has already started. Ten percent of the parishes in the United States do not have priests. In some churches women are already acting as pastors, although they can't say Mass and can't grant absolution. But they certainly do hear confessions! The other reason for hope is that there are a number of Bishops who see this issue as very important and are pushing for it.

Women who want to be priests don't fall into stereotypes, just as there is no stereotype for a male priest. The women have one thing in common: the call comes from God. They have to work on that and it can't be ignored. A nun/psychologist has done a study of women who feel called to ordination, and the results showed that women were well qualified to be priests. The women's movement has brought a lot of good gifts to the Church and to society. Women theologians are looking at Church history from the women's experience, and what is being gradually uncovered is that there have been women called to priesthood all along. Church history was not written by women and these calls were trivialized or ignored. It's said that Saint Thérèse of Lisieux wanted to be a priest.

Married or not married, women should be ordained if they have a call—with proper qualification and training, of course. From the beginning, WOC has had married women members. Why should ordination have a mandate of celibacy? It didn't at first. Jesus had married followers: Peter was married—we don't hear much about his wife but we've certainly heard something about his mother-in-law. Celibacy was only brought in later on, in the Middle Ages, when priests were giving Church land and property to their children.

We are a feminist group, more precisely, religious feminists, but we are not separated in the sense that religion is in one slot and feminism in another. We represent an integration of both. In our Church, there is an impression of women as being sinful. But we see how Jesus related to women as equal to Him. They were His faithful followers and the first to announce the Good News of His Resurrection. We have to overcome forms of dominance, of oppression, of sexism. Our aim is to have women treated as equals.

Saint Paul himself said we are all created equal, male and female. [In April 1988, the Catholic Bishops issued a Draft Pastoral Letter, *Partners in the Mystery of Redemption: A Pastoral Response to Women's Concerns*, recommending the expanding of leadership roles for women at almost every level of the Church except the priesthood.]

There is a possibility that women will be ordained deacons in the Catholic Church. I support that in many ways, but my concern is with clericalism and the limitation on marriage in the diaconate. If a married man becomes a deacon and his wife dies, he cannot marry again; if a single man is made a deacon, he cannot marry at all. There again is this problem with women being the source of evil in some way. I would hate to see women ordained to the diaconate and forced to take a vow of celibacy. An optional vow is fine. Another concern is that if women are allowed to become deacons, the Church may feel it has given us *something* and we should be happy. I'm always afraid of co-optation, of being bought off.

Some of us feel angry. Although I have nothing against the Pope personally, I have a lot of rage at the unjust system in the Church. One of the things the women's movement has taught us is that depression is caused by anger that goes backward in on oneself. The movement has taught us to get in touch with this anger inside us and deal with that, work with that, channeling it into positive energy rather than being destroyed by it. One thing John Paul II does not understand is *the anger of women, that we can be angry and still love the Church as much as we do.* If we didn't care, we'd walk away. Anger at injustice is what compels people to work for justice.

Sometimes I tend to get depressed about it all, but then I say to myself, "Look, the Women's Ordination Conference started in 1975. We've lived through the reign of three popes and we're still here, even though they've told people not to associate with us and done everything they could to trivialize and ignore us. Financially, we've had a rough time, but we're still hanging in." If I disappeared tomorrow, we'd still go on. Deep down, I truly believe that our aim is a gift from God; it's a movement that cannot be stopped. It's beyond us and is self-perpetuating.

General Alexander M. Haig, Jr.

Alexander M. Haig, Jr.

THE "MODERATE" POINT OF VIEW

It is our private schools, be they Catholic or Jewish or Baptist, that have recognized that there's more to learning than simply the facts in the textbook. They have always taught values. Public money for these schools is a matter of right reason.

General Haig is a self-made man whose father died when he was ten, leaving no resources, and he delivered newspapers in Philadelphia, his hometown, to save money to get into college. He grew up to be an army general (Supreme Allied Commander of NATO), the nation's fifty-ninth secretary of state, and a corporate executive (president of United Technologies Corporation). In 1987–1988 he ran briefly for the presidency of the United States on the Republican platform. All of his activities have been bolstered by a moderate's view of man and politics, and a firm belief in the values of Catholicism, the religion of his maternal Irish ancestors, to which he has automatically anchored the conduct of his life.

In December 1987, he took time out from the campaign and sat, jacketless, in striped shirt with monogram, in his business office at Fifteenth and M streets in Washington, D.C. With intensity he answered the questions about his faith, and here are his responses, including views on contemporary morality, Catholics in politics (especially Mario Cuomo), AIDS prevention and the Bishops' Letter on the Economy, which he challenges.

As the author was leaving his office, he had already picked up the phone and said, "Get me Henry Kissinger." He is a man who does not let a moment pass unseized.

I'm very suspicious of being called a conservative. The term "classic conservative" is totally perverted in today's world. The conservative traditionally believed in the *imperfectibility* of man, that is, man cannot be perfect because he has shortcomings. The liberal is more inclined to accept the *perfectibility* of man—that he can be perfect because he does not have shortcomings. That meant that historically conservatives were advocates of restraint on human fallacy. Strangely enough in modern times, the roles have been reversed. You find today most of the liberals wanting bigger government and more regulations, rules and plans from the federal government on the lives of our citizens. In that sense, liberals have become more conservative. In political terms a conservative is more concerned today about the intrusion of the government in the lives of individual citizens. That's why I'm always leery of accepting that handle.

I believe we do have shortcomings and that we need guidelines and rules that will protect us from ourselves. But I am also very optimistic about the nature of man. The human condition can contribute to sounder morality and performance and less inhumanity to each other. So, if I were to choose a label, I would call myself a *moderate*. I don't believe, for example, that you can legislate morality. What I mean by this is that the human spirit is so creative that when you attempt to legislate excessively, morally or economically, people will find ways around it because of the creativity of the human spirit. And in some respects, if those rules and regulations and laws are too ideologically promulgated and too rigid and insensitive, they may produce the very outcome that they are designed to prevent.

Now when it comes to Catholicism, I don't want to fly under false colors. I'm not what one might call a very rigid Catholic. I do seek to live by the tenets of my faith, I do believe in them, and I do try to abide by them. In such contemporary questions as the right to life, I accept the Church's position, not only as a matter of faith, but as a consequence of right reason. I don't know of any fundamental Catholic tenet that I do not accept and believe in. Now, I have to tell you I wasn't particularly pleased with the recent conclusions from the Bishops' Conference on the subject of AIDS and birth control [referring to a statement issued by the U.S. Catholic Conference

Administrative Board in 1987, titled *The Many Faces of AIDS: A Gospel Response,* which spoke of providing, in these critical circumstances, accurate information about prophylactic devices in the schools as a means of preventing AIDS]. I'm more behind Cardinal John O'Connor on that issue. What I'm saying is that there are certain areas where rationalization and excess flexibility are really the "death knell" of principle. There are other areas when they're not.

I'm a great believer in the dialectic of human experience, that is, debate or reasoning based on man's experience, not simply theory. I wouldn't say that I adhere to Immanuel Kant with rigidity, but he had profound wisdom when he pointed out that the flow of history is a dialectic in which you swing from one set of preconceived notions to another, like the swing of a pendulum. And believing in the perfectibility of man (he being a pioneer liberal), he felt the pendulum would become less and less extreme as it approached the ultimate truth, man's perfectibility. I think recent historical experience would suggest that he was wrong, at least in this juncture in history. Since the swing of the pendulum on the liberal side that was begun after World War II and given impetus by Vatican II, we now in recent years are seeing a change. What we are witnessing—under new papal authority, through Church doctrine, encyclicals and so on—is a period of substantial adjustment. I think that this adjustment was overdue, and I welcome it.

I am sympathetic to the pronounced social mission of the Church today, such as promoting justice and defending human rights and helping the poor in Latin America. As a result of the Holocaust in Nazi Germany in World War II, not only the Catholic Church but other religious groups found themselves under criticism. And I suppose there is a basis for it—*the shoe fit.* Of course, the Church has to be involved in social justice, morality, individual freedom. *It has to.* I'm very comfortable with this.

This does not mean, however, that I always agree with some of the positions that various Church leaders have chosen. Take, for example, the United States Bishops' Letter on the Economy [*Economic Justice for All: Catholic Social Teaching and the U.S. Economy,* final draft, published by the U.S. Catholic Conference, Washington, D.C., 1986], which advocated some startling changes in our systems of taxation, private-property ownership and defense expenditure, among others. I took a very strong stand against that document and accepted William Simon's request to join a Lay Commission which promoted some alternative approaches. Together with a lay group of prominent Catholic believers, under the aegis of the American Catholic Committee, we drafted a counter-pastoral letter in defense of our economic system. It was called *Toward the Future: Catholic Social Thought and the U.S. Economy* [published by the American Catholic Committee, New York, 1984]. Some fellow members were William Ellinghaus, J. Peter Grace and Frank Shakespeare. The basic point of our position was to remind our Bishops that capitalism and market economics are *not* an evil. Sometimes they have to be reminded of that because they see all the evils of a system—and too few of its virtues.

Religious affiliation should have no major role in running for office, or in the conduct of an office. Our Founding Fathers were very wise and prudent in the secularization of our government. But that has not always worked the way it should. Way back when I was young, people thought Al Smith was deprived of winning the presidential election—despite his great talents—because of his Catholic religion. I rejoice that Catholicism ceased to be a political issue with the presidency of John Kennedy. Now that the principle of a Catholic becoming president has been established, the less said about one's Catholicism and public office, the better.

Does that mean, however, that when a Catholic is president, his religion shapes his position on issues? The answer to that is *no*. But the "bully pulpit," as Theodore Roosevelt called it, which is the president's ability by virtue of his high office to communicate forcefully, is always going to be a reflection of the president's convictions—moral, religious, philosophic, economic—and they will also be mirrored in the positions he takes. It is important, however, to remember that we are a secular government, and we are a pluralistic society in which there are many personal views and convictions that differ from Roman Catholicism. That doesn't say that I don't believe the Catholic position is a correct one, but it says *I don't have the right to impose that position on those of other convictions.* For that reason, I like to keep religion out of politics. It has no direct place in politics.

I don't mean to imply that anti-Catholicism has disappeared. But I don't think it has gotten worse—the bias has dissipated somewhat. If I were ever to become a front-runner for the presidency, I'm not naïve enough to think that this issue would not surface—in a regional context and in anti-Catholic publications perhaps. [During John Kennedy's campaign for the presidency, 392 different press pieces of anti-Catholic sentiment, with a circulation of 25 million, floated about the country.] On the other hand, I really feel very comfortable today with American society as a whole. It has become less tolerant of such prejudice and more ecumenical in the context of personal choice. Kennedy broke down a number of those obstacles, but not totally. The greatest thing a Roman Catholic can do as president is to be a *good* president in every sense of the word, and if he's a good president, that fact should be quoted often enough to erode bias.

[The following three statements, on issues that still create conflict on the contemporary scene, were presented to General Haig for his reactions.]

Catholics holding political office are conscience-bound to implement the established Church doctrine whenever possible.

As I've indicated, any president has the opportunity to reflect his views through the bully pulpit, but beyond that, no, I cannot accept that statement. No one can enact laws on his own. We are a nation of laws that hopefully reflect a powerful national consensus. National consensus can either be codified by the courts or the legislature. I would not want to see that changed even though from time to time abuse is evident.

A principal aim of the Church in this country is to procure public money for its schools.

It is our private schools, be they Catholic or Jewish or Baptist, that have recognized historically that there's more to learning than simply the facts in the textbook. They have always taught values. Public money for these schools is a matter of right reason. Our public-school system suffers from a lack of values, especially in our grade and high schools. That is why I am a firm believer either in vouchers or tax credits, making it possible for diverse families to seek the private education of their choice. The private-education system in America has come closest to achieving excellence. I think if you were to do an analysis of dropouts and performance, private schools would have a much better record than public schools.

I would like to see an infusion of values in our public-school system. It is one of the victims of that period of liberal excesses in the late sixties and seventies when we expunged values, when we made it improper for a public-school teacher to have a personal, moral point of view on performance, on excellence, on a host of moral issues. Also, incidentally, on national issues. Teachers were discouraged by public-school regulation from teaching the virtues of democracy versus totalitarianism. All they could do was to teach the two systems and take a neutral position. That's ludicrous! These values should be back in. The reason I'm such a strong proponent of the private schools is that they have *never* expunged values. Those who have, have suffered.

Some Catholics are saying that the Church should not take single-issue stands on the taking of human life, as it has on abortion, but link various moral issues that also involve the taking of human life—capital punishment, euthanasia, war. Cardinal Bernardin has compared this approach to a seamless garment where everything flows together and nothing stands out. The rationale is that highlighting one area, as abortion, can be self-defeating.

As I see it, this is designed to water down the approach to the right-to-life issue. My interpretation is that because Catholics in some instances can accept capital punishment, they have no right to be as rigid as they are about taking the life of the unborn. That is replete with contradiction and the thesis itself is designed to weaken an issue that is not simply Church doctrine but a matter of right reason as well as faith. The taking of a human life, in the circumstances of abortion, is *wrong,* morally, and it cannot be adjusted because of the contradictions in taking human life as a punitive action to serve both as a restraint and a punishment for excess criminality. I can't accept that. The Bible is replete with examples of taking life for excessive crimes or in defense of the nation. These are not comparable issues. They shouldn't be confused.

I have repeatedly been asked about right to life and have taken a position. It is consistent with the teaching of the Church, but does not just follow Church teaching. God-given reason convinces me that it is the right position.

Other Catholic political figures have different views. In the case of Mario Cuomo, I find it startling that he could go out to Notre Dame, my former alma mater—I attended Notre Dame but didn't graduate, going on to West Point—and in his speech on abortion, espouse essentially heretical attitudes *against an apparent backdrop of applause and support from the Catholic faculty!* What I really believe about that situation is not a lack of fidelity on the part of the Catholic faculty, but the fact that Mr. Cuomo is such a Svengali and so articulate and so disarming that he could preach heresy without their even recognizing that he was doing so. Governor Cuomo is a dialectician of profound capability. But I happen to be a very close friend of John O'Connor's, and he wasn't fooled by it. And I happen to agree with him. That doesn't mean I always agree with John O'Connor on everything. I am sure we would have our differences, but we worked well together for many years when he was a naval officer.

The Catholic Church today has many problems, but modernization is the most anguishing challenge that it faces. I admit being discomforted by the dropping of Latin from the Mass. And I suppose it's because I was raised as an altar boy whose happy experience with the Latin ceremony was far better able, and is to this day, to turn me away from my day-to-day concerns and let me focus on the ceremony and the celebration that we were involved with. I still have that uplifted feeling when I attend a Mass in Latin.

And I admit frankly I don't like the guitar played in church. I differ from my Jesuit brother in some things. [General Haig has a younger brother, Father Frank Haig, who is a Jesuit priest and former president of Wheeling College in West Virginia and Le-Moyne College in Syracuse, New York.] He is very reform-minded. Well, he *was*. I find that enthusiasm for reform is part of being young, and age and experience modify it somewhat. But don't misunderstand me. I'm not one of these fellows that rants and raves on the changes. It's just my personal preference.

I am half Irish and the other side is Scotch-English. I wouldn't want to say much about the Irish part because I know how to get into a row very quickly. As a child, I served at the altar, and as a young man I was very active in my parish. But most of my adult years have been spent traveling. My life-style has been so hectic— I've lived in many different parishes over the last thirty years—that I've never had very much time for a parishioner's life, or for community life of any kind. And I suppose I could be criticized for that. I go to church. I'm a communicant. For thirty-seven years I've been married to the same woman, and we've been blessed with wonderful children.

Bishop Ricard greeting his Baltimore flock

Bishop John Ricard

THE ADVENT OF THE BLACK BISHOPS

At a Black Catholic Mass, the sign of peace (greeting one another and shaking hands) takes fifteen minutes, not just a half minute as in other churches. People are all over the pews, climbing across one another, kissing, laughing and talking.

Since the 1940s, the Catholic Church in America has inaugurated eleven Black Bishops, more than ever before since the nation began. A new breed of clergy, they possess Black pride and a determination not only to evangelize among unchurched Blacks but to right the wrongs of years of neglect within the Church. Their arrival has infused the religion with a new source of strength, vigor and basis for change. [Since this interview took place, one of the Bishops, Eugene Antonio Marino, has been named Archbishop of Atlanta, the first Black Archbishop in the country.]

John Ricard, forty-four years old, is a leader among them. Born in Baton Rouge, Louisiana, he is descended from a Black Creole family that has been Catholic for generations. He was the convenor of the Black Catholic Congress of 1987. A vigorous man who jogs daily, Bishop Ricard is both an activist and a visionary. Here, he presents the facts about Black Catholics and a Black man's account of what it means to be both Black and Catholic in a white and Protestant nation. Also included is a glimpse of the culture that Blacks are bringing to this faith—the preaching, the instruments and the Gospel song, whose sounds of joy are rattling the stained-glass windows of an increasing number of Catholic churches throughout the land.

Most of the American Blacks who are Catholic today came into the Church as adult converts, even here in Baltimore, which, historically, has had the largest number of Black Catholics. And much of the leadership in the Church came through conversion. Of the eleven Black Bishops, I would say that about half are adult converts. Bishop Moses Anderson of Detroit is a convert, Bishop Emerson Moore of New York City is a convert, as are Bishop James Lyke of Cleveland and Bishop Wilton Gregory of Chicago. It is fascinating how, as converts, they have been able to progress so quickly. The permanent deacons in the Baltimore diocese and a number of the priests are also converts.

In the past decade, the influx of Blacks into the Catholic Church has been marked. Membership has increased by 40 percent and Black Catholics now number about 1.3 million, out of a total of some 53.5 million Catholics. The Blacks themselves number about 30 million. The increase is partly the result of migration of West Indian Blacks of French culture, like the Haitians and others from Catholic islands in the Caribbean, like Guadeloupe and Martinique. But almost half of the 40 percent increase is the result of an evangelization thrust by the Church that took place in the 1960s and 1970's, especially in big cities like Chicago, Washington and Los Angeles.

American Blacks did not take to Catholicism earlier for a very good reason. John LaFarge, the Jesuit historian who wrote in the 1920s and '30s and whose work is still around, said the reason we have so few Black Catholics is *not* that any deliberate effort was made to keep them out. In the early years in America, the Catholic Church was an immigrant church and concerned mainly with European immigrants, protecting the faith of immigrants, fighting the onslaught of Protestantism, which saw them as a foreign invasion. There was little time or energy to think of the Blacks. More precisely, Father LaFarge said, no bold and innovative steps were made to invite Blacks in.

There were a few attempts. The Third Plenary Council of the Black Congress of Baltimore met in 1884 with a call for dioceses to reach out toward the newly emancipated Blacks. It invited religious groups to go into Black communities, and as a result the Josephites came over from Mill Hill in England. [Called originally the St. Joseph's Society of Mill Hill, the Josephites were founded in England by Cardinal Vaughan. It was the first missionary society established for the sole purpose of converting Blacks in Africa and the New World. Josephites came to America to address the issue raised by the Third Plenary Council to reach out to the Blacks. Soon after, they broke off from Mill Hill and became exclusively American.] Another Church attempt to reach out was the establishment of a national collection called the Indian and Negro Collection, which was intended for both American Indians and Blacks and is still collected, bringing in about $6 million annually.

In the 1950s and '60s, with the shifts of ethnic populations, things began to change. Many parishes in big cities that were formerly white—Irish, German, Italian, Polish—experienced shifting neighborhoods and these parishes, with very large churches, found themselves surrounded by communities which were predominantly Black, and non-Catholic. A response to that, a creative response on the part of many, was to say, "Why don't we invite these people to come into the Church?"

By the 1960s and early '70s, the Blacks were coming in in good numbers, especially because the Church had such credibility in terms of civil rights. During the civil-rights strife there was a forefront of strong Catholic participation. Cardinal Patrick O'Boyle of Washington, D.C., who died recently, took a very strong position in terms of integration of Catholic schools in Washington, D.C., and southern Maryland. Much to the chagrin of white Catholics, Cardinal Lawrence Shehan, the Archbishop of Baltimore, who died in 1984, took a rigid position for open housing before the City Council in Baltimore. In New Orleans, Archbishop Joseph Rummel integrated the Catholic schools before the public schools were integrated and excommunicated Catholics who resisted his effort. You had chief shepherds like these at the local levels taking leadership roles on behalf of civil rights. Of course, this created an image of the Catholic Church as *concerned* and this drew Blacks. The Church has had a fairly good record throughout the country in civil rights and is respected by Blacks in that regard.

With the influx of Blacks into the Church and the ensuing needs for plans to meet new problems, the time seemed right in 1987 for a Black Congress. A few years earlier there was a convergence of feeling, a sense that we were ready for a Black Congress. In American Catholicism today, there is an acceptance of group meetings of an ethnic and cultural makeup like this one. Hispanics have met three times: the last being the *Encuentro Terced* in 1985. The Native American Catholics meet each year at the Tekakwitha Conference to charter vision and bring together the collective strains. In recent years we Blacks had had some internal disputes that prevented this kind of meeting from occurring, but then there was a convergence of hopes and we said, *Now is the time*. You might say I was the convenor of the Black Congress and the vision behind it. It was a question of being on the scene at the right time.

Back in the 1920s the Church did not take up Father LaFarge's call for bold and innovative steps to attract Blacks. Now the Black Catholic Congress of May 1987 was taking up that challenge to reach out. Actually there had been five previous congresses, and to maintain that tradition we called our meeting a congress as well. The previous Catholic congress was in the 1890s and was five thousand strong. They had their own newspaper and dealt with issues relating to slave trade, segregated churches, and the need for establishing schools and churches in Black Catholic communities. Our gathering in May 1987 was to articulate a vision for the Church as it extends itself into the Black community. It seems like Black Catholics have an endemic problem: that of being a minority within the Church because they are Black and that of being a minority within the Black community because they are Catholic. So there is a fundamental question of how can we be authentically Black and authentically Catholic. That's not an issue for the Hispanic Catholics because they are so numerous, but it is for Blacks.

We felt we needed to come together and make a bold and innovative statement: *We can be authentically Black and authentically Catholic*. Also it was necessary to bring together the various elements in the Black Catholic movement into a cohesive whole, and in pursuance of this, the Congress discussed and passed a pastoral plan for the Church: A step-by-step process that reaches all levels— liturgy, social action, education—to help the Church as it wishes to extend itself into the Black Catholic community throughout the country. Before, as I mentioned, you had individual efforts of dioceses. Now, we're saying to those dioceses that have not done anything: *This is what we feel is a true and workable approach that we should try*.

Our plan of action encompasses three levels. It looks at the local parish, the diocesan level and the national level. At the parish level, we address issues relating to the life of the Church as expressed in the parishes. Concerned with all aspects, we are looking at social outreach, the local church's liturgical development, and clerical and lay leadership. In each area, we ask: *How can this be activated or revived? How can this be more authentically Black?* At the same time, all action must reflect very clearly the faith and magisterium [the teaching power and function] of the Church.

At the diocesan level, we consider the number of Black Catholics out of the total number of Blacks in the diocese and try to fathom the unique challenge of that diocese to increase the number of Catholics. The New York diocese, for example, has 50,000 Black Catholics but over one million Blacks. How can the Church be a true Sacrament to the community if it does not represent the community fully? When we speak of the Church as being sacramental, we mean, in effect, that the Church as Sacrament represents the embodiment of the Incarnation. If the Church is to be a true witness to the Incarnation of the body, person and word of Jesus to the community, it must then be that full body, it must reflect that full body. If it reflects part, a very small part of that, it's not a true Sacrament to our world and local community. It's kind of a shame to think that in a city we may have a Church that is strong and vibrant and very much alive, and yet a significant part of the community does not feel a part of it. This is true in many areas as, for example, in Los Angeles. Over a million and a half Blacks live in Los Angeles; maybe less than 100,000 are Catholic. It's not that these people just came; they've been there a long time. Under our pastoral plan, the pastor of a diocese would say, *We must as a Church begin to raise these questions anew and look at how we respond to them and accept the challenge.* And, of course, the same would be true on the national level.

On that level, we see the Church as a whole continuing its role—actually it has been quite admirable—of speaking in terms of civil rights and forming coalitions with Black Catholic leaders, as we address the myriad issues of Black unemployment, housing, family disintegration, and so on. We foresee an even larger involvement of the Church in these problems in terms of developing leadership and permanent action.

The next convening of the Black Catholic Congress will be in

1990. We plan to have a meeting every three or four years in different parts of the country.

Father Giles Conwill, a Black priest, said that God and the concept of religion mean different things to Black Catholics and to white Catholics, indicating the differences between the two. Let me attempt to expand on that. You see, we each bring to our understanding of God, into our concept of God, our history and our background, our experiences both historically and culturally. In their Pastoral Letter on Evangelization, called *What We Have Seen and Heard,* the Black Bishops discuss this. Blacks have a more holistic approach to God than lies in the experience of the European. For example, Blacks don't have difficulty in blending the social with the religious. When I first came to Baltimore, there was a social function for me—the Black community was welcoming their new bishop. At one point a piano sounded some chords and everybody put his wine and cheese down. Each person picked up a program and started singing hymns and went into a prayer service. From that we went back to the social. There was a blend of the two, and it was striking. Many whites who were present commented, in effect: *It's interesting how you folks are able to run the two together.* In the Western cultural tradition, there is a strict dichotomy: one does not express one's religious sentiments in public. And that's what we call our holistic approach to God.

Another thing is that Blacks tend to bring emotional expressions to their worship of God without a sense of inhibition. At a Black Catholic Mass, the sign of peace (greeting one another and shaking hands) takes fifteen minutes, not just a half minute as in other churches. People are all over the pews, climbing across one another, kissing, laughing and talking. It slows things down and the liturgy takes longer. You'll also find that the homilist speaks of the *relevant* issues of the day and of the community. There's also much more use of Sacred Scripture, with the homilist frequently using anecdotes from Scripture. Another dimension of Black Catholicism is a sense of community. The Blacks have a much stronger sensitivity to sharing responsibility, to the extended family. Being your brother's keeper has been historically the experience of Blacks, and this expresses itself in various ways.

Another difference between white and Black Catholicism is the understanding of Sacred Scripture. Again, this stems from our

Black experience. Bear in mind that when the Sacred Scriptures were used during the days of slavery, they were introduced to the slaves by and large by the white masters as a way of rationalizing slavery. When the slaves became aware in Sacred Scripture of the experience of the Hebrews in slavery in Egypt, they identified with that and believed that the God who delivered the Hebrews would also deliver us. And they prayed that He would. In Black music and liturgy, you'll find themes from the Old Testament and references to our Ohio River, the river that leads from the North to the South across the Mason-Dixon line, as the Jordan that will set us free, the river the Israelites crossed into the Promised Land. There are references to nonslave America as the Promised Land, free America as opposed to slave America, and the image of Moses that was applied to Black liberators like Harriet Tubman and others. These references are still very much used today. Even the names of churches that you'll find in Black Catholic areas and Protestant communities, like the Beulah Baptist Church, or Shiloh Church, are rooted dramatically in relating the Hebrew experience of the Old Testament to the Black experience of today. These are not abstract historical references that occurred a long time ago, but are occurring in the here and now. In Black worship, there's much more of an integration of Scripture with the themes of oppression and of liberation from oppression and of promise.

I have always thought that the Black Catholics, and Black people generally, play a kind of prophetic role. The prophet is a voice in the wilderness who reminds us of what we're called to be. Because of their suffering, because of their experiences of discrimination in the Church and society at large, Blacks serve to remind the Church, and *continue* to remind the Church, of its authentic call to the Cross and to death and resurrection. In the inner city of Baltimore, the Black parishes that struggle so much with serious difficulties can serve to remind the affluent, the successful and fast-moving parish in the suburbs and elsewhere, and say, *Look, there's more to our faith than security and comfort. This is where Christ is to be found.* The Black Catholic reminds the comfortable, secure Catholic what the real challenge of Catholicism is: *We were called to share. We are our brothers' keeper, our sisters' keeper. We share in the joys and sufferings of all human beings.* That's how we respond to Christ. We weren't called to comfort and security.

*   *   *

The dearth of Black priests is a dilemma. They are much fewer proportionately than white priests—the reality is that there are only about 300 black priests in the country out of a total of 53,000 priests. Most Black parishes are staffed by white priests, and that, too, is a problem reflective of the dilemma we face. In a sense, we're still an expanding Church, a Church that has not yet come to a full realization of itself. There is a tension: on the one hand, total integration and incorporation into the Body of Christ and on the other hand, the need to be Black. Because, you see, fundamentally the Church and the Black community reflect a reality in America, *and that is that integration really does not exist.* You may have a few examples of individual communities—very small communities and very few, as a matter of fact—where some integration exists. But by and large it does not exist in America. We are still very segregated societies. And the Church reflects that.

When white priests tend to Black flocks, questions arise. Are these white priests aware of the levels and differences of Black Catholicism? Or do they address Blacks as they would whites? Without proper training and acquired sensitivity, they treat both alike. But some *do* have acquired sensitivity and are very much aware of these elements.

Actually, when you consider the development of Black Catholicism in terms of the advent of the Black Bishops, a lot of that did happen with the collaboration of Black and white clergies, Black and white leadership. Black leadership was disproportionately more influential, but it *was* certainly relatively small, with only three hundred Black priests. So much of what has happened is a collaboration, just as it is in many parishes. Here in Baltimore we have only two Black pastors and some of our most dynamic priests are white. It is the same in Washington. St. Augustine's Church in Washington, at Avenue V and Seventeenth Street, is all-Black and celebrates a powerful two-hour Black-liturgy Mass, with Gospel music and African vestments, on Sundays at 12:30. Yet it has always been under white clerical leadership and still is. St. Bernardine's here in Baltimore is the same situation. By and large, I'm pretty pleased with the white leadership in Black parishes.

There's a very strong collaborative ministry among lay Blacks in the Church. Mainly, this is the result of Vatican II emphasizing the apostolate concept among laypeople, that is, we are all ministers in the Church. But more than this, collaboration rises out of necessity—out of the nature of the Black Catholic parish, which tends to be in areas like inner-city Baltimore, inner-city Washington, D.C., and the parish is challenged by its very nature to address social issues and problems. It *demands* that lay leadership. You have much more development of lay leadership and participation on that level than you would, by and large, in the typical Catholic parish.

Collaboration and closeness exist also because we haven't had the clerical experience for long. Priests and the clerical separation they bring are new to us. Because of our innate sense of community, it's more of a collaboration with the priest; "Father" is never *up there*, and we are *down here*. Blacks entering the Church from Protestant experience would bring that collaborative, congregational model with them.

However, if the Church is to survive in the Black community, it must develop an indigenous Black clergy and religious. In the past, until the 1950s and '60s, Blacks were barred from most seminaries. The Bishops had a problem which amounted to: *Where shall I put these fellas, and will they be accepted?* There wasn't a real recruitment in the sense of inviting them in. That is the historical baggage. A second issue was the seminary experience itself. Young Black men found themselves in a totally white world. Seminary experience is much more intense than the college experience, where cultural roots can be retained. The seminary created a complete acculturation into European Catholicism. It was very difficult for many Blacks. They came out as white as the white seminarians, with little reference to their Black community. By gaining a vocation, they lost their identity and effectiveness. We still face the question whether seminarians should be trained in an all-Black center or in an integrated one. The issue has never been quite resolved.

Clearly these historical obstacles are part of the reason for the paucity of Black clergy. Today, we're trying to find out how Black identity can be retained in the seminary, so that the person can be effective when he goes back to the Black community. Even more basic, we're addressing the subject of how to sensitize young Black men and women to religious life. We have a lot of catching up to do.

I must add that there is a fraternity, camaraderie that is very real among Black, white and Hispanic clergy. Closeness is very real at that level; and at various community activities, we function as equals. When we speak of the national body of Bishops, the United States Catholic Conference, there are only eleven or twelve of us Black Bishops, compared to the three hundred plus other Bishops, and so it is a bit unbalanced numerically. However, I think you have some very strong people among the Black Bishops, men like Bishop James Lyke of Cleveland, Ohio, Bishop Joseph Francis of Newark, New Jersey, Archbishop Antonio Marino of Washington, D.C., who was vice-president of the Congress, and Bishop Wilton Gregory of Chicago, Illinois—strong leaders, articulate, bright, intelligent, who make their voices heard. I respect that. But the whole body of Bishops comes together in common interest. Many Black Bishops serve on committees of the USCC, as on the Committee for the Development of Liturgy, which is for the entire Church. There is a subcommittee on Black liturgy. But as Black clergy we don't always deal with Black issues because our responsibility as Bishops is for all Catholics. Take myself, as an example. I'm a vicar bishop, and my responsibility is not only to Black Catholics but to the City of Baltimore, which includes every Catholic in it, the majority of whom are not Black. Our responsibility is like that of a mayor of a city.

The Bishops are aware that many of the social problems facing Blacks in urban areas—family disintegration, violence, crime—tend to occur in households without any church affiliation. I believe these problems can be addressed through our faith and Church. Black Catholics tend to function better, families are more stable, and there's less incidence of these problems. It's a sociological fact that people who are affiliated with, or feel themselves a part of, an organized religious structure do better in terms of all aspects of living: they cope better with problems, have stronger families, find better employment. Daniel Rudd, who called together the first Black Catholic Congress at the turn of the century, saw the Church as the answer to the myriad problems the newly emancipated were experiencing. I have the same kind of vision: our faith and our Church, not only as an institution but as a bearer of faith and Good News, can be more effective than anything in addressing these problems.

And I think it's true of other Black religions as well. But the sad fact is that there are many, many Blacks who are unchurched, who belong to no formal religious structure. Our estimation is that there are 10 million of them. Generally speaking, Blacks are religious people, but that is not always translated in terms of church attendance. It is that unchurched group that we're looking at.

To get to a more positive note, a happy one. In the past twenty years, Black liturgy—Gospel music, the use of drums, saxophone and piano (instead of organ), tapping, swaying, animated homilies—has become an important part of the worship of Black Catholics. The best way to experience this is to go to one of the Black-liturgy masses celebrated in many major cities. In Washington, as I've mentioned, there is St. Augustine's where the 12:30 Gospel Mass on Sundays pulls out all the stops. At Masses like this one, you'll hear Gospel music very dramatically and emotionally presented, with soloists and choir taking a prominent role. You'll hear Gospel music used to sing the Gloria, the Lord Have Mercy, the Creed, and other traditionally sung parts of the Mass.

You'll find the use of Black symbols—statues and icons that are Black more than European, such as the Black Madonna and Child, the Black Christ, and the Black Corpus of Jesus, saints, the martyrs of Uganda who died one hundred years ago, icons of Martin Luther King. You'll see vestments made from *kinte* cloth: the wool from Ghana used for stoles and other clothing. They're colorful and typically African—orange, yellow, black. You'll hear the preacher tying the Gospel message to the community in terms it can understand and relating it to the immediacy of their own experience. He speaks of drugs, teenage pregnancies, alcohol. And you would find a warm sense of community, as with the sign of peace, when Catholics shake hands at Mass and bid one another peace. You would think you were in a Baptist church, except that it's in the context of a Catholic Mass being celebrated. Most people are thrilled by all this.

It's hard to ascertain exactly how many Black parishes exist. Catholic parishes throughout the country number about nineteen thousand, and we estimate about two thousand of them are Black. Believe it or not, there has been no central focus to collect all of this data. But the Black Congress is getting to that. What we've done is write to each diocese in the country asking it to identify whether it's Black or white and the pastor who is serving there. The Congress plans a workshop for the purpose of sensitization and conscious-ness-raising. We've had about a 70 percent reply from the dioceses, and on this we've based our estimation.

About half the Black Catholics in the United States attend white churches, which means that they worship in integrated settings. At the Congress last May [1987], 109 dioceses were represented and about half of them were from integrated situations. In places like Kansas City, Rockford and Belleville [Illinois], you might have one Black parish; Milwaukee has more, maybe three. But the rest of the Black Catholics worship in integrated settings.

What happens is that Black Catholics simply move into the parishes. But there are many issues involved as to whether or not they're accepted. In some, they're accepted quite well. My sister, for example, who still lives in Baton Rouge, belongs to an integrated parish: her family is one of about ten Black families belonging to it, and the children go to the schools. But she says that participation on the part of that small minority is minimal. Some raise the issue that what they want in church is *an authentic Black experience*. Generally, in integrated churches, Blacks fight the coldness, the lack of real community and acceptance, especially in certain ethnic churches where the people tend to be more stoic. Where a Black Catholic church does exist, Blacks come from all over to attend the services. They come from everywhere, seeking that authentic Black experience.

In the Black churches that do exist and where the priests are often white, another question arises: Do white priests ministering to Blacks develop the art of effective, spirit-filled preaching? Sure, many of them do. Not too unlike the preaching of a Jimmy Swaggart, for example. Many of the white Baptist preachers speak like the Black Baptist preachers, using Biblical imagery and addressing relevant issues. White priests can do that, too. There are three in this area who do: Father Miller in Baltimore is one. He speaks like that and is very popular with the Black parishioners, providing them with a good positive experience.

If we think that the number of Black Catholics in the United States has grown in the last decade, it is as nothing compared to the fast-growing Black Catholic Church of Africa. Out of 200 million Africans, there are now about 60 to 70 million African Catholics. The fastest-growing segment of the Catholic Church anywhere is in Africa, I believe; in other words, the fastest-growing rate of conversion is African.

A large part of these conversions is due to the foresight of Pope Paul VI when he envisioned the growth of the Church there and appointed Black Bishops and encouraged African clergy and the development of local idioms and liturgy. There, seminaries are bulging at the seams, and as a matter of fact, there is a religious community of African priests who are foreign missionaries to America. Three of them are now in Houston, Texas; they are called the Society of St. Paul from Nigeria and are a diocesan religious community with about one hundred members who serve Black Catholics. They might even go to Europe and help them out [laughs]. It's fascinating. The Church in Africa is very much alive, with many African Cardinals in highly influential positions in the Vatican. Cardinal Gantin from the African country of Benin, for example, is head of the Commission for the Appointment of Bishops throughout the world. Numerically they are very strong; there are fifteen African Cardinals, and almost every major city on that continent has one. In comparison, North America has seventeen.

If you attend any of the synods in Rome or any of the meetings of Bishops, you will see there is decidedly a Third World dominance of Bishops from Latin America, Africa and Asia. The minority is European and North American.

As a priest I would like to be remembered as one who was serious about evangelizing the non-Catholic Blacks and serious about welcoming them into the Church and serious, within the context of our faith, about addressing some of the social problems they have. I would also like to be remembered as a person who served as a visionary.

I have a vision of Blacks less concerned about consumerism and militarism, less concerned about the material. I have a vision of them returning to our roots with a greater interest in the community, a greater concern for the individual and for our spiritual values. Historically, the African experience was decidedly nonmaterialistic and communal. It was alien to consumerism. I would like to see us return to these ancient roots. Martin Luther King suggested this very strongly. He attempted to establish a loving community of nonviolence in a violent world and a community that was truly communal, that saw the value of everybody pulling together and working together for a common good. I would like to see us recapture many of these values. There are hints of them in many aspects of the Catholic and non-Catholic Black community. It would be tragic if we were to become like the rest of America, so concerned with the individual as opposed to the community, and with objects as opposed to the important aspects of life—the spiritual values.

Missionary Sister Melanie in Buena Vista, Colombia, wearing handwoven poncho

Sister Melanie Persche

THE SUN GOD, PACHA MAMA, AND CHRIST

The Indians of Bolivia are a very gentle people. The family and the person, whoever it is, are the most important thing. Even among the poor, with rags on their shoulders, the essential thing is to be gracious and to shake your hand when you meet and when you leave.

In Buena Vista and environs of the tropical lowlands in Bolivia, Sister Melanie Persche, a slender woman from Flemington, New Jersey, teaches children the rudiments of the Catholic faith as part of a reevangelization effort. The youngsters are descendants of Inca Indians, with brown skin, black hair and eyes and, according to Sister Melanie, "the most beautiful manners of children anywhere." In mud huts, backyards and makeshift chapels, teacher and students meet for a brief education in Christ. Wearing a T-shirt and jeans that enable her to mount a jeep or ride a horse, the missionary wends her way to these open-air schoolrooms along uncertain roads that are sometimes flooded over with monsoon rains.

Sister Melanie belongs to our Lady of Victory Missionary Sisters of Huntington, Indiana. In addition to her work with the children, she is helping to establish Christian base communities by teaching local peasant leaders to conduct weekly religious services. Because there are so few clergy, the bishops themselves are emphasizing these communities and are encouraging laypeople to take responsibility for their church; the future falls on them. Sister's personal contribution—aside

> from her assigned work—is to provide encouragement and
> guidance to the women who lead lives of total subservience to
> the men.

John Sigstein, a priest from Chicago, founded our order in 1922
when he saw the need among Hispanics of the Southwest for
contact with the Catholic Church. In the twenties there weren't
enough priests to minister, and parishes were widespread. It was
missionary territory, and he envisioned an order really working
with the people and teaching them. Realizing later that along with
religious ignorance, there was much poverty and sickness, he made
our mission threefold: religious education, social work and home
nursing. Wherever we have missions, our Sisters go into the home
and take care of the sick.

But we have never been an institution. Most religious orders of the
time began by running big schools, big hospitals. Wanting us to be
free of those responsibilities, our founder made us mobile to go
where the need was. Our first missions were in the northern part
of New Mexico—in Las Vegas, New Mexico, a town you've probably never heard of, and in Santa Fe. We still have missions there.

Until the 1960s, we were home missionaries, working only within
the United States. From the Southwest, we spread to the East, West
and Midwest. And we *still* are mainly home missionaries. But in the
early sixties, Pope John XXIII issued a call to the whole Church,
asking each religious congregation to send 10 percent of their
members to South America because of the great lack of Catholic
guidance on that continent. Many Catholics were being lost to the
faith. All over the world, congregations rallied and asked themselves: *Can we do anything?* Our group decided to send two scouts—
two Sisters who spoke Spanish, one being Anglo (white American)
and the other Hispanic from New Mexico. They traveled in several
countries of South America, spoke to the people and made contacts. Upon their recommendation, we set up a mission in Bolivia
because it was the poorest country and most in need of help. It
opened in 1968, on the altiplano, a high area of the desolate

Andean plains, in the mining town of Oruro, with four Sisters in attendance.

When I went to Bolivia in 1979, I lived in this mission. But after we accepted two Bolivian women into our order, the mission became too small and we began looking for another home. We ended up in the tropical lowlands, the other extreme of the country, in the eastern part, in a town called Buena Vista. That's where I'm living now. The two Bolivians made vows and became Sisters. But not having a strong vocation, they didn't stay. Some of the Spanish Sisters have a problem that way. I don't know . . . part of it may be living with Americans. Actually, both sides have to adjust. The cultures and backgrounds are *so* different.

The people of Bolivia are a mixture of Indian and Spanish— some are more Spanish and some, more Indian. By Indian, I mean native people who lived there when the Spaniards conquered South America. The Aztecs lived in Mexico and the Incas in Bolivia and other parts of South America. In our part of Bolivia, the people are *mestizos,* the official racial designation—it means people of mixed blood. Definitely the Incas inhabited the altiplano—Oruro, La Paz and into Peru. A separate group that had conquered other native groups, they kept spreading out and gaining more and more land. In our part of the country, various tribes lived before the Incas arrived, and they are still pretty distinct, despite the mixture of groups. When the Spaniards came, there was another mixture. Today most native groups are pretty well mixed in with the general population. There still are, though, a few groups that live apart and are racially pure.

In the altiplano, where I first began mission work, people are shorter, with wide chests and bigger lungs than ours, the result of adapting to the rarified atmosphere of high altitudes. They're not very tall, about five feet ten inches at the most. In the tropics, people are more slender. Everybody has brown skin, and depending on the mixture, some are very dark brown, others are lighter. Because some Bolivians are descendants of immigrants from Europe, there is a strong European look. After World War II a lot of Germans came and settled and have intermarried with the upper classes. Among the poor, one sees more Indian features. The Indians of Bolivia are a very gentle people. The family and the person, whoever it is, are the most important thing. Even among the poor, with rags on their shoulders, the essential thing is to be gracious and to shake your hand when you meet and when you leave. The social quality of life is very important.

The majority of Bolivians are Catholics. *Relaxed* Catholics. The reason for this can be easily understood. When the Spanish came, their religion was something *you had to accept*. It wasn't a voluntary conversion. This is more true of the altiplano than in the tropics. It was more like, *If you want to get along, you've got to become a Christian.* Until this day many of the religious practices are a blend of their former Inca religion with Christianity. The Sun God, Mother Earth and Christ are all intermingled in the rites and customs. This adds an exotic bite to Catholicism here, but it's frustrating, too.

Local people have a strong love for Mother Earth, whom they call Pacha Mama (peaceful mother). To assure a good crop for themselves, they beseech Pacha Mama with gifts: they might bury the fetus of a llama in the corner of a field as a sacrifice and hope for a good harvest. At parties they like to drink beer, but before they take a swig, they spill some on the ground for Pacha Mama to drink. If they're inside, they pour some on the floor. These are customs of the altiplano. Where I live, the culture is different.

On All Souls' Day (November 2), Christians pray for the dead. In Bolivia, they have a much stronger devotion to the dead than we do. On the eve, they all go to the cemetery, sweep the graves of family members and light candles on the graves. They haul food and place the favorite dish of the deceased on the grave, like an offering. Then they eat and share. Anybody who stops and visits also partakes. Little boys come along carrying bags and they beg to say special prayers for the dead in exchange for some food. Rattling off Our Fathers and Hail Marys, they're rewarded with goodies, which they stuff into their bags. People celebrate the dead by being present and talking about the deceased. When the Sisters and I visit, we ask about the dead person and spend a little time with the family, hearing stories and tales. Trying to keep awake, some stay all night; others give up and go home. Keeping the vigil is considered a sacrifice. All-night vigils are done at different times of the year. On Good Friday, people stay all night in church—it's like a wake for Jesus Christ. All these traditions are very definitely descended from the Incas. On their own Day of the Dead, the Incas would dig up the corpse and dress it in real clothes and carry it aloft in procession. Thus, in praying for a good harvest and other good things of life, the disinterred would join the living.

Our mission with the Bolivians (aside from home nursing and social work) is to put them in touch with Catholicism, not only by instructing the children but by involving the adults as well. We do not concern ourselves completely with the children. In fact, in the United States also, we have come to realize that teaching children about Christ is not always the way to go. Learning from us and then going home to a family setting that is not tuned to religion, they lose whatever they may have learned. Today we put special emphasis on adult education and family programs.

In general, the children receive me very well, with a lot of affection and graciousness. They want me to stay, *not to leave,* and always urge me to come back. Actually, I can do better work outside the school setting. Usually, I go to them *after* school, in the neighborhoods, in someone's front yard. The weather in Buena Vista is so clement you don't need shelter. Or I may go to a little village about an hour's drive away over bad roads. When I arrive there are eighty or ninety kids of all ages, waiting. No matter how often I tell them I only want junior-high-school age, from twelve years and up, when I arrive, there are the five-year-olds, six-year-olds, all the little brothers and sisters of the older ones milling about. I can't send them away. I take them all.

In that village *all* the children show up and I use the public school because classes are in session only in the morning and then I just take over in the afternoon. In another little town, about twenty or thirty children show up and we meet in a mud hut that the townspeople use for a chapel. The kids bring their own benches and stools. We do not have a full-fledged CCD program [Confraternity of Christian Doctrine, providing religious instruction and formation] as in the States. No first-grade program, no second-grade program, and so on. What really attracts the Bolivians is their desire for First Communion and Confirmation. *They love the Sacraments.* They have a sense that keeps motivating them: *I have to make my First Communion.* That's our biggest help—their longing for these two Sacraments.

Since we do have them with First Communion, we make the most of it. In our program, called Family Catechesis, the children come for instruction in First Communion *but the parents have to attend adult meetings of their own.* It's a yearlong program, and that's how we get in our adult education. Not having the staff, or time, to teach the adults ourselves, we prepare Bolivian couples to do the teaching.

They're called catechists. Once a week the parents meet in small groups led by catechists who start the discussion that deals with basic religious concepts, talk about Jesus, God the Father, the Church, the Mass and so on. We hope some of this may develop into what we call *base Christian communities.* In South America, as you may know, one of the aims of the Christian churches is to form smaller groups of committed Christians who will really get to know their faith, live their faith, and be sources of social change. Liberation Theology is what is behind this, and the idea that poverty is an injustice, an enslavement which God doesn't want for His people. He wants to free them from this.

Thus we practice a little bit of Liberation Theology ourselves—by helping people to see, to look at their reality, to ask themselves, *Why are we poor? Why is it that the people in the city are so rich?* We help them reflect on this reality, *their* reality, and to feel confident in themselves so that they can do something and take a step, a little step, forward. If you were to ask me point-blank, "Have you seen any results?," the answer is "No." I can only hope that the direction I'm aiming at is the right one. Perhaps a generation from now, there may be some change. That's the hard part of working in a place like Bolivia—you don't see results.

Our catechists help fill a vacuum created by the paucity of clergy in Bolivia. There are forty or fifty of them and they're trained by us to work in our parish since the priest can only get around to each village about once a month. Every Sunday, they meet with the people for the *liturgy of the Word,* which involves reading from the Bible those sections that you would hear at Mass that Sunday, and then getting them to reflect on the significance of the passages and what they mean for them, in their individual lives. Now these small communities are not even at the point of being eucharistic communities in the sense of having the Eucharist or Holy Communion. Nor can the catechists distribute it. The people are more like catechumens—people preparing to become Catholics—who are still at the level of learning their faith before they can even make a real Christian commitment. Although they are Catholic culturally and by Baptism, they have never been exposed to the teaching that we have. And so we're starting at a level of preevangelization. In effect, we are saying, *Here's the Word of God and try to see what it means in your life.*

About once a month, a priest travels by jeep or horseback to the villages around Buena Vista. Living next door to our mission are two members of the clergy who perform these religious services. One is from Iowa, the other from England. They belong to the St. James Society, an American order that was started by Cardinal Cushing of Boston. It comprises Catholic diocesan priests who leave their parishes and work overseas for five years as missionaries, perhaps because of a secret yen to get away, or to help the poor. Ministering to thirty or forty villages, our two priests celebrate Mass and provide other services. The farthest village is about sixty miles away, and they have to drive on awful roads; sometimes it's like driving through rivers—not like darting along a superhighway.

The little house we live in now in the tropics of Bolivia is made of brick and has a cement floor. It was built originally for priests and when they moved away, the house was given to the Sisters. All the rooms are on one floor: four bedrooms, a living room, dining room, one bath and shower, kitchen and screened-in porch. Because there are always mosquitoes in the house, we sleep with a mosquito netting. Each of the three Sisters has her own room. We schedule everything, and all help with the housework and take turns doing the cooking. At open-air markets we find all the fruits and vegetables we want, and we buy staples by the kilo, equivalent to about two pounds. There aren't many packaged and convenience foods around, but there is a lot of cheese—one kind, mainly, that is made from cow's milk. Since we don't have much meat, we cook our dishes with cheese and soybeans. The three of us being from the States, we end up using as many American recipes as we can adapt—casserole-type things that aren't really Bolivian. It's our own style of cooking. Unlike the Mexicans, the people here don't have a distinct type of cuisine, like tacos. You know, I miss Mexican food—I love it so much. But the Bolivians are strong on soup. They make delicious peanut soup by grinding up peanuts and making it the basis. But it's not as distinctive as Mexican food and I haven't gotten into their kind of cooking.

We don't wear habits. Skirts, jeans, blouses, sandals without stockings are the wardrobe. Rummage clothes, mostly. Somebody might say, "Oh, that looks so nice!" and it's always a surprise because I don't think much about clothes. My hair is short and takes easy care. I am the beautician in our house and cut everyone's hair. But nobody can cut my hair, so I go down to a Bolivian lady in town. Each week we take a day off. For relaxation, we might drive into

Santa Cruz, which is about a two-hour drive, to pick up the mail. Picking up the mail is always a thrill—we have a post-office box there. We eat out occasionally and if there's a good movie, we go. If these things aren't appealing, I just stay home and read. We've had several floodings recently that have ripped apart the main highway and sometimes the highway is covered with water. It's just so nerve-wracking to drive through that to get to the city. I'd rather stay home.

There's a one-hour time difference between the United States and Bolivia. When it's 4:00 P.M. at home, it's 5:00 P.M. in Bolivia. We receive telephone calls at the priests' house across the yard. They call out and we run across. We have a jeep, a Toyota, for the three of us. Each of the priests has a vehicle. Sometimes, if we go to places that are inaccessible, we borrow a horse. When I travel on horseback, I'm always accompanied by someone who gets on another horse or walks. Riding horseback through the swamp or woods isn't at all romantic; it's a necessary evil. The ride is uncomfortable and you get sore if you haven't done it often. One of the priests who drives to a different zone has to cross a river, and since there are no bridges, a villager with two horses waits for him on the other side. He leaves his car and wades across the river and rides horseback the rest of the way.

The hottest it gets in Buena Vista is in the 90s. June, July, August are our winter months when we have very, very strong southerly winds that come in from Argentina. The wind-chill factor is much lower then. It never freezes and it never snows, but somehow or other it just feels very cold. Starting in September or October, we have 90° weather which continues through February and March. The rain cools things down a little. Sometimes it rains all day, day and night, day and night. It's a downpour, a monsoonlike rain. We're in a tropical climate and the rain stays—*it's just steady rain.* The worst we ever had was seventeen days and nights! And then the floods came. There's a big problem with flooding. But I must admit it's very pleasant when it rains. Things cool down. Back home in New Jersey, when there's a little shower I think, *When is it going to really rain here?* I miss the heavy rains of Bolivia.

The closest friends I've made among the people are the cate-chists, the ones we work closely with to make into religious leaders. I'm drawn more to them because of their dedication in building up the Church and their desire to learn. These things impress me.

There are so many things I'd like to say about the culture, especially about the position of women. That makes my stomach churn. People may say I'm coming from the American point of view, but when I go there and see the *machismo* . . . are you familiar with machismo? In so many ways, women are in a secondary position, in the family, in education, in public life. When I see things like that, I just want to say something to change them. But I know we can't go in and say, "This is wrong. Why don't you . . . ?"

Women are expected to stay home and take care of the children. The men are free to go out and do whatever they please. When there's a fiesta or celebration, the men go as if they were single, while the wives are at home taking care of the children. As the men sit and drink beer with their buddies, they dance with other women. People rarely go out as couples. The second injustice is on the educational level. Finances are very tight and sometimes there's hardly enough money for essentials. But if there is a chance for anyone to go to school, it's the boys who go, especially for higher education.

Although there isn't much one can do about changing women's lives in Bolivia, I do try to teach the women their own dignity by helping them to appreciate themselves as people and realize they're just as important as men and equal to them. I take every opportunity to do so, as in classes and meetings. The ladies meet every week to receive surplus goods from the United States. That is their motivation in joining the Mothers' Club. But while they're there, *we teach them.* One Sister is an LPN [licensed practical nurse] and when she attends, she instructs them about nutrition, preventive medicine and first aid. When I go, I teach them religious education but from the point of view of human dignity and human worth. One thing I get across to them very clearly is the idea, *You are not second-class.*

We did this for several years. Then someone said, "Wait a minute. The men aren't around to hear this. So what difference does it make? Perhaps a little, but nothing will really change."

With the Family Catechesis groups that we have now, we make sure that the men are present and try to get the message across to them, too. For some the message is completely new. Believe it or not, some men say, in effect, "It's the first time I realize that my wife is a child of God, just like me."

Vatican Ambassador Frank Shakespeare with Pope John Paul II

Frank Shakespeare

EYES AND EARS IN THAT UNIQUE, UNIVERSAL PLACE

Let us beware of assigning predominantly Catholics to this job. Either this embassy is in the interests of all Americans, or we shouldn't be here.

In the summer of 1988, Frank Shakespeare sat on an ornate Italian chair in his beautifully proportioned office in the Villino Pacelli on Via Aurelia overlooking the hills of Rome. Ambassador to the Holy See, he talked to the author about the new American embassy at the Vatican and the role, position and pressures of the ambassador himself. He explained that since he is only the second man to hold the job, there is no body of reference or anybody to consult as he forms a pattern of procedure in the fledgling embassy. With particular emphasis, he allayed any fears on the part of non-Catholic Americans about this embassy: it has nothing to do, directly or indirectly, with what goes on in the Catholic Church as an institution in America and has no special relation to American Catholics.

After serving as director of the United States Information Agency, Mr. Shakespeare was appointed ambassador to Portugal in 1985. A year later he was named ambassador to the Holy See. In private enterprise he has held various executive positions with WCBS-TV, New York, and with Westinghouse, Inc., in New York. He was also chairman of the Heritage Foundation, a Washington-based think tank, and chairman of Radio Free Europe/Radio Liberty, which broadcasts to the Soviet Union and Eastern Europe. A graduate of Holy Cross College, he is married and the father of three children.

T he question I'm frequently asked is, *Why did the government of the United States decide to send an ambassador to the Holy See and establish an embassy there in the 1980s and not before?* Attempts *were* made earlier. In 1950 President Truman formally proposed to the Senate that the Vatican be made an embassy and actually submitted the name of General Mark Clark as ambassador. But in its wisdom, the Senate decided not to. Truman's suggestion was based on his positive experience of having a president's personal representative in Rome, a man named Myron Taylor, who was not formally an ambassador but more or less a de facto ambassador. The post was started by Franklin Roosevelt in 1939 when he appointed the first president's personal representative to serve for the balance of his term. Presumably, he did so because he sensed the possibility of a great conflagration in the world, that it would be worldwide in its concerns, and he wanted *eyes and ears in the place that is uniquely worldwide in its penetration and influence: the Vatican.* When the Senate refused Truman, he withdrew his proposal and canceled the position of president's personal representative. We went home.

And we stayed home all during the presidencies of Eisenhower, all during Kennedy's and all during Johnson's, until Richard Nixon's, beginning in 1968. Now Nixon was almost the quintessential foreign-policy president, a man with extraordinary experience in foreign policy. When he became head of state, he was cognizant of the serious problems that beset the world and he was involved with all of them. And he had dreams. War was tearing us apart and he had to find a solution to the situation in Vietnam. For a long time, he had thought in depth about the Soviet Union, about the nature of Communism and of the major-power struggle. Wanting to change our relationship with the Russians, he sought to become the first president of the United States ever to visit the Soviet Union, and he accomplished this. Concerning China, a place that fascinated him all his adult life, he sought to open up that vast land and bring her into intercourse with the rest of the world. He visited China. In 1967, there had been a tremendous war in the Middle East, and he felt there was still a problem—the war had settled nothing. In view of this, Nixon, like Roosevelt before him, said in effect: *I need eyes and ears in that unique universal place.*

Thus, because he was a foreign-policy president, Nixon wrapped himself in the mantle of Roosevelt and Truman and proposed to reestablish the president's personal representative. His request granted, he chose Henry Cabot Lodge. Why didn't he propose an embassy? From his own experience when he was a senator, he knew the trouble Truman had in proposing that to the Senate, and perhaps he told himself the only way to get his man in Rome was *not* to ruffle feathers by proposing a full-fledged embassy. When Jimmy Carter became president, he kept the post of personal representative, despite the fact that he was a born-again Christian and came from the South, a region that had serious concern about the appropriateness of our having representation here. He appointed Robert Wagner for the job, a man who had been mayor of New York City. After Ronald Reagan took over, he appointed William Wilson as personal representative, who later became the first ambassador.

Now, I don't think any other nation could have gotten away with the concept of personal envoy. We were a superpower and, as I said, that post was established by Roosevelt very quickly during World War II. Continental Europe had fallen and there were only two countries in the world with the bulwark of freedom—England and the United States. It depended on these two nations to set Europe free. Thus, a personal representative from one of those two powers, the greater power, was a special person no matter what you called him. When the war ended, the United States emerged as a true superpower that had interests all over the world.

The reason the Senate was loath, in the first place, to have a full-fledged ambassador at the Holy See is, I think, pretty clear. That august body, and by extension the American people, have always thought it unsuitable, in view of our concept of the separation of Church and State, to have any special relationship with the Holy See. The reason is that the Holy See has the connotation of being specifically a church despite the fact that it has a legal entity as a state. This attitude was exacerbated by the suspicion that has existed on the part of Protestants toward Catholics in this country. That kind of thinking has waned and Americans are beginning to realize the appropriateness of our official representation at the Holy See, especially since the rest of the world—118 countries in all—has ambassadors there.

For some time our presidents had been toying with the idea that for the benefit of foreign policy, the Vatican is a useful place to have eyes and ears. Finally, in 1984, President Reagan decided to formalize a relationship by establishing an embassy.

Why is the United States here? Before responding to that, let me mention a bit of history. The Holy See, which is the government of the Holy Catholic Church, has been in existence for some two thousand years, and it has seen states come and go; it has seen institutions come and go. By its very nature, it has a long-term vision of human life, a vision that is rooted in the deepest spiritual values of man's relationship with God, his relationship with eternity, and his relationship to the State. It is essentially a moral vision and there are really very few human institutions where that is the infusing value. William Wilson, the first ambassador, said that a moral vision was needed in international relations and that there can be no human order unless it's based on a vision of a person's origin in God. His statement might be taken to mean that we are here in search of that moral vision.

But that is not the reason the United States is here. Although that moral vision is a very important factor, the United States is here specifically because it is useful to us from a foreign-policy point of view to talk about foreign-policy situations with the Holy See. What does that mean, *specifically*? It means that the Holy See has been associated with many countries, many places for a very long time and often in a way that is profound. They know a great deal about what is going on in various parts of the world—the Philippines, Central America, South America, the Middle East, Eastern Europe, Lithuania, the Ukraine. Places like that. The United States being a power that is involved all over the world, it has a great need to talk with people who have deep knowledge about what is going on in different areas. It is in the specific foreign-policy interest of the government and people of the United States to have a diplomatic mission here, *and that's why we're here.*

I'd like to elaborate on this a bit. The 118 ambassadors accredited to the Holy See come from most everywhere in the world, except the major Communist countries. Three Marxist-Leninist states have ambassadors here; they are Nicaragua, Cuba and Yugoslavia. The remaining 115 countries represent almost everyone else. For example, many of the Islamic states have ambassadors here—Iran, Syria, Iraq, Egypt, Turkey—the list goes on and on. Now Islam has a moral vision. Christianity has a moral vision. The ambassadors from Islam are here not because of the moral vision of Christianity but because of the useful relationship between the states that happen to be Islamic and this particular state. It is a pragmatic reason that they are here. Japan has a population of 123 million people; 300,000 of them are Catholic, or one fourth of 1 percent, meaning, of course, that Japan's perception of the world is rooted in another vision, largely one that is not Christian. Japan is here because it finds it pragmatically useful for Japan to have diplomatic relations with the Holy See for foreign-policy reasons. One could give endless examples to reinforce the point that while the moral vision aspects of this unique state are interesting and important, they are not the central reason to have a diplomatic embassy here, for us or any other state.

What, then, does the American embassy to the Vatican do? We deal with *ideas*. This state deals with ideas, with movements of ideas in the world and with a sense of what is happening in various parts of the world. In the long run, that's more important than military or economic power because it's ideas that change the world. If you want to get a sense of what's happening to ideas and values and moods of people and attitudes in various parts of the world, this is the unique observation post because that is what the Vatican officials are specialists in. This embassy has a unique and special mission. It is much more of a world observation post than it is a diplomatic post. It is much more like our embassy at the United Nations than our embassy to France. The United Nations is a world observation post, and that's what this is. It is all very possible, for example, that in our communication with Vatican officials, we might talk about Mozambique on Monday, about Poland on Tuesday, about Nicaragua on Wednesday, about Brazil on Thursday, and about the situation with Gorbachev on Friday. In other words, we talk about situations taking place in the whole world where the officials have knowledge, contacts to a greater or lesser degree, and sometimes centuries of experience. Oftentimes the population itself, as in Latin America, is overwhelmingly Catholic or formerly Catholic, so that they have a deep sense of what's going on in that country in view of the people, the attitudes, the changes and the value judgment, and all of that. This exists here to a unique degree. Now, in order to relate to this world you need a very small embassy of people trained in ideas. You don't need consular offices or military attachés and that kind of thing. You simply need a small group that can relate to ideas. In that sense, this embassy is different from every other embassy we have in the world.

You may ask, *Who do you talk with about ideas?* The Vatican has a foreign office which is rather like our State Department except that it is much smaller. Agostino Cardinal Casaroli is head of it; he is the secretary of state, an office that is equivalent to our own secretary of state. Structured more or less the same way as our State Department or the British Foreign Office, this foreign office has desk officers and specialists in different areas of the world. If we want to talk to someone who knows about the situation of a country in southern Africa, we deal with the specialist who has been following the events in that country and has news that he receives from the nuncios, the Pope's ambassadors to those countries, who know even more. Exchanging ideas and thoughts, we do not use the telephone; 95 percent of what we do is done in person. Three or four members of our staff deal with these matters regularly. Our office being very small, everybody is in on the act, all the time. Everyone knows everything in terms of communication, and therefore we can pinch-hit. While we have presumptive lines of authority and structure, we all play the same game and we all help one another. One of us can do one thing one day, and the next day someone else will sit at his desk.

In reporting back to Washington, we sometimes send as many as four or five cables a day. But there are heavy days and there are light days, as in any other operation. An ambassador goes directly to the president only in an extraordinary situation, and we deal mostly with the higher levels of the United States State Department, with the assistant secretary of state, the undersecretary for political affairs or when the matter is of significant importance, with the secretary of state himself. From time to time, we are in contact with the White House through the National Security Council. Now there are a large number of American visitors who come over here to talk directly and personally with the officials of the Holy See. We facilitate the arrangements for them to talk and, of course, we are present. But the conversation is between the senior official of the United States and the senior official of the Holy See, one to one.

We have a twenty-year lease on our embassy building but we do not own it. [The embassy is housed in the Villino Pacelli, a beautiful Côte d'Azur–style villa outside the Vatican grounds that once belonged to the Pacellis, the family of Pius XII.] Leasing our embassy buildings is a grave mistake. Throughout the world, the United States leases 75 percent of the residences of its ambassadors. Not buying is stupid—that's a tough word to use—but it *is* stupid because if we are going to be in a place for decades and perhaps centuries, we should buy it. What a scandalous waste of money of the people of the United States that our government takes short-term leases for the majority of the diplomats' residences! We have 5,700 residences throughout the world for our senior diplomatic officials and because three quarters of them are short-term leases, the rent goes up every year or every two years. There is no doubt that this newly established embassy will be here for centuries, yet we rent this chancery, we rent my residence and the residence of every officer assigned here.

As Vatican ambassador, I am faced with two tremendous challenges. One is the result of the anomalous, unique position of this particular embassy. It is like no other. Intricately woven into its existence is a great sensitivity not only on the part of the United States but on the part of the Vatican itself. Very simply put, the Holy See does not want to become contaminated with the superpowers, and the United States does not want to become contaminated with the Church. My challenge is to try to find answers to the question: *Under these peculiar circumstances, what is the appropriate relationship between this unique universal place, the Holy See, and the United States, which is unique at this point in history as the superpower of the free world?* The United States embassy to the Vatican in 1988 is not like the embassy of any other country because we're not like any other country. Let me amplify that. The United States is truly involved almost everywhere in the world, and its role is extraordinary. If there is to be a disarmament arrangement between the East and the West, what that really means is that it is between the general secretary of the Soviet Union and the president of the United States. Many nations have ships in the Free World, but there's only one real navy in the Free World and that's the U.S. Navy. We're involved with Third World debt: a very great deal of it is held by U.S. banks. We have 345,000 troops forming almost the whole bulwark of the NATO Alliance, that is, troops present in Europe—the shield, if you will, against communism. There is also a nuclear shield, which is essentially the U.S. nuclear shield.

Since it is a brand-new embassy in this special place, what do we do to determine what is the appropriate relationship? Remember that in the bureaucracy of the State Department, there is nobody who has ever served here and thus there is no accumulated knowledge there or in the White House or in the Senate concerning the place. Just the fact that you have had to ask me basic questions in this interview shows there is no body of knowledge one can refer to. Facing this totally new situation, we are setting the precedents, we are setting the ground rules, we are setting the procedures for what the relationship will be between these two very important sensitive entities, the United States of America and the Holy See.

The other challenge of my job is for this embassy to try to communicate and feed back to the United States the perceptions, the information, the judgments on so many important places in the world that exist here in this universal place, so that those who make foreign-policy decisions in the United States can weigh them. This involves talking with knowledgeable people here, assessing what it is that they believe and know and think, reducing that to something which is useful and readable for those in policy positions back home and getting it to them, so that along with all the other information they have, they may incorporate this new information into their decisions.

This embassy has nothing to do at all, directly or indirectly, with what goes on in the Catholic Church as an institution in the United States. *We stay totally out of it.* Even beyond that, this embassy has not, and must not have, any special relationship with the 28 percent of Americans who happen to be Catholic. We represent the generic interests of the government and the people of the United States. The fact that there is a particular Catholic connotation in terms of the Holy See is something that we stay away from. In the formal sense, we represent the interests of our country and of all the people, including Protestants, Jews, everybody, as we should.

Now, on a worldwide basis, more or less the same thing is true. In other words, we have to distinguish in this embassy very carefully what is Church and what is State. We deal with the Holy See *as a state*. We deal with information and ideas that have to do with the whole movement of people as it affects foreign policy. We stay out of anything that is Church as Church. This is an area that involves a great deal of sensitivity and judgment because the issue can get cloudy. We must be constantly aware of our purpose to stay out of the realm of the Church both in its worldwide aspects and, most particularly, as it affects the United States.

I see the Pope a good deal: at meetings I shake his hand, and that sort of thing. But one-to-one private conversations with him are rather like one-to-one private conversations with the president. Let's shift it back to our country for a moment. There are, I would guess, about 150 foreign countries represented in Washington. Their ambassadors rarely sit down alone with the president, whether it's Reagan or Carter or Nixon, because he is a very busy man and because 99 percent of all matters are handled at different levels, appropriately so. Indeed, it is rather unusual for an ambassador to meet even with our secretary of state. Certainly he meets with the assistant secretary of state, a desk officer, or a specialist. The popular image is for an ambassador to go into the Oval Office, sit down alone with the president, and work it out. No, it's all done through normal working levels, and that's exactly the same here at the Vatican. As the U.S. ambassador, I would see the Pope in a one-to-one meeting only in an extraordinary circumstance. If it's an important matter, I would deal with Cardinal Casaroli, the prime minister and number-two man, or with Cardinal Silvestrini, the foreign minister. Normally, I deal with Cardinal Silvestrini. When a junior is here, he works with Cardinal Silvestrini's juniors, desk officers or specialists. That's the normal hierarchical arrangement.

My being a Catholic helps a great deal in my job, but it is something I have to be careful about. It helps because if you're brought up a Catholic, you have a natural sense, developed in you through the years, as to what the Church is all about, what the Holy See is all about, what all the titles—cardinal, archbishop and so on—mean. You have an idea of the way Rome thinks and you bring to your job an instinctive knowledge that would be quite difficult for an outsider to acquire quickly.

But let us beware of assigning predominantly Catholics to this job. Either this embassy is in the interests of all the people of the United States, or we shouldn't be here. And if it is to represent all of us, by what logic would we assign just Catholics to this post? Presidents have a tendency to do this because prominent Catholics who happen to know the president ask for the job. To be assigned as ambassador to the Holy See is like getting the Congressional Medal of Honor. All presidents will be under huge pressure from their most powerful and dearest Catholic friends who want to be ambassador to the Holy See.

We must be careful. Imagine how we would feel if all our ambassadors to Israel were Jewish. After a while, we'd say, *What is that all about? Do they have some special in on that? Should our embassy in Tel Aviv represent all the people in the United States, or is it something just for Jewish people?* I would respectfully suggest to future presidents that they must be sure to mix it up. We must not make this a Catholic ghetto or a Catholic post. It is an assignment for all the people.

Father McNeill, beleaguered adviser to homosexuals

Father John McNeill

THE HOMOSEXUAL IS ALSO A CHILD OF GOD

In the old days, many priests advised a gay man, "Find yourself a good woman and marry her. You'll get over it." Which is nonsense. Those marriages frequently ended up in the divorce courts of the Church.

In a church environment hostile to homosexuality, Father John McNeill has chosen as his particular mission to seek the spiritual health and emotional well-being of men and women who are either active or latent homosexuals. A Jesuit priest and himself a homosexual, he is the first member of the Catholic clergy to publicly challenge the Church position against homosexuality. In 1985, he published *The Church and the Homosexual,* a rational and compassionate reevaluation of the subject based on Scripture and current psychological research. It created a worldwide sensation and for this and other writings, and for having defied a Vatican directive to remain publicly silent on the subject of homosexuality, he was dismissed from the Jesuit Order early in 1987.

Father McNeill helped form Dignity in New York, a group of Catholic homosexuals who do not insist on celibacy for themselves. His ministry also involves retreats and workshops for all gay Christians who come from various parts of the country to attend them. A psychotherapist and teacher as well as priest, he currently practices psychotherapy in New York City, where he also teaches at the Institutes of Religion and Health and at the Union Theological Seminary. This interview took place in the library/office of his West Side Manhattan apartment, where he unfolded the story of his own life—and the influences that came to bear on his choice of mission.

After I was ordained and working on my doctoral thesis in Europe, I became totally aware that I was a gay person. I was fully conscious of my gay feelings. It was during my year of tertianship—a time of spiritual renewal and strengthening for priests, when we are supposed to nail down our spiritual life and attain peace, once and for all—that I experienced extraordinary struggle. Looking back, I realize these feelings were there since childhood, but I had been able to deny and repress them so that they never really became a problem. Now it was necessary to deal with them in some conscious way.

During World War II when I was a United States Army private, these feelings had become a source of some distress. But then, the major issue of my life was to keep alive and survive the hellish conditions of a prisoner-of-war camp in Germany, which pushed everything else aside. I had gone to Canisius College, the Jesuit school in Buffalo, New York, and finished one year. The war was on, and at the age of seventeen, I decided to enlist in the army in a specialized-training program. This training lasted only three months because it was really a hoax to bring seventeen-year-olds into the service since they couldn't be drafted. We were immediately trained as infantrymen and shipped over to Europe—ten thousand seventeen-year-olds sent in as replacements for the American casualties of the initial invasion. I went in as a rifleman with the 87th Infantry Division and fought the Germans right on the border between France and Germany.

After a month of combat, I was captured in the Battle of the Bulge and spent the last six months of the war as a prisoner of war in Germany. The Americans had control of the skies and were getting closer, and because the smell of Allied victory was in the air, the Germans were afraid of prisoner uprisings and kept us in a weakened state by starving us. I entered the army at about 140 pounds and came out weighing 80. All we had to eat on a typical day was one small potato and some thin soup. After the bombing raids over Berlin, the Germans sent me to dig out the bodies from the ruins and take them out to lime pits outside the city. All through the last days of the war, until the Russians arrived at the outskirts, I was a rankless, starved prisoner of war moving bodies to the lime pits.

From those war days, I date my vocation to the priesthood. One experience in particular stands out. We were sent outside the city to a farm run by the SS, where mink were raised. A Polish slave laborer, under guard, was mixing mash for the mink, a blend of vegetables for their feed. We were starving and he could see that because we looked like skeletons. When the guard's back was turned, he risked his life by throwing us a few potatoes. I signaled thanks, and he blessed himself. This slave laborer became a symbol for me—someone whose faith was so strong that he courted instant death for some strangers, and did it out of love for and belief in Christ. He had the guts to act according to Christian principles in the face of Nazi authority.

Since I had always seen myself as a coward, this man's act strengthened me. It gave me the courage to do what I think Christ would do in a given situation—even if it cost me my freedom or my life. The fundamental religious symbol for me—true religion—is *courage in the face of death.* It has become the theme of my life. Just this morning [June 29, 1987], *The New York Times* printed a report on yesterday's annual Gay/Lesbian Pride Parade in New York and titled the story:

HOMOSEXUALS PARADE IN THE FACE OF DEATH

As Grand Marshal of the parade, I gave a speech. The *Times* quoted me on this very point, to wit: "Our primary task these days as gay people in the light of the AIDS epidemic is to learn how to celebrate life in the face of death." It all rose out of that war experience.

Coming back after the war, I was in and out of hospitals. My stomach had closed and needed to be forced open. The condition was aggravated by beriberi and yellow jaundice. It took two years to get back on my feet. As my health improved, I returned to Buffalo and went back to Canisius College. After graduation in 1948, following my resolve to become a priest, I entered the no-vitiate of St. Andrew-on-Hudson, which belonged to the Society of

Jesus—the Jesuit order. Incidentally, in addition to the three vows that priests take, the Jesuits take a fourth vow of direct obedience to the Pope, thus removing them from the jurisdiction of local Bishops. They are responsible directly to the Pope.

The *novitiate* begins a young man's education for the priesthood. It is a two-year period spent almost exclusively in prayer and spiritual reading and formation, which leads to first vows. I took my first vows as a Jesuit in 1950. Two years of *juniorate* followed [a period of study in which classes in Greek, Latin and other disciplines are given in preparation for the study of philosophy]. After that there was a three-year period of studying philosophy at Bellarmine College in Plattsburgh, New York, where I received a Licentiate in Philosophy (Ph.L.)—a degree just below a doctorate, which allows you to practice or teach in that area of study. I enjoyed every minute of philosophy and decided to become a professor in the discipline. The *scholasticate* came next, a two-year period of teaching. I was sent to Canisius High School in Buffalo, where as a teenager I had flunked the entrance exams, and spent two wonderful years there teaching Latin and English literature. I was not yet ordained.

The next four years, from 1957 to 1960, were spent studying theology at Woodstock Seminary, the oldest Jesuit theological institution, which was then in Maryland. At the end of the third year, I was ordained to the priesthood by Cardinal Spellman at Fordham University in New York. A year later, I received a Licentiate in Sacred Theology (LST) and was sent to Europe by my superiors to do the *tertianship* at a monastery in Ghent, Belgium. Tertianship is a third year of novitiate, and like the first two years, it is spent in prayer and meditation. At this point, as I've said, my homosexual feelings became a real problem.

Leaving Ghent, I went to Louvain University, a Catholic institution in Belgium and one of the best schools of philosophy in Europe. There I continued to study philosophy over a four-year period and to work on my doctoral dissertation on Maurice Blondel, a Catholic philosopher who was silenced by the Church in the early part of the twentieth century. They forbade him to publish anything further under the threat of condemnation. I didn't know it then, but I was soon to follow in his footsteps. Repeating that pattern, when my book *The Church and the Homosexual* came out, I was silenced by the Church and ordered not to publish on that subject in the future. But let me tell you the events that led up to this.

After tertianship, when it became obvious to me that I had to deal with my homosexual feelings on a conscious level, I returned to the States. My superiors assigned me to teach at LeMoyne College, a Jesuit school in Syracuse, New York. When I went there, I became intensely aware of the gay situation. Gay students started coming to me for help, and I began to read up on what was available in the way of advice. I was looking for good psychological and pastoral guidance, *but there was nothing*. It was one of those subjects that everybody was afraid to deal with. For two years I spent all my spare time reading everything on homosexuality that I could get my hands on—psychology, sociology, pastoral studies, works by Catholic theologians, Biblical studies. I searched the world over.

A fellow Jesuit gave a major talk at Fordham University, which condemned homosexuality as a sickness and homosexuals as destructive. The evidence he presented was unconvincing. You see, I perceived my homosexual feelings as *feelings*. They weren't sickness, they were just a different kind of sexual attraction and they did not prevent me from growing spiritually and psychologically, from maturing and being healthy.

At that time, there was a big fight going on in the American Psychological Association concerning new empirical evidence that disproved the belief that people who grow up gay are mentally ill. The evidence came before the association and after an internal struggle, it decided to remove homosexuality from the category of mental illness, placing it in a different category. This basically said if you are *in conflict* with your homosexuality, then it's a mental problem. The concept thus arose in psychology that the health of gay people depends upon their ability to live with, and accept, and be comfortable with, their homosexuality. If they are accepting, they are healthy.

Now, the teaching of the Church is that *you are to see it as an objective disorder and you must deny and repress it.* The Church wants you to feel great discomfort. I saw the Church's teaching as leading gay people into extreme psychological disorder. The more you conform to the Church, the unhealthier you are. I began to think there was something wrong here. What is bad psychology has to be bad theology, and vice versa. The Church should listen to this new evidence which further showed that *no one chooses his sexuality, no one has a choice.* It's not that a man or woman can decide "I'm going to be gay" or "I'm going to be straight." You are one way or the other. Following Church teaching amounts to denying yourself any intimate relationships.

In the old days, many priests advised a gay man, "Find yourself a good woman and marry her. You'll get over it." Which is nonsense. Those marriages frequently ended up in the divorce courts of the Church. Homosexuality is grounds for invalidating a marriage. I found so much pastoral advice based on sheer nonsense and doing real disaster to a lot of people.

New psychological evidence indicates that the only way to live comfortably with yourself as a gay person is to accept your homosexuality and hopefully to enter into a committed, meaningful relationship with somebody with whom you can live happily, each taking care of the other until death. Now, the Church would say, *That's a sinful state.*

But consider this. I've discovered that some of the Catholic men and women who are gay go out, get drunk and have sex with their own sex. On Saturday, they go to Confession (or did) and receive absolution because they can say, "I was drunk and feel terrible about this and would like never to do it again." They do the same the following week and so on, and we end up with compulsive, promiscuous people who become alcoholics. *But who are in good standing with the Church.* On the other hand, you have gay men and women who go out, meet someone, live together and commit each other to a monogamous, faithful relationship. They can be excellent Catholics and Christians doing excellent work. These people would be told by the Church: *You must break up your relationship, or we will refuse you absolution.* I said to myself that there was something unrealistic about this.

With such a background of reading, observation and thought, I took the bull by the horns and wrote a series of three articles under the general title "The Christian Male Homosexual." I sent them off to a conservative magazine called *Homiletic and Pastoral Review,* which among other things, dealt with questions and issues that come up in counseling and Confession. The magazine accepted the articles and published them in the June, July and August 1970 issues.

Obviously there was a real hunger among priests/confessors for rational advice on how to deal with gay suppliants. The articles got an excellent reception also because they appeared in a conservative priests' publication. In view of this, the Church wasn't disturbed by them in a sense, but they provoked a lot of discussion. You see, in doing the articles, I found some new Scriptural evidence that there was nowhere in Scripture a real condemnation of *loving* homosexual relationships. There were condemnations of many forms of homosexual violence, promiscuity and rape, and the use of homosexual activities in the old pagan religious services. But there was no place where a genuine, loving relationship was dealt with, never mind condemned. The conclusion I drew was a bombshell: to wit, *There were no real grounds, either in human nature or in Scripture, for the Church's two-thousand-year-old tradition of condemning homosexual relationships.* The entire code of sexual ethics as put forth by the Church was thus challenged.

From 1970 to 1975 I was assigned to teach at Woodstock College in New York City. Here Avery Dulles and Walter Burkhardt, two famous theologians who were members of the faculty, urged me to continue my research and expand the articles into a book because they felt there was a real need. I continued studying the issue and developing insights. That was how I came to write *The Church and the Homosexual,* which finally led to my dismissal from the Jesuit order. The book took direct aim at the Church's record of homophobia, which was no longer supported by either Biblical or psychological evidence. I challenged the Church to reconsider its position. The empirical reason was that it was destroying the lives of hundreds of thousands of people and out of compassion, if for no other reason, the Church should stop and say, "What are we doing?"

While writing the book, I discovered there was no ministry at all for gay people in New York City—in all of this huge metropolis, let alone the Catholic Church. New York is the mecca for gays from all over the country. If you grow up gay in Omaha or Buffalo or Cleveland, you cannot live there as an adult. You move away because you don't want your family and friends to know. Every gay person grows up an orphan. So you come to the Big City that is very attractive because of its anonymity. You can be gay here without the folks at home ever knowing. Gays come here by the millions. There were a half million people demonstrating at yesterday's Gay/Lesbian Pride Parade, and they are the half million that can afford to be public and walk around the street without fear of losing their jobs. The others are hidden.

Consulting with a group of psychiatrists, psychologists and priests, I decided to begin a ministry to gays, using my own time, over and above my teaching. We opened a New York chapter of an organization called Dignity. Actually, my articles on homosexuality had spurred the creation on the West Coast of this group, which comprised homosexual Catholics who do not insist on celibacy. As time passed, the Church began to feel a menace from Dignity because we were challenging their position against homosexuality. People in Dignity were making a judgment of conscience that they had a right to a permanent relationship, just as some lay Catholics might feel free to practice birth control. Gays could live in good conscience and still receive Communion in Church. So the Church sought to come up with a ministry for gays that would strictly adhere to Church teaching. Father John Harvey founded a group called Courage whose concept is to give support to gays to live a celibate life. To belong to Courage, you have to commit yourself to a life of total abstinence and you have to agree that homosexuality is evil. Father Harvey runs weekly meetings of Courage here in New York. In Dignity, we accept all people wherever they're at. If they want to be celibate, we'll support them in that. And we support those who are in a relationship.

But gays who hang out in bars looking for easy pickups are another question. This can be a self-destructive life-style. We see it as a question of individual conscience. We don't substitute ourselves for the judgment of conscience of the individual gay, but we support him in trying to interrelate his life-style with his faith. The ideal in sexual relationships is that there should be no sex apart from a committed loving relationship. That includes both committed gay love and committed heterosexual love. This is precisely the theme of my book, *The Church and the Homosexual*.

Upon publication the book became a media event. I was on *The Phil Donahue Show* and *The Today Show*. My publishers sent me on a tour of thirty cities and arranged for newspaper and TV interviews. It was an immediate success. The book sold forty thousand copies and came out in many different languages, including Italian (it was being sold right in the Vatican), French, the Scandinavian languages, German and Spanish.

Rome panicked. The Congregation of the Doctrine of the Faith issued a statement that, in effect, did two things. It removed the *imprimi potest*, the official permission for publication that the General, head of the worldwide Jesuits, and the Provincial, head of the Jesuits in New York, had granted the book. The reason for removing it was that the book differed from and challenged the traditional Church teaching. This was a reprimand to the General and the Provincial who were thus advised that they should never have given the *imprimi potest* in the first place, despite all the advice from theologians. Secondly, Rome silenced me. I was ordered to be silent on the issue of homosexuality and sexual ethics.

When silence is imposed by the Church, it means that the person on whom it is placed cannot address certain issues in public. What I heard was that I should not talk about homosexuality in any public media, i.e., on television or in newspaper interviews or in lectures, but I was still free to minister to gay people, give retreats and workshops, preach to Dignity about such issues as spiritual problems, freedom of conscience, and emotional disturbances. Since the situation was not cut-and-dried, I took to heart the motto, *Odiosa sint restringenda.* This means that hateful things are to be narrowly interpreted. A canon lawyer once quoted that to me and said it was a principle of canon law, which is a set of laws governing the actions of the Church. Applying this principle to my case, I could narrowly interpret the limitation on my freedom and feel free to do anything that was not explicitly forbidden.

I kept testing that limit and did a lot of talking and speaking. I even published again and wrote an article for a book of essays called "Challenge to Love: Lesbian and Gay Catholics in the Church." My subject was not the ethical issue but rather the contribution that gay people make to humanizing society. It was a strong plea for recognition of the fact that gay people make a very important contribution, and a very loving one, to human society as a whole. The main argument was that many gay people are involved in human services out of all proportion to their numbers—in teaching, counseling, working with the sick, retarded and blind. I speculated as to why that was, and my conclusion was that the love the straight person normally pours into the family, the gay person pours out through his work into the community at large.

Rome was very upset. A new order came. Now I was told that I could not address the homosexual issue in speech or *in writing,* and I could not address it in the psychological, as well as the ethical and theological, aspects. The biggest blow was being blacklisted as a teacher. I had been a professor of philosophy, theology and ethics most of my professional life. Now I was boycotted from the Catholic-school system. Around 1974, six years after the book's appearance, my work with Dignity and ministry to gay people were increasing. Cut off from teaching, I asked permission of the Jesuit Provincial in New York to go into full-time training as a psychotherapist and it was given. I began training at the Institutes of Religion and Health in New York City. Founded by Dr. Norman Vincent Peale and associated with the Marble Collegiate Church, the school trains clergy of all denominations as psychotherapists. After four years of postgraduate study, I was accredited as a psychotherapist.

Today I have a full-time practice in psychotherapy—my office is here in this apartment—and teach theory of psychoanalysis to clergy at the Institutes of Religion and Health. Thank God, it's a non-Catholic school and I can teach there. Most of my ministry to gays goes on, including retreats and workshops in various ecumenical retreats, like Kirkridge in the Poconos. For the last twelve years I've given three or four retreats a year there for gay and lesbian Christians.

Most priests who are gay do, I think, live out their commitment to celibacy, so it's not an issue really. Some gay priests have left because they can no longer in conscience serve in a church that hates gays. You see, in its actions the Church is violating the Gospel. If gay priests stay in the Church, they are implicitly accepting the Church's attitude, and a lot of them end up sitting on that couch, telling their story and the dilemmas they face. I'm hoping they stay in because if they leave the Church, there's no hope for change. They have to stay in and become a lobbying force.

The orders from Rome silencing me had been getting harsher, and one came that was the harshest and most stripping. I had given a talk entitled "New Dimensions and Christian Freedom," which dealt with the freedom to be born again, with therapy as a kind of rebirth process. The speech displeased the American Bishops. To my knowledge, they asked Rome to act. Let me remind you that they themselves could not take action against me. As Jesuits take a special vow of direct obedience to the Pope, they are exempt from the jurisdiction of local Bishops. When the Bishops appealed to Rome to do something, Cardinal Joseph Ratzinger, who was then head of the Congregation for the Doctrine of the Faith, called in the General and said he had been told I gave this talk and that I had greatly upset the local hierarchy. He was issuing a new order that forbade me to minister in any way, public or private, to homosexual people. The General said the Cardinal demanded that I end my entire psychotherapeutic practice, but he, the General, would allow me to continue if I formed a whole other ministry.

My ministry to gay people was my whole life. What sense would it make to stay in the Jesuit order and not be able to speak at a gay liturgy, or even attend it? After forty years of priestly work, *this was suicide they were asking me to commit.* God was calling me to this ministry. People needed me, and they could not be abandoned at this point. I notified the General of my decision. Eventually, the Superior General of the Jesuits, Father Peter Hans Kolvenbach, asked to see me while he was on a trip to the United States from Rome, in October 1986.

I was fearful of this meeting and the outcome. And as it turned out, the General made it quite clear that if I were to continue the ministry, it would be incompatible with the mission of the Society of Jesus and he would be obliged to dismiss me from the Jesuits. He first reminded me of the special vow that Jesuits take of direct obedience to the Pope, and the Pope was definitely against this ministry to gay people. My response was that I had prayed for guidance and could not in conscience give up the ministry.

It so happened that a month later, the Vatican issued a letter on homosexuality—I call it the Hallowe'en letter because it came out on October 31—ordering the Bishops of the world to put out of the Church any gay group that does not fully conform to Church teaching. As a result, Cardinal John O'Connor of New York put Dignity (the New York City chapter) out of St. Francis Xavier Church, where meetings for gays were held. Aside from the ban, the letter made homophobic attacks against gay people and statements to the effect: *Homosexual rights are unthinkable* and *Homosexuals should not be surprised if violence erupts against them because they seek unthinkable rights.* It was a hateful letter in the name of the Pope and totally contradicted the spirit of the Gospel. Homosexuals are at a critical point. Because of the fear and hysteria over AIDS, they are in real danger of serious attack against their liberty, their well-being and their very lives. When you get a letter from Rome aiding and abetting such attacks and saying practically the same things, somebody has to speak up.

I held a public news conference. Strongly objecting to the letter,

I made a strong statement that it would go down in history as a terrible thing for which the Church will have to repent and do penance. Sometime later I received a decree of dismissal from the Jesuit Order for disobedience. I appealed the dismissal. Cardinal Hamer in Rome responded to my appeal. He wrote that certainly the Church was aware of my deep concern for the homosexual, but that I was seeking solutions that were not in keeping with the teachings of the Church. He also acknowledged receipt of letters I had sent which were written on my behalf by people whom I had helped. He said that their testimony did not alter the facts on which the dismissal was based. Therefore, the Church did not find sufficient reasons to retract the decree of dismissal from the Society of Jesus and he confirmed the decree.

What is my status today? I am now officially dismissed from the Jesuit order. There are some financial worries. I am sixty-three years old. Although secular priests may receive Social Security if they contribute to it, Jesuits take a vow of poverty whereby these payments are considered a violation of that vow. So I will not be getting Social Security. But I am hopeful. My health is good and there is my teaching and practice as a psychotherapist.

I am still a priest. I am not excommunicated and could continue to act as a priest. A Bishop would have to accept me into his diocese and grant me the legal right to exercise my priesthood. But the chances of that are dim. The condition of entering would be, once again, giving up my ministry to gay people and that is not possible. I think God wants me to continue it. I will work in a nonofficial capacity, giving talks, retreats, workshops, practicing psychotherapy, and teaching at the Institutes of Religion and Health.

But I miss my activities as a priest. My identity as a priest goes back to when I was seventeen years old and a prisoner of war in Germany. It is my purpose in life. Being cut off from my fellow Jesuits is also painful. But the community is only a block away and they make me feel welcome. I go over to have dinner and attend community liturgies. They're interested in my work and are supportive of it.

I'm taking the months of July and August this year [1987] to write a book. It's eleven years since the first one. This book will deal with the spiritual life and being gay and will comprise all the homilies, talks and workshops that I've given over the past ten years. The contract with Beacon Press was signed Friday; they are scheduled to have the book out by October 1988. I just settled on the title: *Taking a Chance on God.* I love the title. It came to me all of a sudden and I said, "That's right. *That's it.*" Later it dawned on me that I actually had a beautiful old ballad from the forties in the back of my mind. Do you know it? [In a sweet tenor voice, he sings several lyrics from the song "Taking a Chance on Love."]

Charismatic Annemarie Schmidt

Annemarie Schmidt

DID YOU EVER HEAR A WOLF SING?

When I first went to the Catholic Church here, it was like a tomb. It was not the same Church I had grown up with in Czechoslovakia. I cried out because the pain was so great in my heart.

Charismatic groups within the Catholic Church gather together in homes or church halls to sing and worship the Lord, study and read the Bible, and pray for one another. They often speak in tongues. Sometimes the leader of the group is believed to have extraordinary healing powers, granted by the Holy Ghost, which have been known to cure major illness.

Annemarie Schmidt is a charismatic who lives in Milo, Maine. While attending a charismatic retreat near her home, she herself was cured of a serious lung condition. An American citizen, she was born in Czechoslovakia into a family of wealth: her father was a baron with landholdings in the high mountains of her native land. In childhood, she had two great loves: the Virgin Mary and the animals of the mountains, including a pet wolf whom she reared. In 1946, after a series of war experiences that deprived her of home and family, she married an American soldier and came to the United States.

The saga she relates is that of a European believer/turned American Catholic/turned charismatic—a woman of joy who found the Church in this country a cheerless place and Catholics a people who bury their emotions. Through her own participation in conducting charismatic gatherings, she finally witnessed "the Lord bring forth their feelings through the outpouring of the Holy Spirit."

I grew up with the wolves in the mountains of Czechoslovakia on my father's land. In that country we cherish our wolves. Man has made an ogre out of this animal, and he's not. He is one of the most intelligent and beautiful creatures imaginable, with human qualities. A wolf mates with one mate all his life. Only one mate. If that mate dies, that is it. The wolf has territory that another wolf will not trespass upon—unless he is invited. I remember once a wolf from another pack came to our wolves' part of the mountain. He stopped and called out. Wolves have a funny "yip" when they want to visit. If our wolves did not give him a signal to pass the borderline, he would go away. He would not trespass.

The packs we knew usually consisted of what I, as a child, called "aunts" and "uncles." The "alpha" wolf—he is the leader—and his lady would go hunting together. But they hunted only for food and never killed unless they were hungry. We had very severe winters in Czechoslovakia when they could not hunt, so we supplied them with food. They would sit on the ridge, and by their sounds, they would let us know they were hungry.

"Where is my food?" the wolves would ask.

Never, never, did they touch one of our sheep, *not ever.*

I had a pet wolf whose mother died giving birth. An employee of my father's, the man responsible for the preservation of the woods and animals, brought the wolf cub in a basket to our house. A very tiny creature, he looked as if he were going to die. I asked to look after him, and Cook prepared a formula—I don't know what she put into it—but it was just right because the cub lived. I would take him, basket and all, to bed with me (it was very cold, you know) and feed him every two hours. So, I raised him; his impression of me was of a caring person, a mother. I thought surely that when he got to be a year or so, he would leave. And I *wanted* him to leave, I wanted him to be free. *He never left me.* As he grew up, he was always allowed in the house, and he slept in my bed. In wintertime he climbed underneath the covers. I didn't dare let my mother know. His name was Prince and he was my best friend. When I would sing, he would sing. Have you ever heard a wolf sing? He was beautiful and grew to be huge, weighing about 180 pounds. He was with me for nine years, and then the Germans shot him. A soldier had threatened me, and Prince went for his throat.

The snowstorms in the mountains of Czechoslovakia are so thick you are surrounded by whiteness and can't see a thing. But I was a good skier, and always eager to go skiing. During a blizzard, we were staying in the apartment above my father's factory and knowing my proclivity, my father said to me, "Don't go out skiing today. We are not going home in the storm and will stay here overnight."

Thinking I could make it home before the storm hit its peak, I disobeyed, put on my skis and left. The storm seemed to hit its peak right at the spot where there was a deep drop. I couldn't see a thing and lost all sense of direction. Frightened, I started praying, speaking in tongues—glossolalia, as it is called here. The people of my native village all spoke in tongues; it was nothing unusual. During my childhood, it was my prayer language. You use words that you yourself don't understand. What happens is that the Holy Spirit is allowed to pray through you. The language comes from deep within your heart by which the Holy Spirit prays directly to the Father. Our gray matter has nothing to do with it. I started praising and worshiping and singing, as I used to do sitting before a little shrine to Mary that had been built in the mountains. I still speak and worship in tongues. People say I'm crazy but that's all right. I don't mind that as long as it is for Jesus.

Suddenly out of the blizzard I saw a nose, then a face. It was Lady, the mate of the leader of the clan of wolves in the mountains. These wolves were close enough in territory to feel at home near my shrine. When Prince and I sat on top of the rock, they would come and stay below. When I sang, they sang. I used to say my singing hurt their ears, and they were drowning it out. What I really thought was *They are joining me in praising God because they are my brother wolves.*

I knew it was Lady because of her face, the shape of her muscles. She put her nose right onto mine and made a funny sound on her insides. I held on to her fur and she led me to her den where the tribe was with their young. They were smart enough to keep out of blizzards. That night they stayed around me to keep me warm. The blizzard didn't stop. The second day Lady became very agitated. I thought it was my presence and tried to explain to her that I couldn't go out yet.

"You know that, Lady. I know I'm in your way."

I was playing with the cubs and really thought that she had had enough of me. But I had read her all wrong.

With beautiful amber eyes she watched me and put her head on my lap. I petted her. Somehow the wolves had managed to catch some mice and they had their meal. Naturally, they didn't invite me but I never wanted to be invited to that. After she ate, Lady began walking and her hair was rising. "Now don't get ugly," I thought to myself. "I'll go as soon as I can." But that wasn't it.

Suddenly she disappeared and came back with a mouse. Where she got it is a mystery. She brought the mouse to me, still warm, and laid it on my lap.

"No, Lady, I can't eat that."

She sat looking at me for a moment and then took the mouse between her jaws and crunched it, as if tenderizing it. Holding the limp body between her teeth, she came close to my mouth, as I said, "Go away, Lady, I don't want that thing." She dropped the limp body and grabbing it, I threw it to the cubs. Naturally, the little ones went right after it. She got very upset. Lying down on her back, she exposed her breasts . . . for me. I did not partake. It occurred to me to eat some snow, that this might please her. I went to the entry and managed to scoop up a handful of snow, brought it back, and ate it in her presence. She calmed down.

When the storm let up, Lady began tunneling a way out and came back. She looked at me as if to say, "You can follow me now." I crawled out after her and found I could see where I was going. Digging out my skis, I went home.

Some years later, the leader of our wolf clan showed me another example of a wolf's compassion. After the war, broken and desolate, I returned to Czechoslovakia to look for my family. But there was no one left in the village. I went up to the hills to the little shrine I used as a child—that private place for me and the wolves who used to gather nearby. On the hillside I saw the wolf who had been the leader of the clan. He was old now, and alone—his lady must have died. I sat on my rock, and the wolf, who had never allowed me to touch him, came up to my rock and put his big head on my lap, as if to say, "I'm here. I know you hurt." When there were no human arms to hold a hurting person, God's creature had the sense to come.

Has anyone in America had the experience of petting a wolf, of hearing him sing, or of being allowed by him to observe and love him? God has given us the animals to care for. Why have we been so nasty? In many countries, the wolf has been made the enemy of man and because of this, the wolf has become secretive and afraid because man is afraid. When man is afraid, he gives off a scent that the wolf does not know how to handle and *he* becomes afraid. You see, God in His love for mankind has given us so many animal friends to love, and we don't do it. The animals know. They sense love and will respond to it. In most of the world, love is missing, and this is true of many people in the Christian churches as well.

When I first went to church here, it was like a tomb. It was not the same Church I had grown up with in Czechoslovakia. I cried out because the pain was so great in my heart: God has given America so much and we are not appreciative enough. I did not see any of the joy and love that my people had for one another. Here the faces were closed. They looked straight ahead, never turning to the right or to the left. At that first Mass, I felt a longing for Czechoslovakia. At home we would greet one another on the steps of the church and give thanks to God that once again we could see one another, touch one another. Instinctively we knew that if we could touch one another, it was the touch of God, the touch of the Father, and if one of us had pain in his heart, the spirit could feel that pain and we would cry *with* one another, console one another. And then we would go inside the church, into the vestibule and into the Father's house, before the table, to worship with joy and freedom of spirit. Sometimes the Masses lasted five hours.

The Church in America reminded me of the Catholic Church in Germany after the war. It had the same joyless spirit. But I could understand it *there* because of all that happened to the people under Hitler. They had forsaken the God they knew and took to their bosoms a new god of militarism, a new army, shouting "Heil Hitler." Broken, they now came to church for solace and they were in pain. But there was no one to lift them, to hold them when they cried. In my new country, there was no imaginable reason for an attitude like the one in Germany. I began making excuses for my brothers and sisters and said to the Lord, "Well, I think it's because they are a young nation." But then I began to question it. "Dear Father, what has happened here? Every church is the same. Have you not poured out your Holy Spirit as you poured it out upon my people?"

I discovered that the situation was aggravated by the attitude between different groups of Christians—the Catholics and the Protestants. In small towns and elsewhere, Protestants and Catholics seemed to hate each other. *But they both said they loved Jesus.* How can they love Jesus and hate one another? It seemed that Protestants never understood what Catholics do, and we never told them. They thought we were pagans, and they were afraid of us. When I started speaking to Protestant groups, these realizations came to me. The Mass and the Rosary were their greatest horrors because they did not understand them. We needed to pray that the Holy Spirit would come and fill the hearts of all people and kindle in them the fire of His love and to love Him the way He needs to be loved.

After my dreadful war experiences, I looked upon this land as the New Jerusalem. The Lord had chosen for me to come here through my marriage to an American soldier. When the Korean War broke out, he was sent to Korea and I came to the States with our young son. When I saw the words *In God We Trust* inscribed on American dollars, I was deeply moved. God has given us so much in America and we are not appreciative enough of God's grace towards us.

After my husband returned from Korea, we were sent to Germany and stayed there for four years. With World War II memories still painful, I did not want to go. I prayed and thought, "Lord, is there a reason?" There was. We went back and through the Red Cross, I put in tracers for my parents. I had such hope that they were still alive. Truly they *were* alive, and living in exile behind the Iron Curtain. With our constant requests, they were finally able to come to see us, but they had to leave people behind as hostages in case they fled. The Russians who were holding young people as hostages, told my father, "If you do not return, they will be shot." My children had the wonderful experience of seeing their grandparents for the first time. After the visit, my parents went back.

These situations—the great suffering of people behind the Iron Curtain—do not come out in American newspapers. Their hardships are not reported, and thus Americans have no idea of what life is like there. Some time ago I got a letter from a friend who was very dear to me and still living in Czechoslovakia. She wrote:

Dear Annemarie:

It is a very difficult time for us. We need your prayers, we need your singing to God because at this moment we cannot sing and praise and worship the Lord as He needs to be worshipped. It has been forbidden for us to go to Mass. We must be silent: we come and go in silence.

A few days later I got a telegram from a woman we both knew who told me that my friend had been killed because they found the Bible on her person. Desolation filled me. Here I was selfish and safe in America, secure in our faith, going to Church whenever I wanted and reading the Holy Word anytime. I felt like a traitor to my country. My heart ached at the thought of life under Communism, where praise of God is forbidden. This further added to my pain at America's indifference to God's gifts.

You have received so much. You have the fullness of His love. Pope Paul VI spoke these words to us. We have taken the benefit of His love, accepted it, but we are not living it. People of Christ need to pray and fast and come to God in repentance that we have not taken His gift seriously. Think of God, the Father, as a very precious good Daddy who has all the gifts packed and ready for His children. But the children don't accept the gifts, and if they do, leave the boxes unopened. They might say, "Oh, what pretty wrapping," but never ask, "What did Daddy put in that box for me?," never opening the door to their heart to allow the Spirit to enter. As Jesus said, in effect, *The Holy Spirit will come and he will teach you the truth. He will be your Paraclete [intercessor]. He will be your guide. He will be your helper.* We have not allowed that Holy Spirit to take over. Mary did. She received the fullness of the Spirit and she received Jesus. Jesus has to be born in us, too. Jesus has to come into our hearts and take flesh.

Beginning in the 1960s a few Americans who felt bereft of love and spirituality came together for prayer. They beseeched God, praying in effect, "There's got to be more, there's got to be more." They started searching Scripture and studying the Acts of the Apostles. As they prayed, God heard them and the Holy Spirit touched all of them. And for many the Spirit was released. You see, in my country we receive such gifts at the time of Confirmation and the laying on of hands, and we are blessed with the gifts of tongues, of prophecy, of healing, all the gifts that the Spirit has. Now, suddenly, the Spirit came in here. What came to life was the Charismatic Renewal.

The first time I came in touch with the Charismatic Renewal was when we came to Maine in 1972. My husband had left the army because of my ill health. For years my lungs had been troubling me since the phosphorus in the bombings of World War II had damaged them. They had finally capsulated. With not enough air to oxygenate the heart and the body, I was placed on twenty-four-hour oxygen. Despondent and frightened, my husband made a pact with the Lord. For years I had given a good deal of time away from the family to the local church, helping in any way I could. My husband prayed: "If you leave her here on earth with me and the children, I will give her to you."

My husband had recently fallen in love with the state of Maine and the people. On a hunting trip, he had walked into a church and people greeted him. They reached out their hands and said, "Welcome." They were average types, but the goodness of God had been allowed into their hearts and the gift of hospitality of the Holy Spirit was in them. Using not just their lips, they sang with their hearts. He loved them instantly and decided that was where he was going to retire. My daughter Katherine found the college of her dreams in Maine: the University of Maine at Orono. Everything pointed to Maine as the place where we should settle, and we bought a house in Milo, which is out in the boondocks away from big cities. It is very beautiful up there.

With my health getting worse, it was difficult for me to walk from one end of the house to the other. I carried an oxygen machine, but even that didn't help much. There was no feeling in my hands and legs, just numbness. Each day Kathy came home from classes to check in on me to be sure I was still alive. Then the Lord finally led me to a community of charismatics at St. Paul's Center in Augusta. It was there that I found the two things that were my most precious gifts: health, and people who were not afraid to express their joy to the Lord and cry "Alleluia." After entering the center's meeting hall, I stood in a corner with my oxygen bottle. People were afraid of this paraphernalia and I did not want to disturb anyone. With Mass about to begin, they were praying over a sick baby.

I said to the Lord, "Thank you for blessing this child. I know that you could heal me, too, if you wanted to. I'm grateful for whatever happens."

I felt a powerful heat come into me, a burning, but it did not hurt. For the first time, I could breathe without pain and knew the Lord had done something. In that moment I was completely healed and have not used the oxygen since. That was thirteen years ago. After my health was restored, my husband concluded his pact with the Lord: "I give her to you because you gave her back to me. All I ask of you, now, Lord, is that she can be home one day a month to clean the house. The rest of the time you can have her to do your work, to do anything you want of her."

The months that followed were beautiful and full of joy because I had been cured. We started a prayer group in our own parish with the same priest who had conducted the retreat at St. Paul's. Five of us came together every week to pray and give worship and thanks to God. But more than anything, I wanted to find a special way of showing my gratitude to God for being well again. One night I heard these words spoken to me very clearly and precisely: *Go to my people and speak of my love for them. I do not want my children to fear me but to love me and know me.*

My immediate reaction was to answer, "Lord, I can't do this. I do not know how to speak English well."

His response was *Go.* I prayed, and feeling a bit more confident, said to the Lord, "Nobody knows me. How can I go anywhere? You will have to open the doors. If you want this ministry to go forward, I'll sit in the car and you go in there and talk to them."

The Lord took care of it. A priest in a village near Milo, Father Rokus, asked me to come to his church and speak to the Ladies' Sodality [a devotional group]. Since I knew many of the ladies, that was no problem. Also, as a result of the ecumenical movement that had been ignited, some Protestant churches began calling me to speak and share my faith with them. Thus slowly I found my ministry, and the way to show appreciation to God for restored health.

Throughout the country, the Charismatic Renewal, which took a fundamental, emotional approach to religion by reading and discussing the Bible, singing, praying for the sick, was taking root. Participants became full of joy and the Spirit. But trauma took place when they attended ordinary church services and had to be quiet and subdued. They could no longer sit still in church. The results were devastating. Many Catholics left the faith and went to the Assemblies of God Church, not understanding their own religion. In Maine, the clergy tried to bring some order out of this chaos. I was asked to be coordinator for the Bangor area. Aware of the mess that existed, I didn't want to do it but finally agreed. One very important change we effected was to insist that the pastor or priest of the parish be present at every charismatic meeting or retreat so that he would be better able to deal in church with the uplift and fervor his parishioners were experiencing.

Despite these difficulties, the Catholic Church was becoming alive and prayer groups were being formed. In my area the Lord started a Charismatic Renewal group that sponsored "Life-in-the-Spirit" seminars, with twenty-two people in the group, including myself. Our team is called Children of the Cross. We do our Charismatic Renewal work by going into the parishes on weekends and holding seminars. The priest has to be involved, or we do not hold the meetings. Consecrating ourselves to the Lord to do this work, we have a special adviser, Father Paquette. The people on the team are just wonderful. They all hold jobs and have only a short weekend for themselves. But they give up that time and whenever a priest requests the seminar, we go into the parish. If we're not called, we don't go. Nothing is charged. We do ask for a place to put sleeping bags, and the parishioners have always provided: *I can take two home. I can take three home.* We have eight speakers who give talks on "God's Love" and other subjects, with the team circulating among the people and asking questions, like *What did you hear in that talk that you can relate to your own life? When have you felt the nearness of God?* You'd be surprised how many people never think of these things. We also eat together, have community together and worship together.

Praise, worship and release are the power of our charismatic meetings. Through them, people have been healed. Marriages have been put together again. People have become stronger in their faith because suddenly the Holy Spirit was released in them. They had the Spirit but didn't *know* and now they are able to give to God what God has given to them. They can open their hearts from the inside and say, "Lord, come in." It has been phenomenal.

Father Edward Malloy talking with Notre Dame students

Edward Malloy

HIGH-CALIBER EDUCATION IN THE MIDWEST

Catholic higher education has tremendous strength. There is no other part of the world with such an extensive and high-quality Catholic network of schools.

In June 1987, at the age of forty-six, Father Edward Malloy, C.S.C. (Congregation of the Holy Cross), succeeded Father Theodore Hesburgh as president of the University of Notre Dame in Indiana, one of the youngest men to hold that position. Nourished completely by Notre Dame, he obtained his undergraduate and master's degrees in English at the University, played on the basketball team (he still plays with the students every Monday and Wednesday nights), and served as associate provost assisting in the administration and development of all academic activities. At present, he is also a professor of theology.

Nothing pleases Father more than to talk about Catholic higher education in this country. He is a fluent and enthusiastic explicator of the subject. On these pages he explains exactly what a Catholic education is and gives a revealing sketch of a great Catholic university at work, Notre Dame: its operation, costs, curriculum, objectives, and hopes for the future. Born in Washington, D.C., he is the author of two books and numerous articles and reviews. The areas of specialization on which he writes, outside of education, include matters of social justice, the quality and distribution of health care, substance abuse and sexual morality.

Ａs a minimum, a Catholic education tries to address the preparation for life of the *whole person,* which includes, of course, skills
of various kinds, how to think, read and write, how to approach
scientific experimentation with comfort at a level appropriate for
the particular age group. In addition, a Catholic education tries to
prepare people in terms of values and in the implications of what
they're learning to everyday life, including decision-making. Obviously such a training also includes a concern and preparation for
a life of faith and worship and Christian service. That preparation
involves book knowledge and a participation in the worship life of
the community, that is, seizing opportunities for Christian service
to help people in need. I think *all* of these components are relevant
to a Catholic-school education.

A big difference between a secular and a Catholic education is
that in the latter, teachers and students usually share the *same*
religious background, which is not true of secular education. Another difference is the public and forthright way in which matters
of faith are addressed in the Catholic system that is not possible in
the secular system. Here one can talk about religion in general or
in a neutral way, but not in a committed sense. That's the advantage: that commitment in Catholic education that is both open and
systematic.

Now I don't claim that a Catholic education is always satisfactory.
But in the schools I know best, I *am* satisfied with the quality of the
education experience. I refer to Notre Dame, of course, and to St.
Mary's College, which is right next door here, and to Georgetown
and Catholic universities in Washington, D.C., my hometown. The
better Catholic colleges and universities are doing a good job.
There are some marginal schools in higher education that may
have lost their identity or may not have sufficient resources to do
the job well. But it's not for lack of goodwill or effort. Some schools
have a certain life cycle; not *every* school should continue to stay
open.

We read every day that Catholic schools are closing. They are
financially impoverished; there are too few clergy left to teach; and
so on. Then we remember the remarks of Father Theodore Hesburgh, my predecessor at Notre Dame, who said that Catholic

education in America is a monumental success story. Now, which view reflects the true picture? Without a doubt, I think Father Hesburgh's and for the following reasons.

Totaling approximately 235 colleges and universities, Catholic higher education has tremendous strength. There is no other part of the world with such an extensive and high-quality Catholic network of schools. That is, indeed, a tremendous success story, and I think we need to appreciate that. One reason we were able to grow to this point was the dedication of religious men and women who founded the schools and have been very instrumental in their development through the years. In the past two or three decades, we've seen a decline in the number of these religious administering and teaching in these institutions. On the other hand, we've developed a bank of talented lay men and women who have always been there but now are more actively involved in leadership roles. In many cases, they're doing an extraordinary job. At the level of higher education, many good things are happening. With a growth in the relative affluence of the Catholic population, we've been able to derive from our graduates sufficient financial support to be able to sustain the effort and even to dream greater dreams for the years ahead.

But this happy view is of *higher* education. With our primary and secondary schools, the picture is more negative. Because of the uneven geographical distribution of the Catholic population, the schools have suffered. Availability of religious men and women to teach has fallen, and religious communities that invested their existence into providing continuity for the ongoing life of the schools are themselves diminished in numbers. The costs of education, particularly at the secondary level, are very high, and in the absence of state and federal support, a greater pinch is placed more and more on the average parent's pocketbook.

Historically, there is a difference between Catholic colleges and the lower schools, which may partly account for their status today. Unlike the colleges, which have been owned and operated by religious orders like the Dominicans and Jesuits, Catholic elementary and high schools are owned by the Bishops and managed by the pastors in the dioceses. Back in the eighteenth and nineteenth centuries, when Catholic churches and parishes were beginning to be established, the Protestant model, also called lay trusteeism—in which the people who built the church owned it and hired the pastor—went against the grain of the Roman system. After a flurry of problems, it was established that the Bishop owned the institutions within the parishes and the pastors managed them on behalf of the Bishop. This system was to include schools as they were built. The rationale was to convince the people of the parish that they should support the parish and the institutions within it. It was *their* parish, and the schools were no different from the Church or any other aspect of local parish life. Once that idea became established, no one was going to buck the tide and the Church has stayed with it to the present. Up until recently, these parochial schools did very well.

Even today, some of these lower schools are full to capacity. Unlike an earlier time, the students are not children of immigrant Europeans—the Irish, Germans, Italians, Poles. Rather, they are Blacks, Hispanics and Asians who have added a new vitality to a waning system. The parents, however, are often not in a position to pay the tuition. How then does the Church manage to maintain these schools?

Depending on the diocese, one way is by the distribution of funds from wealthier parishes to poorer parishes. Another is to have special fund-raising efforts, particularly in the inner cities. In some areas there has been such dynamic leadership that it has been able to get a level of support from friends, many not Catholic, just because of the worthiness of the cause. Also, some Black and Hispanic parents are appalled by the nature and conditions of education in the public-school system and are willing to sacrifice to send their children to parochial schools. My hometown of Washington, D.C., is like that. And there are a lot of middle- and upper-middle-class people, especially Blacks and some Hispanics and Asians, who are desirous to keep the parochial-school system going for these reasons, as well as for a chance to pass on a certain set of values and religious traditions to their children.

Regarding state and federal help for our Catholic schools, I don't know what the future has in store. It is a constitutional question and a legislative one at the same time. To my mind there is nothing incompatible between government support and a parochial-school system. Catholic schools have not only contributed *variety* to American education but certain good qualities of management. Because we have less bureaucracy, the schools are run more efficiently. The environment is safer and the learning situation healthier. The state ought to provide some degree of support. Theoretically I understand why pure civil libertarians object to that, but I don't agree with that judgment. In our colleges and universities, we have enjoyed a long tradition of state and federal support for certain aspects of higher education. I don't think that has been detrimental to anyone, and it has certainly been very helpful to us. I see no reason that couldn't be extended down to the secondary and primary level.

On the level of Catholic higher education, a subject I am more familiar with, one of the most exciting things that has happened is the change to lay control of many colleges and universities. Lay control simply means that lay boards take over control from a clerical board. Now remember, it isn't lay control vis-à-vis the institutional Church—Bishops, the Vatican, or anything like that. It simply involves control of the institution by laypeople rather than ownership by a religious community. Notre Dame was the first large university, along with St. Louis University in Missouri, to be placed in the hands of a lay board of directors. Since our inception, we had been owned by a religious order, and at the time of our decision to change, we felt that we did not have sufficient resources to own and staff the university perpetually in the way we had in the past. Reality required a much more shared responsibility—one that we felt was appropriate to the time and, in fact, I think it has worked out that way.

Incidentally, practically all the 235 Catholic colleges and universities in the United States are chartered by the state. Their degrees are authorized by the state and then approved by regional and crediting agencies. Although our institutions have no financial support from the state, they do have federal support. The Supreme Court has ruled that unlike private primary and secondary schools, private institutions of postsecondary education—junior colleges, colleges and universities—are eligible for federal support because the religion that is taught or practiced is not thought to be catechetical but rather scientific exploration and, therefore, providing support for the institutions is not in violation of separation of Church and State. In practical terms, this means that the federal money comes to us usually through federal programs supporting higher education in general, such as financial-aid packages and support for research of various kinds. In some cases, the construction of facilities may be connected to research purposes. It isn't like the federal government pays our salaries or contributes to our endowment. The aid is for some *specific* purpose for which we are eligible, as are private and public institutions of various kinds.

Today many of our Catholic colleges and universities are independent and autonomous. By that I mean we are not owned, run, or governed by the Roman Catholic Church through its normal administrative structure, such as the Bishops, for example. Now many people are taken aback by the fact that these institutions are independent and autonomous. What must be remembered is that within the cultural context of our life and activities, we are *very* Catholic. I spend more time talking about how Notre Dame is Catholic and about the comfortable and mutually supportive relationship we have with the institutional Church. Actually, it's only when you have a crisis or controversy that the subject of our autonomy comes up. I think anybody who spends time at Notre Dame and does not think it is a Catholic university would have to be blind to death. It is overwhelmingly a Catholic university. But that does not mean that everybody on campus is Catholic. There are aspects of life here that resemble what goes on in any other university. But pervasively, something distinctly Catholic characterizes our worship, our values, our attitudes and our approach to education. And the *look* of things: I am a Catholic priest, I lead the liturgy, I counsel, I participate in the Sacraments—all of this reveals instantly to people that I, personally, and the institution I work in, are Catholic because of all these things that go on here.

Aside from being president of Notre Dame, I teach classes in theology. I am a moral theologian or Christian ethicist: both are terms for the same thing. Since Vatican II, the discussion that has taken place in the Church about the different aspects of theology has been healthy. We've had some excellent material: books and articles which, I think, have advanced theological speculation and pastoral practice. Some missteps and expressions of opinion have not won the support of peers and others. If you know the history of theology, that's not unlike the past. The impression exists, particularly in America, that theology was always the way it was right before the Council. That's a myopic historical view, and all that has been happening is that more people in the United States have become better educated and, therefore, capable of engaging in reflection and study of what are sometimes very complicated issues.

Through their education and reading, they are discovering that some theology is good theology, and some is bad, and they have to learn to tell the difference.

Concerning my plans for Notre Dame, I could talk forever. But I've identified a number of priorities, and let me tick them off. One is to give appropriate stress to our research effort and to our graduate programs. Historically, we've been known as a fine undergraduate institution, with selectively good graduate programs. What we are trying to do now is upgrade *across the board* and see for which of our graduate programs we can do this most quickly. We are particularly well situated to make our kind of distinctive contribution to the world of learning and culture, and I would like to see us pursue that as wholeheartedly as possible. A component of this contribution is that, in addition to the kind of technical training we can provide like everybody else, we can talk the language of values, and about the ethical issues related to the practice of the various professions *in a public way.* In general we can appeal to the importance of that dimension of education. In my meetings with corporate leadership, as well as other educational administrators, I find that they think Notre Dame has an advantage in that regard, that we should take some initiatives and that's what we are trying to do.

We just recently announced a major effort to increase our minority enrollment and the presence of minorities in our faculty and administration. With our goal of a 15 percent minority enrollment by 1992, we have just targeted $12 million of our endowment for purposes of financial aid for minority students. Another plan is to develop an awareness of the international dimension of education. We have a number of foreign-study programs in which we are trying to concentrate a lot of attention on the teaching of foreign language and culture, as well as on giving people a firsthand experience by bringing scholars and students from other parts of the world to Notre Dame. We want to awaken the recognition that we're economically in an interdependent and competitive world.

One recent change concerning courses has been an addition to the core curriculum that we felt was vital to the general formation of an educated person. The core curriculum used to require one course in either history or social science. Now we've added another requirement: one course in either literature or fine arts.

Of course, we will continue to emphasize an aspect of our education that is perhaps its greatest asset: our concern for the whole person, including spiritual development and training. That has been a reason that people have invested so much money, spent so much time and effort, in supporting Catholic higher education. Our people have always taken family life as a very high priority, as well as an investment in civic and leadership organizations and charitable works of various kinds. Now, certainly, others consider these priorities also, but I think our people have always taken them as the hallmarks of a Notre Dame education: the emphasis on family life, public service, and charitable works. And it is one reason we have such a high percentage of graduates who want their children to come here; 25 percent of our students each year are sons and daughters of graduates.

No college is immune from certain internal problems, such as the failure to provide proper guidance and advice on choice of courses for careers. We've had the problem. After careful study, we put into place a new position in the College of Arts and Letters which oversees the whole outreach to students and the quality of instruction and academic advising. Other colleges at Notre Dame have followed suit.

Precisely because of all the positive aspects of Catholic higher education today, a special challenge faces the Church leadership and theologians. That is to help Catholics who have a good education and are bright to understand the nature of their religious heritage and the problems it faces today. Catholics are better educated and many families are into the second and third generations of college-educated people. With so many Catholics in the professions and positions of leadership, their socioeconomic backgrounds have changed dramatically. At least, they now comprise a higher percentage of upper-middle-class and upper-class Americans on the basis primarily of the role they play in the economy and in the professions. As a result, Catholics have become very sophisticated and tend not to accept religious arguments given simply on the basis of authority. In view of this, the Church must be persuasive and have good reason for holding a particular position. These educated Catholics may be liberal or conservative or in the middle; some are more vocal than others. The challenge is to face the needs and questions of *all* of them.

To my mind the area that the United States stands out in is education, especially higher education. In this we are the best in the world. Students have flocked to this country from all over and continue to come here in greater numbers than we can absorb. I think it is appropriate for us to continue to focus our attention as a nation on this component of our overall institutional setup. But it costs money. Costs are a problem for all of education. Our tuition this year (1987–88)—tuition, room and board—is $12,500. That's a lot, but compared to our peer institutions, it's quite low. One of the reasons American education is the best is that we have invested in what it takes to be great. What we are trying to do here at Notre Dame is continue to provide the very best professors, facilities, computers, libraries and all the programs required to have a great university. That requires huge amounts of money and we are involved all the time in extensive fund-raising. We have the eighteenth largest endowment of schools in this country, and yet even with that, our tuition costs are fairly high if you look at what people make and what portion of their income tuition is. We try to package financial aid and loans and work-study programs to make it as affordable as we can.

I'd like to talk briefly about the notion of a Catholic university. In my opinion a Catholic university—the catholicity of a university— is a function of no one dimension of its life. It includes the courses in philosophy and theology which are required and the quality with which they're taught. It includes the kind of research that we do and the particular value-oriented focus that we take on it. It includes the social-research programs that we put in place to encourage our students and faculty and staff to make their contributions back to the communities in which they live. And it includes the worship life of the campus.

But one of the problems that we have is that a percentage of outside observers tend to focus their attention on only one aspect of what it means for us to be Catholic. It depends. People get upset at something that is taught in a theology course or at a remark made in a lecture or, if their focus is entirely on churchgoing, whether students go to church or not. In other words, when one spends time here and observes the University in action, I think it would be awfully hard for them not to appreciate that this is a Catholic university in the full sense of the term. And that we are *fully* a university; we're not a seminary, we're not a boarding school of a narrow sort. We observe principles of academic freedom. We have a diversity of people here, including non-Catholics who, I think,

Activist priest Elizondo (in raincoat) meeting opposition at a function at San Antonio's City Hall. Mayor Henry Cisnero (right) blocks his entry.

Father Virgilio Elizondo

THE COMING CHURCH OF THE HISPANICS AND MESTIZOS

A stranger in my own land, I began to experience guilt. Why was I not like the other children who spoke English and ate sandwiches instead of tortillas? Why was I different, outside of things?

By the year 2000, Mexican-Americans, combined with other Hispanic-Americans, will comprise the major portion of the Roman Catholic Church in the United States. After being ignored for decades, this large body of believers is being welcomed by the Church.

Father Virgilio Elizondo, rector of the Cathedral of San Fernando in San Antonio, Texas, is a trailblazing American clergyman who has done more than anyone else to bring about this recognition. As a prime force in the Hispanic movement of the Southwest and as founder of the Mexican American Cultural Center, he has struggled to correct the distorted racial views of Hispanic Americans held both by the Church and the civil authorities, and to right the many wrongs perpetrated upon them. Raised in the Mexican community of San Antonio, he has lived his life between two cultures, the Mexican and the Anglo, and his work is enriched by a deep understanding of each. Committed to his faith, he still insists that Hispanic religious practices that differ from the norm must be understood in their economic and historical context—and be accepted.

Lecturer, feminist and writer, he is the author of a book called *L'Avenir est au métissage (The Future Belongs to the Half-breed)*, which was published in France, with a preface by Leopold Senghor of the L'Académie Française.

T here is a saying that before there was San Antonio, there was
the Roman Catholic Church. The very name of the city comes from
the first Spanish missionaries who arrived at the banks of the local
river centuries ago on the feast day of Saint Anthony of Padua.
Celebrating Mass on the riverside, they named both the land and
the river after the saint. I would go a step further and say before
there was a Texas here, there was the Catholic Church. The fascinating question is whether this was part of Spain or of Mexico or
a republic. Now, of course, it's part of the United States, and
whatever it may be next, the Catholic Church was here, is here, and
will be here. Several nationalities have flown their flags over this
area but the Church has been present all through and has admin-
istered to all.

I was born in San Antonio. My parents were married in this
cathedral where I am now the rector. My mother's people came
from Mexico City during the great revolution in Mexico around
1910. On my father's side, it seems—and I would underscore *it
seems*—the family has always lived here, but some members went
back to Mexico after the Mexican-American War because they
saw it as a Protestant-Catholic struggle and did not want to live in
a Protestant country. In the early 1900s, during the great
depression in Mexico when living was very difficult, my father
was sent back to Texas to live with uncles who were still here. He
met my mother at one of our social clubs which, incidentally, are
still active.

My childhood was full of joy. In the Hispanic community in
which I grew up, there were no problems about identity or belonging. My father and mother ran a vegetable-and-grocery store
which became a kind of center for community life. Women would
come in, linger over the fruits, exchange news and gossip while the
men drank beer in the back and talked pleasantries. At home, the
atmosphere was entirely Mexican. We lived in a small house—my
parents, sister, mother's mother, whose name was long and
memorable—Dona Maria Manuela Petra Paula Ester Fernande del
Castillo widow of Peimbert—father's father, Don Antonio, three
canaries, two cats and two magnificent German sheepdogs called

Kaiser and Tarzan. I heard Spanish spoken everywhere and I did not understand English, but there was no need for it. Although we lived well outside the political limits of Mexico, Mexico was *in us*. Our early religious instruction was supervised by Mexican nuns who were hardworking, gay and smiling, educating us carefully with advice and rewards.

This paradise of my early years came to an abrupt end the first day I attended a Catholic elementary school run by German nuns near my home. It was in a German parish where the pastor still told the Mexicans who came to church:

GET OUT! THIS IS NOT YOUR CHURCH.

In the school, Mexican children were tolerated but not welcome. The years that followed were like purgatory. Hearing English was strange, and it was hard to study in a language I barely understood, in an environment that was so odd, so alienating. Accustomed to our own Mexican dishes, the food in the cafeteria—sauerkraut and knockwurst—struck me as bizarre. The Sisters never smiled, and I can still feel the raps on my knuckles with the ruler. The classes were endless. I got bored and flunked first grade.

A stranger in my own land, I began to experience guilt. Why was I not like the other children who spoke English and ate sandwiches instead of tortillas? Why was I different, outside of things? It was no doubt the result of experiences like these that I faced throughout my growing-up years that led my life in the direction it has taken. And that is an ongoing effort to help Hispanic Americans achieve equal political, educational and economic opportunities and social acceptance.

Perhaps the most important thing I've done, born of that frustration, is to establish the Mexican American Cultural Center (MACC), which was founded to research the needs of Mexican-Americans and respond to them. In 1971 I started the center with Archbishop Flores, who was then Auxiliary Bishop of San Antonio. We were joined by other Mexican priests. Based on our experience, we were convinced *beyond any doubt* that none of the institutions of Roman Catholicism was responding to the needs of these people. The seminaries, in particular, were not responding—I don't think they're responding even today. The crisis was *not* that we did not have vocations to the priesthood, but rather that the seminaries did not understand the young Mexican-Americans who came in to become priests and were driving them out. It all springs from the differences between Irish-German Catholicism, which has dominated the Church, and Latin-American Catholicism.

Our work at MACC was motivated by two conditions, one outside the Church and the other within. The first was the fact that universities were not prepared for, and therefore not properly educating, people from the Mexican-American environment. And the second was that seminaries did not accommodate Mexican-Americans, or provide programs adequate to meet their specific needs. Very simply put, the primary institutions were not bothering to serve us. When the Irish and the Germans, the Polish and the Czechs, first came to the United States, they found similar situations, but institutions were quickly set up to serve their needs. Boston College and Notre Dame were established in answer to the education problems of the poor Irish immigrants whose children could not get into Harvard or Yale. Nothing was ever set up for the Mexicans. They were banished, so to speak, to the margins of the Church. I don't say this with malice. Goodwill there was, but the facts are facts.

There were, of course, many aspects of the Mexican-American scene that MACC concerned itself with. The need for identity was one. Our member-priests felt that something had to be set up that would enable us to look at ourselves *and tell others who we were.* A lot of other people had been telling us who we were. Who are Mexican-Americans? we began to ask ourselves. We're not just Mexicans living in the United States, and we're not mainline Easterners. In other words, we had to search for a self-affirmation that would provide a view of ourselves that wasn't quite what the others were saying. This came on very strongly after the 1960s, the years of the War on Poverty when so many people descended on us to do surveys on the "minorities," using terms like "culturally deprived" [smiles]. Not knowing anything about us, they were making studies and presuppositions all over the place. We decided to study ourselves.

At one point, we opened a Pandora's box of complaints. Seeking to find out what were the pastoral needs of our people *from their own perspective,* so that the Church could respond, we started asking them questions.

What do you think of the Church, the priests, the nuns?
What is wrong with the Church?
Does it really take care of your spiritual needs?

We may have asked the questions, but they did most of the talking. Mainly, we did a lot of listening, intense listening. Pious churchgoers, who had never opened their mouths, spit out words of great anger. It was a painful process for the priest because often, you know, the one that provides the ear is the one that gets all the flak [laughs]. We were ready emotionally, but we didn't quite expect the answers:

If you really want to help, why don't you get lost?
The Catholic Church has suppressed us long enough. If the Hispanic people are down in this country, it is because you have cooperated with the exploitation.
We are pushed around by our pastors.

After our initial research of inquiry and listening, MACC formulated programs that would inform Hispanics generally, and still other programs that would inform Anglos (white Americans, for lack of a better word) on how to work with Hispanics. A good example of this has been our attempts to persuade the Church to retain Spanish in the liturgy and explain why this is so important to Hispanics. In religion, language is crucial. It must be expressed in words that people understand. We've had many Anglo priests who say, "Well, since they're here, they should learn English." All of us agree to that. Every Hispanic community should have an English school attached to it, and I'm working to have one set up here. But our point is: *Don't force people to learn English in order to go to Confession and use the liturgy. Don't force people to learn English to understand what's going on as you anoint them while they lie dying.*

I contend there is more difference between Latin American Catholics and U.S. Catholics than between U.S. Catholics and U.S. Protestants. At MACC we also work to clarify these differences for the non-Hispanic world. I'm not speaking of dogma or doctrine, but of that which touches people's hearts and the ways by which we express our faith. We *want* Americans to understand the faith expressions of our people; we are legitimately different.

Let me give you a few examples. In our faith expression, we like to involve not only the individual but the collectivity. In Holy Week, our processions comprise a whole community. In our eyes, the U.S. celebration of Holy Week is empty—it's almost like you sucked out the meaning. We like to dress our statues, we like to walk together in the streets, we like to relive the event from the inside out. At noon on Good Friday, we set up outdoor speakers because we cannot get all the people to come into the Church. They prefer to sit around outside. It's the way they like to celebrate, in the open with others, socially.

To the Mexican-American, the home is very important. They often have altars and shrines in their homes and pray there instead of going to Mass. Since the Church requires attendance at Mass every Sunday under pain of mortal sin, non-Hispanics cannot understand this custom and some say we're committing mortal sin. In the main, I would say not. What has to be taken into account is that for the majority of Hispanic Catholics it has been a physical impossibility. In Mexico City, for example, a church may celebrate seventeen or eighteen Masses on Sunday and *they're all packed*. You can't get one more person in. Now, only 11 percent of the city's population of 13 million goes to Sunday Mass. If 1 percent more were to go, where would you put them?

Since getting to Church on Sunday is not feasible, there has never been an insistence on it. That's why for us home religion is so important. You won't find a single Hispanic house without an altar and shrine where people put themselves in the presence of God each day. For us it's a whole different constellation of what it means to be a good person. I would like to add a postscript here about the whole question of committing sin by emphasizing that God is merciful and God's mercy is always greater than man's sin.

The average Mexican Catholic does not fit into categories of liberal or conservative. In our religious expression—our baptisms, processions and so on—we're probably more conservative than the conservatives. In fact, the way we celebrate our religion makes some liberal Catholics sputter, "I thought you were liberal. How can you do all that stuff?" In thought and understanding, however, we consider the liberals too conservative. For one thing, we have never shunned Liberation Theology. Having made it our own, we've had no problems with it and ask, instead, "What took it so long to come forth? This is where it should be." We are at ease with the Cesar

Chavez movement and the civil-rights advocacy that made some conservative Catholics shudder.

How we celebrate the liturgical cycles shows other instances where we differ from the average Catholic. The Feast of the Dead is a major event for us and is more important than the Feast of All Saints because of our concept of death, our playfulness with death. When somebody dies, that person hasn't left us, and we don't hide the corpus. The dead person doesn't leave the community, he simply lives in it in a different way, and closeness continues. I myself feel a deep sense of togetherness with those in my family who have passed away. They're not dead—they're present in another form.

People are quick to label somebody else's faith practice as superstitious but never see their own that way. Among the Irish, German and Italian Catholics, it's somewhat common practice now to order Masses for their dead *to be said somewhere else.* The Mexican Catholic also wants Masses said, but he wants to make sure that his Mass is said when all the family is present to celebrate it. Now one could say these Masses celebrated afar are popular superstitious practices. But one of the things we're trying to do at MACC is to be very reserved about name-calling. Instead, we ask, *How do they see it from within? What is the meaning for them from within?* It's an exciting period because we may be on the edge of a breakthrough of understanding between Hispanic Catholics and American Catholics. The Latin American Catholic is bringing into U.S. Catholicism a deep sense of the mystical, of the symbolic. We may be more into the sense of sacred mystery. This is the difference. Our relationship with statues and imagery is much closer to the Byzantine Church, with its icons, than to the Western Church. There are many aspects like this, and we at MACC are just beginning the investigation. The past ten or fifteen years of our research of selfhood are just the beginning. We've never looked into ourselves before.

I mentioned briefly Liberation Theology. The entire story of Liberation Theology is simply the awakening of the consciousness of the poor, along with the realization that the Church had not played any significant role in the elimination of poverty. Instead of being uplifted by the force of Mother Church, the people of Mexico were held down and exploited. It was the enslaved being within each of them crying out in pain and God hearing the cry, seeing the suffering, saying, *I will save you. I will liberate you.* It is Jesus moving around in impoverished countries which are in great social up-heaval and saying, in effect, *I have come with sight that the blind may see, that the prisoner may be free, that the poor may be liberated.*

Liberation Theology didn't start in a cathedral, overseen and coddled by a phalanx of priests. It started because there weren't enough priests, because in Latin America, the Church's failure meant that poor people had to share a single, vastly overworked priest. In some places, one priest was assigned to eighty thousand people. People needed the community and spirituality of a church, and so gradually, guided by religious leaders but in some ways independent, groups of ten to thirty believers formed basic Christian communities for prayer and discussion and support. Today these communities are seen as a new inspiration for the Church, the pillars of the New Church, the Popular Church, the Church of the People. It is not anticlerical. But the absence of the clergy has brought about a freedom of thought that gave people a desire to rethink what it means to be a Christian. And that is always dangerous.

Poverty is not beautiful; it is not to be glorified. How, then, do we help people out of poverty? The other question is, How do we help people out of affluence? It may be a more profound question. Another aspect of Liberation Theology is the consciousness that the kingdom of God begins amongst the poor and it is they who are called to offer something new to everybody else, including themselves. It is their realization that they are the active subjects of ministry and that they are waiting to be ministered to. In understanding this theology, one must realize that it begins with the people themselves. The starting point is their living faith experience. Western scholars are frightened by this. They bury themselves in the library with books and develop their treatises. Since Liberation Theology begins among the people, the creators, it doesn't have any precepts.

What are some of the practical aspects of Liberation Theology? In San Antonio, the whole COPS movement [Communities Organized for Public Service] in which grass-roots people have organized themselves in certain areas to tackle the issues of the city that affect their neighborhoods. For the first time people who have had no power now have formidable power to go to City Hall. It's People Power. This is all part of Liberation Theology, but the phrase isn't important. These people have never even mentioned it or know the meaning. Even the theology isn't important. The reality of liberation is important as they begin to realize they don't need a course in political science to analyze a political situation. It's fascinating to see men and women who once were scared of City Hall now walk in there, not scared at all, and ask to see the mayor.

By the year 2000, 50 percent of the Catholic Church in America will be made up of Hispanic Catholics. Because of this the Church has already begun to change and is now accepting the reality of pluralism and is finding ways of working with it. The whole Hispanic movement in the Church has awakened the Black Church. It is interesting how minority groups within society provide motivation to one another: the Black civil-rights movement in a way ignited the Hispanic movement in the Church and now—I could be wrong—the Hispanic movement is igniting the Black Catholics. They are saying, in effect, *We can be Black and Catholic, we can retain our clapping, our hallelujahs, and our amens.*

One big change is the way Catholicism views itself in this country. The Mass is no longer the sole province of English or Latin. Pope John Paul's Mass in Los Angeles was celebrated in thirty different languages. Phenomenal! And his whole affirmation of the pluralistic nature of Christ himself: his saying, in effect, *Today, we must admit Christ is Anglo, Christ is Hispanic, Christ is Japanese.* To hear the Pope saying that Christ is all these different ethnicities! By such emphasis a new element of ethnic acceptance has been brought into the Church. It is based very much on Church teaching, on Church documentation and Scripture. Our own Church is telling us now that we must respect the culture of people. It's *not* just that Father Elizondo wants to do his thing because he likes all this Mexican stuff.

Thus, the Church is opening her eyes to a new vision of pluralism. But I would not stop there. It is imperative not just for the Church, but for America, to begin to dream of a new mission. I'm dreaming of an America without borders, a pluralistic continent *without boundaries.* Why do we need borders? As we approach 1992, the 500th anniversary of the discovery of America, why not consider something totally new? As we near the second half of America's millennium, why not envision a really "New World" without political boundaries?

Yesterday, in San Antonio, a business was raided by the U.S. Immigration Service for hiring Mexicans without documentation. Yet American business can set up shop right inside the Mexican border and hire all the Mexicans they want and pay for a whole day's work with what they pay in one hour on this side of the border. If the American company can go on that side and set up shop, why can't people come on this side and work? Why even maintain the border? The question of a true pluralistic society is not just a Church question, it's a continental question. From another point of view, consider that people are beginning to move to all parts of the continent. You have more and more U.S. people retiring to Mexico. You have more and more U.S. businesses operating in Latin America because it's more profitable for them—they don't have to give as many benefits to workers, pay as high wages, and so on. They pay the worker better there than he would be paid elsewhere, but still much less than he would be paid here.

Europeans are learning this—and I think we can learn from them—in order to survive. Today they are working for a Common Market, a Europe without borders, with a common currency. They have learned that in order to survive, they have to unite without national boundaries. There is a massive campaign going on: THINK EUROPEAN. Realizing they can no longer THINK FRENCH, THINK GERMAN or THINK SPANISH, and still survive, powerful groups are urging a union of all Europe without national borders.

THINK AMERICA—that's the kind of slogan we need here, from Argentina to Canada. Remove all borders. As we approach 1992, the new world would really be the "New World" then.

There has always been incredible joy in the religious celebrations of suffering people, and that includes the Hispanic. All over Europe they have beautiful celebrations, but I find that normally they're dead. This is true in some U.S. churches. Even with a lot of preparation, they have an emptiness. But at a Mass in Peru, Africa and other places where people are really struggling, when they're in church, they're in contact with life. They are celebrating the fact that in spite of everything around them . . . it's almost a defiance of all the forces that threaten to destroy them. In church, they dare to rise, speak, sing. In Black churches, especially, there's a tremendous insight into this; church is the one place where they can *be*. It is the same with Hispanics in their own churches—remember every other institution is in somebody else's place. THEY REJOICE. And when visitors come, they are most welcome. We share the concept of God with one another.

Beyond this, I think among Mexicans especially (I'm not saying this isn't true of others—it's just that I've studied our culture more), there's a profound sense of jubilation in general. On this point, we've had long sessions with psychologists and psychiatrists. We ask, *How can a people who have been battered back and forth and put down and oppressed maintain a joyfulness of living and being alive?* You hear joy and celebration everywhere, humor everywhere. In Monterey I heard someone talking joyfully in the street to a friend who had just lost his job.

"What are you so happy about? You know I lost my job."

"Why should I be sad? Should I be sad about your being sad? Why make double trouble? It's bad enough losing your job."

What it amounts to is affirmation of life, in spite of life. What is the basis for this? I think, I think, as far as the Mexicans go—and my psychologist friends agree with this—it is Our Lady of Guadalupe. This devotion started when the Mexican nation was at its worst in relation to the Spanish conquistadores. Mexico had been conquered, destroyed. It was horrible and the people, the native people, did not want to live. They told the missionaries, in effect: *If you really love us, let us die. Our temples have been burned, our cities razed, our women raped. Now you tell us our gods are false. If all this is true, then why live? Let us die.* It is in this context that Our Lady of Guadalupe first appeared to the Mexican people.

She came as an apparition to an Aztec Indian named Juan Diego at the site of the shrine of the ancient mother goddess Tonanci in Mexico City. She requested that a temple be built there in sight of the mother goddess. For many years the Church opposed this devotion but the devotion imposed itself—people responded by the thousands. They saw in it a message of resurrection, a summons to life, a recall from their death wish. *You are not to go back to your old ways but to follow the new way.* How she transformed a conquered beaten populace into jubilant human beings may be gleaned from a prayer that has been recited by Mexicans for centuries. Addressing Juan Diego directly, Our Lady says:

Hear and let it penetrate your heart, my
dear little son.

Let nothing discourage you, nothing depress
    you,
Do not fear any illness or vexation,
    anxiety or pain.
Am I not here, your Mother?
Are you not in the folds of my mantle,
    in the crossing of my arms?
Is there anything else that you need?

It was the rebirth of hope, the collective resurrection of a people. To this day, if you go to the Basilica in Mexico City at any time, you will find eight or nine thousand believers. And in the United States the biggest religious celebration among Mexican-Americans is the feast of the Virgin of Guadalupe on December 12.

In the Mexican spirit, there's a sense that life itself is a gift. Before anything else, life is a gift to be celebrated.

Donna Hanson with Pope John Paul II after she addressed the
Pope

Donna Hanson

THE POPE LISTENS

Your Holiness, please let me know that you are also willing to walk with me. . . . In my cultural experience, questioning is neither rebellion nor dissent. Rather, it is a desire to participate and is a sign of both love and maturity.

In the fall of 1987, the eyes of the world were riveted, via television, on a slim laywoman who, with great composure, appeared formally before Pope John Paul II in San Francisco. In her address, she described how Catholics in America feel about certain vital issues that have become priority subjects, often clouded with misunderstanding between the Church in Rome and her American progeny. Providing an important moment in the "coming of age" of the laity, she spoke so simply and eloquently that afterward, the Pope clasped her hand and said, "Yours was a good talk." Following this interview, the talk appears in its entirety with Mrs. Hanson's permission.

Homemaker, mother and professional social worker, Mrs. Hanson is typical of a contemporary Catholic laywoman who manages a family, has a career and is deeply involved with the Church. At the time of her address, she was chairperson of the National Advisory Council (NAL), an important and prestigious group comprising sixty-five laypeople and religious, which advises American Bishops on ecclesial and civil affairs. For seven years she was executive director of Catholic Charities in the Diocese of Spokane.

I began the address to Pope John Paul by saying that I could speak only from my perspective and that I did not represent all of the Catholics in the United States because of the diversity within that group. However, my hope was to reflect what I heard in the consultations on Church matters and in the many conversations with family, friends, vowed religious, Catholics no longer active in the Church, and Jewish acquaintances.

As chairperson of the National Advisory Council, I was asked to make this presentation. I spoke as a woman, wife, mother, social minister and volunteer chairperson. The issues mentioned surfaced at meetings of laypeople from throughout the country who had gathered in different regions in preparation for the Synod on the Laity in Rome. [A Synod is a gathering of bishops that meets in Rome to discuss items of concern to the universal Church.] I attended these meetings, one in Belleville, Illinois, and one in San Francisco. From them I was able to gain a perspective on the issues that the laity was concerned about in various regions of the country. A total of 200,000 people were involved; and I read summary reports of these collaborative efforts. All of this research, reading and reflection became background for my talk.

Having spoken before the Holy Father and exchanged a few words with him afterward, I can say from experience that he is very warm, and he listens intently. He has a unique depth. It is also apparent that he is a very strong person. I had actually met him earlier in the year in Rome. There had been a consultation, also concerning the Synod, that was held at Rocca di Papa outside Rome with two hundred people from all over the world. I had the opportunity to greet him briefly and mention that I would see him in San Francisco. From that visit, I knew him to be a person who is open, accepting and supportive of meetings with the laity. He had approved the structured dialogue for his visit in the United States. Actually, I saw my appearance before him in San Francisco in a very positive light—as a growth opportunity in shared responsibility and collaboration in the international Church. I felt it would be like having coffee with a dear friend, speaking honestly as I would sitting down across a table to share one's heart. It was like a genuine opportunity to dialogue, to talk with him personally. And the actual experience bore all of this out.

Professionally, I have a master's degree in social work and am employed by the Diocese of Spokane where I am secretary for social ministries. As such, I am one of five secretaries of the curial staff, each responsible for one of the following: evangelization, ministry formation, Catholic education, business affairs and social ministries. This means that I am directly responsible to the Bishop and am the person primarily in charge of coordinating and implementing goals and objectives in the social-service area. I attempt to share Gospel values with the people on my staff and in our parishes so that they may more easily reach out to their brothers and sisters in need.

As an employee of the Church, I minister both in the Church and in the world. I testify at Washington State legislative hearings, and attend meetings held by the secretary of the Department of Social and Health Services. In other words, I work within the Diocesan structures and civic and state governmental entities, bringing Gospel values *outside* the Church structure, impacting those in the public arena.

In personal terms, I consider what I do as wife and mother as my primary ministry. For my husband and myself, we are now at a transition point. Our older son is a sophomore in college and our younger son will enter in September. By the fall of 88, both children will be living away from home. I often think of the statement that the best thing a mom can do for her children is to love her husband; it is indeed very true. The reverse is also valid: the best thing a father can do for his children is to love their mother. This love provides the foundation. As members in a family, we have different gifts and different talents, but we have been able to support one another in professional and personal ways. Consequently, each of the four of us has been able to pursue individual interests.

Looking back, I realize I did not begin my career hoping to accomplish anything specific. After receiving my master's in social work at St. Louis University, I accepted a job in Spokane and moved there. I had done my practicum work—the supervised practical application of studies in a work situation—in Belleville, Illinois, Catholic Charities and accepted a similar position in Spokane. My faith has always been important to me. My mother was a convert: she converted just before the birth of my older brother. I was the second child. Many of our family celebrations centered around the

Sacraments and rites: First Communion, marriage, the wake and funeral Mass. I grew up in Paducah, a small town in Western Kentucky, part of the Owensboro diocese. In high school, on Sunday mornings I taught religion-education classes in a mission parish about thirty miles away. They needed someone; the pastor asked if I would do it and I did. At that time, and perhaps because of my volunteer efforts, some of my teachers encouraged me to become a nun. It was at a time when we were told that being a nun was the "ultimate" vocation for a woman; that if you were not good enough to become a nun, then you could always be a wife and mother. But I was not called to that vocation; I felt called to be a wife and mother. It is now wonderful to recognize that *all* people are called; that there are different vocations and that each is important.

Although I grew up studying the traditional Baltimore Catechism and had graduated from college at the start of Vatican II, I consider myself a product of the "living out" of the Council documents. I had a very formal religious upbringing. Every day we went to Mass before school. On Sunday morning the family went together to Mass, came home for a big breakfast and then went back to church for the 4:00 P.M. Benediction. It was part of the fabric of our lives; lots of pleasant memories of my childhood are walking together, and children skipping along the way. After Benediction, we would stop for ice cream. I would often get excited, run and drop the ice cream on my black patent-leather shoes. Those are fun memories, family memories. The times when there were weddings and First Communions were special days because grandparents, aunts, uncles and cousins would come to our home. Family and celebrations were all woven together.

I think that what made it relatively easy for me to make the transition from the traditional religion of my childhood into the Church of Vatican II was my graduate social-work education. I was trained to identify with where a person is, develop communication skills and be open to diversity. The training began in 1962 and lasted two years: schooling and Vatican II just came together. As the documents of the Council came out, they made a lot of sense to me. It was not that I sat down, read them carefully and pondered their meaning. Rather, they dovetailed with my lived experiences as wife, mother and social minister.

In 1969, after working two years in Catholic Charities and the same amount of time for School District #81, I was asked by Bishop

Topel to be the first laywoman to serve on the Diocesan Catholic Charities Board of Directors. At that time, it did not seem all that revolutionary. In hindsight, I recognize that that was an implementation step from Vatican II and a very significant thing for him to do. With three new members, including myself, the nature of the Board changed and what had once been a group of people who met once a year became a group meeting monthly, struggling with ways to respond in a deeper fashion to the needs of the poor.

Nine years later, I was asked by Bishop Topel to be the executive director of Catholic Charities. Priests had held that position for the first sixty-five years in the diocese. I had chaired the Board, worked part-time as associate director and had the academic credentials. Asking a woman to be director was revolutionary at the time but I did not realize that. In accepting the job, I did not set out to be a mover and shaker. I simply had the credentials, the experience and it just seemed logical for me to say yes.

In 1982, I was appointed by the Bishops of Region XII (Washington, Oregon, Idaho, Alaska, and Montana) to become the laywoman representing our geographical area on the National Advisory Council (NAC). I was subsequently elected chair-elect, actually spending one year in that position and two subsequent years as chairperson. Serving on the Council is truly an awesome experience because of the responsibility of advising the Bishops on both episcopal and civil matters. The Bishops accomplish their work through two groups: the National Conference of Catholic Bishops (NCCB), which deals with episcopal matters, and the United States Catholic Conference (USCC), which deals with the civil issues. Together these two groups deal with virtually all major questions concerning the Catholic Church in the United States, and the NAC members serve to advise them. The NCCB deals with such issues as Priestly Life and Ministry, Doctrine, and Canonical Affairs. The USCC discusses civil matters like Social Development and World Peace, Education, and A Policy on Political Responsibility.

The National Advisory Council, a product of Vatican II, was founded with the idea that *everyone* in the Church shares responsibility since its members, both clerical and lay, contribute to the decision-making. It includes six Bishops who serve on the administrative board of both the NCCB and the USCC, six priests representing geographic regions of the country, three women religious appointed by the Leadership Conference of Women Religious, three men religious (priests or Brothers) appointed by the Conference of Major Superiors of Men, twenty-six lay men and women representing the thirteen geographical regions, and eighteen at-large members, including two Bishops who are not on the administrative board. The remaining sixteen at-large members are selected by a committee of the Council to assure diversity of age, ethnicity and geography.

The Council meets twice each year, just prior to the administrative board meetings in March and September, in a retreat center just outside Baltimore. Before gathering, we study the documents scheduled to go to the Bishops for their civil or ecclesial consideration. Topics we have dealt with include the Pastoral Letter on the Economy, the Pastoral Plan for Hispanic Ministry, and a document on the role of the pastor, called *A Shepherd's Care*. The professional staff for the various committees come to the center to make a presentation and engage in a dialogue. Generally, on major topics, we have small group discussions. We take a "profile vote," with choices ranging from *strongly agree, agree, disagree, strongly disagree,* to *abstain.* The chairperson presents the results of the profile voting on each item to the administrative board, offering explanations when the voting is unusual or a large number abstain. The work of the National Advisory Council is confidential, going only to the Bishops. The general population does not know about the NAC because our recommendations are usually incorporated into the overall document without reference to source, or they are referred to the proper committee and are incorporated into their overall work plan.

Because it has helped to democratize the Church, to be more inclusive of all the "people of God" in a very direct way, the NAC is a very positive result of Vatican II. This trend toward inclusiveness within the Church has given the laity a much wider participation. As I mentioned in my talk to the Holy Father, laypeople comprise 98 percent of the Catholic Church in the United States; I think that percentage is generally true throughout the world. My hope is that in the future, laity will become much more involved in all Church matters: in their parishes, their community, the state, the nation, the world. The documents of Vatican II make it very clear that we are all called to serve because of our Baptism and if we believe that, it is almost like saying, "Well, why not?" We could virtually change the face of the world if we took the Gospel and really tried to live it. It is my hope that laypeople everywhere will see the opportunities to share their value systems with others: in their daily lives, in their homes and in their professions. I am not talking about preaching religion but rather about living the Christian life. *By their fruits, you will know them.* Integrity, honesty, commitment, compassion—these qualities speak out, not because of words we use but because of the actions of our lives.

There are so many good things going on in the Church. We get caught up in what the media present or what may be taken out of context, and we react as if that were the reality. We find ourselves going down a road and we don't know quite how we got there, or whether it is really where we want to be. The Church is on a pilgrimage. When Christ was on earth, He was with us in person: He could explain and share the parables. But we are finite beings and today we are faced with all kinds of new questions. All of us, generally speaking, are trying to grow in understanding in the light of our culture, which is fraught with new problems. In medical ethics, for example, new scientific discoveries, new equipment, appear daily; ten years ago they were not even a wild dream. Even a few years ago, could we imagine the moral problems posed by equipment that can maintain life indefinitely? This is the type of question we are struggling with: we have Christ's message right here with us to help us face things straight on. Our pilgrimage continues. . . .

I was in Rome in October and walked across St. Peter's Square in the twilight. The lights were just coming on and the water in the fountains was cascading, splashing onto the piazza. A thought went through my head: *You are here at the heart of Christianity.* Suddenly, I stopped and said to myself, "No. Christianity is inside me. It is not a place, *this* place. Rome is beautiful and this is a unique moment for me. But I carry Christ with me wherever I go." As we all become more aware of that, it is more challenging . . . and yet, it is infinitely easier.

[On September 18, 1987, Donna Hanson spoke these words in San Francisco, before an attentive Pope John Paul II, as the country watched and listened.]

We, the American Catholic laity, 98 percent of the Catholic Church in the

United States, welcome you to our land of rich diversity. I speak to you this morning from my own perspective: woman, wife, mother of two sons, social minister in Catholic Charities, and volunteer chairperson of the National Advisory Council to the National Conference of Catholic Bishops. In preparation for today, I have spent much time in consultation with my lay sisters and brothers. They were pleased to be asked their opinions: it is now my hope to give voice to their dreams and desires.

The microcosm of Church represented here today gives you some perspective of my difficult challenge. In this assembly of three thousand are people from virtually every profession, culture and ethnic diversity in the United States. To this assembly we bring different political perspectives and varied experiences of church. We are young and old, rich and poor: we are unique yet unified in our love of Christ and His Church. Although our loyalty to the Church is deep, we are committed to call her to even deeper Gospel faithfulness. Unity, not division, is our goal; service, not power, is our mission.

The Native Americans, the original inhabitants of our land, provide me with a central theme for today. Their wise counsel is: "Never judge another's life until you have walked in their shoes for a day." It is my hope that today we may walk together.

On our journey, I would like to tell you about our unique American culture. I would like for you to know how our experience and tradition has helped to form us in our faith and continues to impact us in our families and in our parishes.

Your Holiness, the United States Declaration of Independence expresses the country's founding belief that all men, women and children are created equal. The reason that my great-grandparents emigrated to this country was to escape the famine in Ireland and persecution in Germany. Yet, as I grew up in the southern United States, I watched my father and his compatriots build a church so that the Black Catholics in our community could have a separate place of worship. In 1960, I saw billboards that proclaimed: "Why Bible-reading Christians could not in conscience vote for John F. Kennedy for President."

From these early life experiences I, like so many others, learned to question immigration practices, civil injustices, religious persecution. Today, my culture compels me to continue questioning those in leadership positions. I question them about public policies related to abortion, development of nuclear arms, the exploitation of our environment. Not to question, not to challenge, not to seek understanding, is to be less than a mature, educated and committed citizen.

When I come to my Church, I cannot discard my cultural experiences. Though I know the Church is not a democracy ruled by popular vote, I expect to be treated as a mature, educated and responsible adult. Not to question, not to challenge, not to have authorities involve me in a process of understanding is to deny my dignity as a person and the rights granted to me both by Church and society.

Your Holiness, within my circle of friends, there are those who are ranchers and those who are city dwellers, those who are politically conservative and avant garde liberals, some who are traditional and some who are progressive Catholics. I rejoice that within my culture there is room for this incredible diversity. The challenge before the Church in the United States is to be welcoming of these same diversities. Can we be as inclusive as Christ who reached out to the woman at the well, who invited a tax collector to be His apostle, who brought the centurion's daughter back to life? Can we reach out and be more inclusive of women, our inactive clergy, homosexuals, the divorced and all people of color?

Your Holiness, the diversity in our culture is mirrored in our families. We are traditional families, extended families, single parents, widowed, and divorced. In our families, we often struggle with the tensions between Gospel values and the excesses of our society. For many newly formed families, there is the challenge of being a loving spouse, while at the same time making responsible decisions about parenthood. In our young families, we often juggle the demands of homemaking with the need for employment. In our growing families, there is the challenge of helping our young adult children understand their sexuality, as well as appreciate the dangers of drugs and alcohol. In our maturing families, there is the balance of nurturing our grandchildren while caring for our frail, elderly parents.

Your Holiness, in our parish communities, we are also experiencing significant change. The lay members of our Church are now among the best educated and the most highly theologically trained in the world. Yet, we hunger for spiritual education and formation. We long for structures in which to truly share responsibility. As the pastors in our immigrant churches worked alongside of us to develop labor unions and the most comprehensive Catholic school network in the world, we were building both Church and society from the bottom up.

Today, our parishes are in transition. Many parishes do not have a resident pastor. Eucharistic celebrations are limited and our people cannot regularly receive the Sacrament of Reconciliation. Lay ministers are involved as never before, but full acceptance by both clergy and the people of God has not been realized.

At the same time, in other parishes, the pastors, deacons, women and men religious, and professional and volunteer lay ministers work side by side. They experience the needs of the people and together they respond: with housing for the elderly, with shelters for the homeless, with immigration counseling for the undocumented. They reach out in love: in peer ministry to the engaged, married, widowed, divorced. They reach out in hope: in bringing the Eucharistic Christ to the homebound. They reach out in faith: in study and reflection on the Word of God. They create small communities of faith; they take Christ into the marketplace; they are the Church in the world.

But how does all of this come together for those of us here today? I began by suggesting a walk. My request now is that you permit me to walk with you.

Let me walk with you so that I can understand the challenge of being Peter's successor. Let me share the burdens you carry as you reflect on the pain of your people: persecution in your beloved Poland, starvation in Ethiopia, consumerism in the United States.

Let me walk with you as you seek to preserve orthodox teachings and challenge the world with Gospel values. Let me also be at your side as you plead for peace on every continent.

Let me walk with you as you prepare for the Synod on the Laity. I know that we in the United States are not representative of the majority of people in the world. At the same time, I know that our concerns are universal: family, spirituality, collaboration.

Your Holiness, please let me know that you are also willing to walk with me. Accustomed as I am to dialogue, consultation and collaboration, I do not always feel that I am heard. In my cultural experience, questioning is neither rebellion nor dissent. Rather, it is a desire to participate and is a sign of both love and maturity.

Walk with me. My family experiences continually remind me that examples speak louder than words. To become the Family of God, it is imperative that both we parents and the Church witness the Gospel we preach. Above all, we must be just, compassionate and forgiving.

Your Holiness, please walk with each one of us. As you, we gladly give our lives in service to the Church. As you, we seek forgiveness seventy times seven. Yet we know that we are a pilgrim people, that we are individually gifted, and that the Holy Spirit speaks uniquely to each one of us. We are all Children of God: may we continue to walk and talk together?

Father Max Brewington of Wichita

Father Max Brewington

THE TROUBLED, LONELY PRIESTHOOD

I never let my heart confront the issue of whether I could live as a single person, like the man in the Simon and Garfunkel song who slept alone while everyone else slept in pairs.

Many of the 53,500 Roman Catholic priests in the United States are overworked, lonely and sexually troubled, according to a report issued in December 1988 by a panel of Bishops comprising the Committee on Priestly Life and Ministry. The report made clear that there exists a serious and substantial morale problem among priests in general.

Father Max Brewington is a case in point. When the author attended Sunday Mass in St. Thomas Aquinas Church in Dallas, Texas, she was struck by the intelligence and ultra-conservative views of the homilist, Father Brewington, who was on leave from Wichita. She requested an interview and he complied. Part I is a result of that first meeting, in which he speaks of his life as a clergyman, his thoughts on the contemporary Church, his love of reading, and his warm relations with people—a life he seemed to find both rewarding and fulfilling.

Some months later the author requested a photograph of Father Brewington and learned of an astounding turn of events in his life. He agreed to a second interview, and the story of those changes are told in Part II. A profound source for reflection, his experience bears witness to the inner doubts that are not uncommonly the secret burden of a priest's life.

PART I

The background from which I come is mainline, midwestern Protestant. My father was reared as a member of the Church of Christ and my mother was a Methodist. When I was six years old, my mother began taking instructions in the Catholic faith because the questions that she had concerning religion—about God and the relationship of man to God—could not be answered by any of the Protestant clergymen she knew. I became Catholic when I was thirteen. I was already practicing a lot of Catholic things, like serving at Mass until the priest realized I was Protestant. My conversion was not an earthshaking event; I had no profound conversion experience. But the fact that I did not grow up in the faith has some influence on me. Even at thirteen, I knew that this was different from anything I had studied, and the Mass was different from any other religious service. I found the Mass *then*, as I find it *now*, the most refreshing, the most solemn, the most Godlike thing that we do as human beings.

My great hope is that I, and people like me, be considered simply *Catholic* and not called traditional or anything else. Words like traditional and liberal are used so often these days that after a while, they break down—the meaning they would otherwise have crumbles. I have some young friends in southeast Kansas who, for the most part, are all traditionalists and quite intellectual—many of them, like myself, are converts. One of them calls himself a radical Catholic in the sense of being radical in embracing today the fullness of what the Church represents and what it teaches, and he chose that title in order to challenge the labels that so often are attached to us. But for lack of something better, I would say the title of conservative fits me.

Revealed religion is suffering because the world has become less religious or, simply, irreligious. This is something that has never occurred before in the life of man. I'm referring to systems that are enacted, or behavior that is based, without any reference to religion at all. The ancient Romans and Greeks, among whom the Church first called members of her body, were not irreligious. They were superstitious, they were pagan, but they were not *irreligious* people.

They acted, they fought, they wrote with the view—at least, an over-the-shoulder view—that God or the gods were about. I'm not sure that occurs much these days. As this breakdown of religion takes place, with more and more people considering God to be less and less of an influence, or none at all, in their living, then we begin to see the Church separated from more and more people. The Church is still here in touch, and she has not changed her position. *She is here.* It's the fact that there is this motion away from religion that seems to cause a perception that the Church is not in touch with the world. The world is moving away from the Church; it is not the other way round.

I can't speak for the Holy Father and don't know what he experienced when he was here in September of 1987. Some of us were hoping that he would see what we see every day. We were hoping that he would see it so that there could be no mistaking the fact that this process of irreligion has occurred. And not only in this country but in many civilizations in the West. Religion has broken down; religious values haven't any influence on the day-to-day living of people and on national policies.

But I do not feel hopeless, being for the most part a cheerful sort and not a person that finds glee in doom. I enjoy people and want to do everything possible for their sake. However, it is discouraging to watch certain Catholics ride roughshod over the traditions of the Church. They claim they're sincere, and I do not doubt their sincerity, but it doesn't prove anything. When speaking of his contemporaries, H. G. Wells and G. B. Shaw, both agnostics. Chesterton said that he never once doubted their sincerity. All it proves it that the sincere man can be dead wrong.

There are a few heartening signs. Although we've lost contact with the richness in the liturgy that was ours—the Latin language, Gregorian chant—people will surprise you. At St. Thomas Aquinas parish here, for example, every now and then the celebrant at High Mass on Sunday will invite the congregation to sing the Our Father in Latin, and many will join in. After all this time, they haven't forgotten the Latin! I remember once giving a tour of the cathedral in Wichita, Kansas, to a group of families with young children.

As we stood before the altar, a little girl about three years old came up to me, tugged at my cassock and whispered, "Father, Father, can I go stand next to the treasure?" [She was referring to the Blessed Sacrament, or consecrated Host, which is the body and blood of Christ.]

The Blessed Sacrament was reserved in the transept of the church in a magnificent altar that was sanctuarylike. She *knew* that this was a special place. I'm disappointed that this kind of spontaneous devotion is diminishing. Ronald Knox, a convert from the Church of England—his father was an Anglican bishop and he himself was an Anglican priest—once gave a homily, a meditation on the Blessed Sacrament. He said how sad it was that the pieces of furniture most frequently missing from the parish church were the parishioners and the parish priest. If our devotion is such that we believe this is the Blessed Sacrament, our God present, His body, blood, soul and divinity, then yes, we should be there in church and not just infrequently. Empty churches bother me a great deal but, again, I temper that. Somehow God is involved. There are priests who are more relaxed than I am and who go along with the flow of things. But the priests I know, my friends, share the same sort of anxiety.

Although the Church may be in dire need today for new prophets and heroic followers, there are few who are called to the heroism and the incredible activity of someone like Saint Paul, who was knocked from his horse and made the apostle to the Gentiles. I don't anticipate being knocked from a horse or knocked off my bicycle. What I hope to do is to continue to be a good priest, to teach the truth, to encourage people to be steadfast in faith, hope and charity. I don't know what I'll be doing twenty years from now. Monsignor Hughes, the director of the seminary I attended, kept reminding us over and over that wherever we are, we are doing the work of God. If it is in a small parish with a handful of souls, or in a large parish with two thousand families, we are doing the work of God, preaching, teaching, and hearing confessions.

I enjoy teaching and have taught religion to sophomores at a Catholic high school in Wichita. At Thomas Aquinas, I spend a great deal of time in the school answering questions, moderating behavior. An important part of the life of the Church in the United States is our established system of schools. The parochial-school system in America is a miracle; it is such an incredible gift. And if there is to be a revival of religion and religiosity, then it has got to begin with the young by giving them knowledge of the faith as well as providing examples of virtue and developing character. The proper education of the young—it is the great hope for Catholicism today.

A good prospect for Catholicism is the coming back into the Church of a lot of young adult Catholics. Where have they been? *They haven't been anywhere.* They didn't join another church. For one reason or other, they just quit. A Franciscan friend calls them the Happy Pagans. Now that they are establishing families and having children, they foresee some of the difficulties that rearing a family in the modern world involves. And so they are returning to the place where they know they have a solid foundation. And the Church continues to have converts. I have an instruction this evening with a young woman who has never been baptized in any church. At Thomas Aquinas, I've had five private instructions and received five into the Church. So that in little places, here, there— besides the schools—you find reasons for hope. There's life in the Church and always will be.

Another encouraging aspect is the fact that in America and the world, the Church is being infused with new blood—the energies of Hispanic Americans, Black Americans, American Indians, and the many peoples of Asia. They are bringing in vibrancy and vigor. And in view of these new races of every coloration, if white supremacy dies out, that would not distress me. I wouldn't be a bit surprised if the Pope of the near future turns out to be a Black African Cardinal. Fine with me. I would storm the gates of hell for him just as I would for John Paul II. There are some very capable and holy men on that dark continent who could easily ascend to the throne of Peter.

I enjoy being a diocesan priest, even though it's hard work and often exhausting. If God has given me any intellectual gifts, it's a challenge for me to use them in a way that is understandable on a parish level. Of course, there have been times, even when I was a seminarian, that I've wondered if contemplative life might have been more suitable. But I so much enjoy people and that's what this business is. It isn't intellectually a burden for me to handle the mundane, day in and day out. There is always my reading and study. I have a complete collection of Cardinal Newman, almost everything written by G. K. Chesterton, Hilaire Belloc, and many of the modern authors. I'm still working on St. Thomas Aquinas and the *Summa Theologica.* And the homilies and addresses of the

Holy Father, many of which are gems of devotion and faith. Not the encyclicals, but the many talks he has given. What he writes is profound intellectually, but with his fine mind, he is able to write in a way that is understandable to the great mass of people.

May I mention my hope that Roman Catholics in this country recover the intellectual heritage? That we be not frightened by intellectual things? This is a hope for *all* Americans, actually. With my high-school sophomores, I would insist that they answer test questions with full sentences, with nouns and verbs. If their answers started with "Because . . ." I would not give them credit. We need to regain the ability to write a sentence. And a love of learning for itself. Whether you become a computer operator or a math teacher, there's nothing wrong with having a liberal education. There has got to be a certain broad base, a general-education process. When I was growing up, memorizing a stanza, knowing the parts of speech and using them correctly were great satisfactions. If people aren't capable of using language well, they won't want to read and will miss an awful lot in life. They won't have access to the wise men who have lived in the past—Greek authors, Roman poets, Shakespeare, or one of my favorite writers, Saint Thomas More. Before he was executed, they put him in prison, thus taking him away from his family, a punishment he found severe. But the severest pain came when they took away his books so that he couldn't read, and his writing instruments so that he couldn't write.

PART II

[This addition to the interview, in which Father Brewington explains why he left the priesthood, was taped nine months later over the telephone. The question-and-answer form has been retained to emphasize the immediacy of the talk.]

Father, what happened?

What happened, Linda, was that I finally recognized that I was struggling with these issues and that there was no longer any reason for me to refrain from at least confronting them, asking the questions that I knew I had to ask.

What issues are you referring to?

Chiefly, that my mind and my heart were going in two distinct, different directions. Something that I've thought all along . . . my being influenced toward the Church because I was the eldest child in my family and because I was told by a priest, when I was a sophomore in college, that I had a vocation to the priesthood and that if I didn't accept it, I could go to hell. And because another priest, whom I admired a great deal and still admire in some ways, told me that some day I could be a Cardinal of the Church. Those things took control and I never let my heart confront the issue of whether I could live as a single person, like the man in the Simon and Garfunkel song who slept alone while everyone else slept in pairs. I hate to sound so flippant about it but when I was a child, all I ever wanted was to be married and have a family and live in the country near a large city where my wife and I could raise our children with hard work and provide them with culture and wisdom, and somewhere along the line I forgot that. I talked to the rector of my seminary in September, who is now a canon lawyer, and he wanted to know how I was doing and . . .

When did you leave the priesthood?

My last day was May 31, 1988. In September, a couple of months ago, I called the rector of my seminary, who is in Florida right now, and he asked me a few questions and then I told him what this priest had told me when I was in college and he said, "How come you never told anybody that when you were in the seminary?"

You mean the comment about your becoming a Cardinal?

No, no, no. The remark the priest made that if I had a vocation and didn't accept it, I would go to hell. I told the rector, "Well, I really thought that was precisely how God would get me." And he said, "Max, God doesn't work in that way. You've been fighting this all along?" I said, "Yes." "My God . . ."

In other words, it frightened you to the point where you thought, I had better become a priest or else?

In a certain sense, I was compelled. I felt myself frightened and hid it well and did very well as a priest. I was always considered a gentle confessor and a good preacher, compassionate and empathetic, but I finally confronted the fact that my mind and my heart were at cross-purposes and I had to ask the questions. Six months before leaving the priesthood, I started seeing a therapist, a very competent therapist, once a week and we went through the whole agony of it. My therapist was, first of all, able to assure me that I was quite normal and very sane and, perhaps, one of the strongest persons she's ever known in the sense that I was able to endure it for so long.

How long were you a priest?
Eleven years.

What did therapy do for you?
I discovered through the process of therapy that I had acted so often simply to please others without taking any regard for myself and that as a matter of fact, there's nothing wrong with having a healthy self-regard and that's the thing that began to trigger ultimately the idea that I could, in fact, leave the priesthood successfully, that is, I could do it in a healthy fashion without suffering any spiritual damage; that by taking this step of leaving the priesthood, I was not de facto condemned to hell.

Was she a Catholic therapist?
She was not a Catholic therapist. I was inquiring about a good therapist in the city of Dallas and was given two names, a man and a woman. I called the man first—he was at Baylor Hospital—and his phone was busy, so I called her [laughs] and her phone was not busy, so I began to see her on a weekly basis through the end of May. It was very fruitful, very fruitful.

Was it only during therapy that the thought of leaving the priesthood occurred to you?
It had occurred to me before in the sense that it would pop into my mind; it would be a kind of darkness, that idea, and I would say to myself, "Max, what the hell are you thinking about? You've been praying as a priest, you do well as a priest, why would you leave?" That question became so burning . . . and certain experiences I've had throughout my priesthood exacerbated it. I shouldn't tell this on a dear friend of mine, but I had a wedding, almost a year ago today. Two very dear friends—I had given the bride instructions— were getting married, and during the wedding preparations everyone became very friendly, myself, the bride, the groom, and maid of honor and other members of the wedding party. And then at Thanksgiving a year ago, I was in Oklahoma City and stopped by

to see this young couple, and the maid of honor, who lives in Atlanta, happened to be in town. She and I went out to a play and then we went to dinner and had a few glasses of wine. She had had enough wine and was bold enough to say this to me, "Max, how the hell can you be a priest? You're the most adorable man I've ever known in my life. When my mommy saw you in the wedding pictures she said, 'Oh, Kathy, why can't you find some nice guy like him?' " This kind of remark from the opposite sex had been addressed to me so often in the course of my priesthood. I was once called *drop-dead good-looking* by a clerk at Neiman Marcus. I was in my collar and had asked her where the stationery department was, and she said, "Well, Father, go on the escalator and when you get to the top, follow the hall awhile . . . And *you're drop-dead good-looking. Do you get hit on often?*" Finally, I started asking myself, *Why does this happen to me?* That's one of the issues I discussed with my therapist.

Did the clerk mean, were you sexually approached?

Oh, yeh. Women flirted with me openly. So finally I had the courage to confront these issues because I had sublimated them and driven them deep into my subconscious. And I began to ask the questions, *Can I continue to live as a priest? Is this what I'm meant to do?* With the help of the therapist, I decided there's nothing at all wrong with being a normal human being. I can still serve God in a variety of ways.

In our first interview, you appeared as a priest who was pretty sure of himself. Now I'm wondering if you felt you were on the spot and had to answer in a way that you thought I was expecting you to answer.

You mean, according to the "party line"?

Yes, according to the party line. What I'm hoping, Max, is to use the first interview as it is because I believe it's perfectly valid and in tune with your feelings at the time, despite what has happened.

Oh, yes, and I still mean those things.

That's it. I have to know whether you were just saying them because they were the party line.

No. I'm still quite conservative intellectually and theologically. Someone once described me as being somewhere to the right of Attila the Hun and that's still true in the sense that I have no difficulties with dogmatic and moral positions in the Church. I just finally had to confront the fact that I made a mistake fifteen years ago when I went to the seminary and that the mistake was that I didn't have enough courage to admit at least two things: first of all, that I was at the seminary to please a priest who had told me that I had a vocation. I admired this priest and thought he was a friend of mine, and when he told me that if I didn't accept it, I could go to hell, that put a lot of pressure on me. Secondly, I didn't have enough courage to admit to myself that I was, in fact, human and somewhere along the line I had forgotten what my childhood dream was, namely, to be a father and husband. The things I said in our interview I would repeat. I still believe them to be true.

My leaving was ultimately a personal issue—I came to a point of greater understanding about myself. It had nothing to do with the quarrel I'm having with the Church, which concerns a private opinion about the nature of celibacy and the priesthood in the United States. Celibacy is only a discipline. It is not part of the essence of priesthood. And it could be changed. Now I doubt if it will be, but it could be.

The permanent deacon at St. Thomas said to me, "Max, you've done a lot of good for God and I'm sure He's not going to forget that. The only thing I regret is that we've lost another good priest." It seems now that it's the good priests who are leaving, not the bad ones. The ones who can survive *outside* are the ones who are leaving. The ones that remain, you can't imagine their doing anything else. And there's also, quite frankly, an increasing number of gays that are going to the seminary. I've heard numbers as high as 50 percent of the present population in the United States seminaries are gay.

I am a bit discouraged by the conduct of the American Bishops on the contemporary scene. They don't seem to know where they are going. They seem to have no plan, nothing in view. And they're going off willy-nilly in various directions. The phrase I like to use in describing this is that they're arranging the deck chairs as the *Titanic* sinks. They're running around issuing letters about war and peace, the treatment of women, the poor—all crucial issues, certainly. But the churches are standing empty. Seminaries are being filled with gays. Which issues are more crucial to the life of the Church?

One thing I've discovered by being out is that it's a lot tougher *out here* than most priests think. Being a priest is an easy life in a lot of ways. I mean, people *do* things for you. You don't have to do your own laundry. You have a housekeeper to cook your meals, keep the house clean, turn off your phone in the middle of the night. But I'm reminded of what Goethe said—nothing is more dangerous than solitude. It robs you of so many human qualities. Cardinal Newman wrote a homily called "The Love of Relatives and Friends," in which he said the same thing, in effect, that the virtue which we all hope to have, namely charity or love, is the one that demands the most practice. So often I've seen priests never practice charity or love because they live alone and don't have anybody to practice it on, day in and day out. So many things are taken care of.

In your own mind, is your status as a Catholic as strong now as it was?
Oh, yes. I'm a Roman Catholic. I'm going to live a Roman Catholic and die a Roman Catholic. When the time comes for that, I hope to marry a Catholic woman and we'll have Catholic babies who will go to Catholic school. My canon lawyer did suggest that I do have a case: I can petition Rome and perhaps be dispensed from my vows, which would, in essence, permit me to marry without any danger. My status now is that if I should marry, I would be in the same position as a divorced and remarried person. I would also not be able to receive Communion on a regular basis or receive any of the Sacraments unless I were in danger of death. I'm under vows, just as a married person is under vows.

What do you foresee as a profession for yourself?
Right now I'm in a training program for an insurance company. I've taken their battery of tests and scored very well on them. They think I can learn this business and be successful at it. I'm still struggling in that regard and don't know if this is the right one yet. I plan to take some aptitude tests next week. My major in college was pre-law with a minor in biology. I have long entertained the idea of being a lawyer. The first thing is that I have to make some money and right now I'm not making much. I won't get a paycheck probably until the end of December and that has put me under a great deal of stress, both emotionally and financially.

Do you have a girlfriend?
I did what my therapist called "power dating" in June; that is, I was dating three or four different women a week. Seeing as many

Lisa Pettinella (left) with her sister Lynn

Lisa Pettinella

HOW A HIGH-SCHOOL GIRL REACTS TO HER RELIGION

When it comes to sex, the Sisters never say "Don't do this" and "Don't do that." They teach in ways that lead you *to choose not to.*

Catholic teenagers may be baptized but act as if they are heathen, and getting them to Mass on Sunday is often a hassle. They claim the Mass is boring, and it appears that God has no relevancy in their young lives. For this indifference, Catholic schools and parents are blamed: they have fallen down on the job.

But there are pockets of America where teenagers *do* go to Mass and *do* practice their faith—and usually under the influence of both family and school. Even if Mass palls, they have a personal relationship with God that sustains them. Lisa Pettinella of Hamden, Connecticut, is one of these young people. She is a sixteen-year-old whose Italian ethnic roots still nourish a live, palpable and personal faith. This belief is further bolstered by the high school she attends, the Sacred Heart Academy in Hamden, which is run by nuns called the Apostles of the Sacred Heart of Jesus.

Modest yet self-assured, Lisa is an attractive florescence of this education: she is much involved in the Christian life, is acquiring knowledge, and reacts very naturally to her religion. True to her age, she looks at the world with concentrated vision, as through a telescope that focuses only on small areas. Certain issues—premarital sex, abortion, AIDS—draw quick responses; others—ecumenism, Vatican II, the Pope—draw a blank. But the foundations seem to be in place: the Catholic faith is her steady companion and good friend, part and parcel of her life.

I don't think it's hard being a Catholic. You *choose*. Not among different religions—whatever faith your parents are, you're brought up in that. I mean you choose the *kind* of Catholic you want to be. There are different extremes that people go to. You could be the sort of person that's Catholic on the outside: go to church, go to Confession once in a while, toss money in the collection basket, and that's it. That's your way of being a Catholic. But there are other people who take it more to heart and really try to make Catholic values part of their own nature. These are people who aren't going to be influenced by what goes on around them, by the violence and sex on TV and in the movies and by what other people say and do. They're still going to feel the same way. I think that's how I am.

Following the rules doesn't bother me. Every religion has rules; you just can't go around making your own. You need something to follow. Everywhere you go, anything you do practically—driving a car, playing baseball, standing in line—you follow rules. They're necessary. Now whether you choose to follow them or not, that's your decision. Right now the rules don't bother me but maybe as I get older, that will change.

Very often what my religion says, and what I as a person believe in, coincide. So it isn't always a case of accepting what the Church says *on faith*. Abortion, for example. Can I tell you something that happened in school? I was sitting on the floor in biology before class with my friend, Christina Ruenhourst. If anyone ever had her own ideas about things, it's Christina. She's a person who believes that in certain circumstances things are okay and in other circumstances they are not. We had just come from religion class where we talked about abortion and being very much against that, I voiced my objections. Christina said, "Do you feel this way because that's what the Church teaches?"

"To tell you the truth, that's not the reason. It's not because the Church says it's wrong. It happens to be what I believe in, and so the Church and I agree."

The Church doesn't shape *all* my ideas.

Having gone to Dunbar Hill School, a public grammar school, before coming to Sacred Heart, I can honestly say I like the atmosphere of Sacred Heart better. You get to know everybody. Now that's not saying you're always together and get along perfectly. It's just a much nicer atmosphere. You don't have to worry about having the boys to impress—no boys up there [laughs]. You miss that. . . . But it's a lot easier to talk in the classrooms without embarrassment, to say things you wouldn't say before boys. The classes are not big, about 25 or 30 students: the whole school has about 470. There's a lot of warmth between the Sisters and the girls. In a public school, it's harder to form a relationship with a teacher. There are so many kids always around and the teachers face a whole different group almost every hour, all day long.

Just because the bond between teacher and student is stronger, that doesn't mean that the Apostles—we sometimes call the Sisters that—draw a lot of girls into the order. The last time one of them entered the Sacred Heart novitiate was about three years ago. Actually, a sister of the girl who entered also belonged to the order. But when a girl *does* enter, I'm sure that the atmosphere at school has a lot to do with it. Everybody thinks about joining at one time or other, but I would never join. It's not my thing. I want to be a lawyer.

I think Sisters have a hard job. They've given up their freedom—no, no, I can't say that because that's what they *chose* to do. Their job, their calling, is not the most popular one; girls who become nuns are in a minority. You don't see your friends hopping about for the job, waiting to sign up. And there are so few Sisters and so much to be done. Yet although they do have a hard job, the way they impress people, the way they reach people, is very effective. They strike me as women who really want to be *where they are*. They're rarely bitter, or anything like that. On the whole, they're good-natured. It's hard to say how old they are—the Apostles enter the convent right after high school and they always keep that shiny-faced, fresh look.

My parents and their parents and all my ancestors have been Catholic. My father's sister is an Apostle. We're Italian in origin. My father's father was born in Italy, but the rest were born here. I lost him about two years ago. He came from Tocco da Casáuria, a small town in the Abruzzi in central Italy. He used to tell me that they make *Cent'Erbe* in Tocco; that's a popular drink that means one hundred herbs. He was very proud of *Cent'Erbe*. I also lost a grandmother three months ago. But I still have two grandparents. My maternal grandparents were very devout. I think they said three or four Rosaries a day. Weekdays, Sundays, they went to Mass all their lives. As for my other grandparents, I would say that my grandmother is more outgoing in her beliefs. My mom has special devotions to certain saints and to Mary. Like after Mass, she always goes into Mary's chapel.

I go to church every Sunday. This Lent I went to Mass every morning. That was also to pray for my grandmother who had just died. I like to think my faith is strong. Among my friends at Sacred Heart, I seem to be freer about it. I mean, I'm more apt to talk about it. Now I don't mean to imply my friends and I just sit around and talk religion. It comes up very little. And I'm not the kind of person who gets excited when things happen and says, "What a mess! Let's go pray." It does help—saying prayers—but I'm not this little person who just sits there all the time being holy.

For Confession I go to the same priest every time. It's not that we've established a friendly basis—I don't go that often that he could get to know me. It's more like he doesn't single me out. He's more relaxed and doesn't pounce on something that's said. Sure, if he doesn't understand, he'll ask questions. I don't mind that *from him.* It takes time to get comfortable with one priest and get to know how he will react. It's much harder when you have to turn around and switch priests for some reason.

During this past year I decided to do some service work for the Church and signed up with the CCD to help instruct public-school kids in religion. [CCD is the Confraternity of Christian Doctrine, a program that provides religious instruction to all Catholic children in public schools.] I had wanted to do this for a long time, ever since I went to Rev. Daniel J. Barry Junior High and saw older girls come over to Barry for instruction on teaching these kids. I started working one hour a week as an aide to the regular teacher and tested the kids on prayers.

At Sacred Heart, we have four years of religion. In the freshman year we study the basic elements of the faith, sort of a review of the catechism. In second year we study the Sacred Scriptures and some of the history of Catholicism, particularly as seen through the lives of saints. By the third year we're much more into general themes, like death and resurrection, prayer, sexual and Christian responsibilities. The last year the Sisters talk about the options we have in adult life, and we also study Christian morality and human actions, conscience and things like that.

There is one girl in our class who is not Catholic. Her name is Andrea Gayle and she's Pentecostal. Once in religion class we were discussing how Mass is celebrated, with the people sitting or standing quietly, and she began telling us how in their services there's a lot of movement and clapping. Besides that, they gesture with their hands and sing a lot—very different from ours. I'm impressed with the way she can quote the Bible. She refers to a certain passage and says, for example, "In Ecclesiastes, Chapter 27, verses 2 to 5, it says . . ." There aren't too many of us Catholics who can do that.

In the classroom, I'd say that the Apostles are moderate in their outlook. But outspoken. One Sister especially—she has a class in religion—says what she has to say and talks freely about things. We discuss current problems a lot—drugs, alcohol, sex. Just recently we had a speaker who came and talked about AIDS and ways to protect yourself. When the girls went back to class, that Sister started talking about it and told the girls that *with abstinence, you don't have to be protected.* This sort of statement also shows how the Sisters feel. They're not encouraging us to run out and go with every guy . . . you know. But they don't cry hell and damnation either. The Sisters never tell us, "Don't do this" and "Don't do that." What they try to do is teach in other ways so that *you'll* choose not to. They communicate indirectly. Like getting speakers. We had a woman who lives across the country come in and talk to us about teenage pregnancies. The unspoken lesson was the *results* of sex: What happens afterward? What happens to the individuals themselves? By not forcing things down our throat, they try to teach us *how to choose.* And they never talk about protection from pregnancy or AIDS because that would imply that you can do it as long as you're protected.

I am very active in the pro-life movement. [This movement is dedicated to preserving and fostering respect for life and to supporting the human rights of everyone, especially the unborn, the ill, the aged and the mentally and physically handicapped.] Our branch here at Sacred Heart is called Heartbeat. What it deals with is not only abortion but a Special Olympics program for the mentally and physically handicapped. We deal with the elderly at the Whitney Center, a place for people who are retired but don't live at home for some reason. We are also involved in a house that is being established for teenagers who decide to keep their babies. It will be called Life Savers. It's an old house that is being fixed up. We've already gone there four times to help clean it.

Just recently one of the Apostles took us to a pro-life workshop on abortion to hear a doctor from New York. He was Dr. Bernard Nathanson, a non-Catholic, who used to be a leading abortionist, having performed over 75,000 abortions in New York City before changing sides and joining the pro-life movement. He was absolutely phenomenal. He said that when he was at a medical convention some years ago, a doctor friend, who specialized in late-term abortions, demonstrated a new, easier method of operating for this kind of late abortion. First, the woman was given a needle with a chemical substance and told to go back to her room and return after a certain time. By then the baby's body, which had been immersed in the fluid substance, had become soft and malleable inside her, like the body of a dead chicken, kind of squashy, but still firm enough to grasp and remove from the mother. Dr. Nathanson, who afterward made a movie, *Eclipse of Reason,* about this type of abortion, was very upset at witnessing this—the deliberate destruction of an almost fully formed human baby—and came to realize that abortion of any kind was an unnecessary act against life. In that moment, he discovered his true feelings and the person he really was; a doctor who loved and venerated life and wished to preserve it.

Artificial contraception is something I can't accept. You can't deny life or the possibility of a baby coming into the world. If you protect yourself against getting pregnant, that's still denying life. The economic factor—where does a family get the money to feed and educate another child—there are ways you can manage that. As for the rhythm theory, maybe as long as you're not using anything artificial . . . but I haven't thought about that. I'm not really sure.

I don't know much about the Pope, I'm sorry to say, and don't know what Liberation Theology is. I've never heard of ecumenism until you just mentioned it. Let me ask you a question: What makes the different Christian churches want to become one Christian Church? We all don't have the same beliefs. We do believe in one main God and Jesus, but I think it will be kind of hard. Even though the common belief is still there, the *way* these people practice is important. Are we trying to say that these people aren't going to practice the same way?

Vatican II is familiar—we discussed it in Church history last year—but I don't know too much about it. I remember it was a meeting but can't tell you this or that about it.

I'm comfortable with my religion and am not searching around for a better one. I may struggle to be a good Catholic but it's not like I'm looking for another faith. What you get out of anything is what you put into it, and I'm putting in as much as possible. At least, I think so and hope so. That doesn't mean just going to church on Sunday. It means living your religion, not trying to be the perfect person, but acting according to how your religion says and how you've been brought up. If you can combine religion with how you've been brought up, that will make you a stronger person. I was brought up in a churchgoing family and with rules, but not with rules that were too hard to follow. If you have a little bit of both—I mean religion and home and stuff—it gives you a lot in life. What being a good Catholic amounts to—I mean not only to others but to yourself—is *self-respect,* and by your actions, you show whether you respect yourself or not. When you do something bad, it shows you don't think much of yourself. Besides, your actions are going to stick with you—what you do is going to have an effect on you. Being a good Catholic is making the most of yourself, respecting yourself. And you try to take good actions because you would suffer if you do wrong things. I believe there is someone higher than me who allows me to do this; you know, who gives me the free will to respect myself, to respect others.

Brother Jeffrey (second from right) at an ecumenical meeting with Dr. John Deschner of the United Methodist Church, Dr. Gayraud Wilmore of the Presbyterian Church and Dr. Paul Crow of the Christian Church

Brother Jeffrey Gros

ONE CHURCH FOR ALL CHRISTIANS

With the Lutherans, enormous progress has been made on the issue of the Papacy. Who would have thought two decades ago that we'd have a common statement on papal primacy and papal infallibility which both Catholics and Lutherans could set their names to?

High above the Hudson River near the tower of Riverside Church in New York City lies the limestone, nineteen-story building of the Interchurch Center. A symbol of the tremendous growth of ecumenism in America, it reflects the effort of many Christians to unite the varied churches of the Protestant and Eastern Orthodox traditions. The National Council of the Churches of Christ in the USA (NCCC), which is a primary national expression of the ecumenical movement and comprises thirty-two different churches or communions, has its headquarters at the center.

Through one of NCCC's many offices, the Commission on Faith and Order, the Catholic Church has been participating fully, since Vatican II, on the common aim of theological dialogues and Christian unity. For twenty years, the staff at the commission's offices has included Roman Catholics, among them, Sister Anne Patrick Ware, Father David Bowman, and Brother Jeffrey Gros, the present director of the commission. An ecumenist extraordinaire, Brother Jeffrey brings to this reconciling movement an enthusiasm and vitality that are catching.

Not a priest, not a layman, but a Brother, Brother Jeffrey here speaks on the two subjects closest to his heart: first, the

rather remote, not widely known order of men called Brothers, who live apart and devote themselves to the mission of
teaching, and secondly, ecumenism across this nation, its
meaning and effect on the average Christian, and why a
Brother, rather than a priest, was selected to a top ecumenical
post.

A Brother is a layperson who lives in community with other
men for the sake of a spirituality of mission and for the sake of
focusing exclusively on that mission. Our community, the Christian
Brothers of St. John Baptist de la Salle, is three hundred years old
and was started in 1680 in Louis XIV's France for *service to the poor
through education.* Our founder discovered that in order for the
Brothers to stay with the poor and stay with teaching, it was important that they follow the ministry of the Gospel in a special way
by having a prayer life together and a community life together. In
addition to this vow of service to the poor through education, we
have the traditional vows of poverty, chastity and obedience.

But we are not priests and we are not involved in the
sacramental ministry of the Church. [A priest is authorized to
give people the Sacraments, which produce grace and nourish
Christian life. The Sacraments are Baptism, Holy Eucharist
(Communion), Penance, Matrimony, Anointing of the Sick,
Confirmation and Holy Orders.] Our ministry is the ministry of
education, which we think the Gospel ranks as necessary as the
sacramental ministry of the priest, not competitive with it. If our
Brothers were to be in the sacramental ministry, there would not
be the time and the focus for their spirituality on teaching and
education. We have not had a priest in our order for those three
hundred years, even though our founder was a priest. If
someone desires to leave and go on to the ordained ministry or
to the married state, he may do so by getting permission. But we
don't accept ordained or married persons into the community.
We live a common life: we pray together, study together, work
together. We form or train our own people through the

novitiate, but since we are educators, we have an academic rather than a seminary training.

Brothers have the same calling as the Sisters of the Church, and the same life-style. But with one important difference. Because we are men religious and small in number, we don't seem to be as burdened as they are by present tensions in the Church. Let me give you an example. Originally, our Brothers came to this country as parish teachers. I live in Good Shepherd Parish in New York City with a community that teaches in the parish grade school. But most of our Brothers prefer a ministry that is independent and free from parish control. Less than ten percent of our Brothers in this country are in a ministry where they work with a diocese or parish directly, and our educational work does not need to relate directly to the structures of the Church. When we teach in diocesan and archdiocesan high schools, we preserve independence. On the other hand, Sisters who teach often collaborate more closely than we do. They are part of the local structure of the Church and exist in parish relationships.

We are subject directly to Rome. The Bishops do *not* approve our rule; Rome does. Of course, we have a working collaboration with the Bishops as we teach in their dioceses but, as a community, we relate to the Congregation of Religious and Secular Institutes in Rome. Changes in our rule have just been approved by them. Vatican II suggested updating of the rules of orders and congregations and we, of course, complied.

I should point out that although the Christian Brothers are independent, lately there has been increased collaboration with the diocese. For example, one of our Brothers has just been appointed as a lay pastor in Kansas City. Historically, our separation from Bishops has created tension. But since Vatican II called for renewal within the religious orders, we are working hard with the Bishops to provide collaborative models of ministry so that we can be more supportive and serve the people of God better. Brothers are now working in diocesan roles, but these are still a minority. We tend to work better independently as educators.

We do wear a habit, though not always in informal situations. [During this interview, Brother Jeffrey was dressed in sweater, shirt, tie and slacks.] In fact, our habit is something like the one worn by our founder, St. John Baptist de la Salle, in the eighteenth century. The collar has two strips of white cloth suspended from it;

my Protestant friends say it's just like the Geneva tabs that Presbyterians have. We wear a long robe with no belt, usually black, and in tropical countries, white. Laypeople are impressed by the habit and separate themselves from the Brothers *because of the habit.* And that's why in certain contexts it's less helpful to wear it because our task in the Church has been to promote the role of the laity, all of us working together equally on the basis of our Baptism. In other words, the habit should not become something that separates members of the Church but rather should be a symbol, in a sense, of what we all stand for.

My interest in ecumenism, which Vatican II defined as "promoting the restoration of unity among all Christians," started in childhood. I grew up in Memphis, Tennessee, where Catholics are about 5 percent of the population. To be a Catholic there is to be someone in a minority who looks around and sees that everybody else is Baptist. We often joke in Memphis that there are more Baptists than people! I grew up in an environment where from the time I could talk religion, I was in dialogue with other Christians.

In 1963 I was a young Brother teaching biology in a high school in St. Louis, Missouri. *Time* magazine published a piece about the Roman Catholic Church's new participation in the ecumenical movement as a result of Vatican II. This impressed me. Across the street from the high school was a Protestant establishment, the Concordia Seminary of the Lutheran Church–Missouri Synod. Hoping to discuss the *Time* piece with someone at the seminary, I walked over and happened to meet a professor, Dr. Arthur Carl Peipkorn, whom I later learned was involved in history and very ecumenical. He couldn't have been a better person to meet. As Vatican II moved forward and set up a dialogue with the Lutherans in 1967, he was one of the Protestants to be in dialogue with our Church.

And so I began to learn about other Christian churches. In 1964 my community asked me to go into theology. Our Brothers had not studied theology before; we tended to teach high-school religion and secular studies. I went away to study at Marquette University and did my master's thesis on the ordained ministry of the Presbyterian Church and how Catholics might understand the priesthood among Presbyterians. After this I did my doctorate in theology at Fordham and ended up being quite well prepared for ecumenical work.

Before going further, may I mention that ecumenism is just one of the many things that happened as a result of Vatican II? It was such a wonderful inspiration for renewal in many, many areas of the Catholic Church. For more than the twenty years since Vatican II ended, all our dioceses and parishes throughout this country have been inspired with a spirit of renewal and the reforms of Pope John XXIII and Pope Paul VI who immediately followed him. My advanced degrees prepared me not only for the spirit of ecumenism but for Church renewal of all kinds. For example, I went back to Memphis and worked very hard toward building a new kind of diocese patterned after the model set up by Vatican II. This was in 1971 and we started the diocese with a "pastoral office" instead of a "chancery office." There were full-time directors of liturgy and religious education. Parish councils in every parish were established at the same time as a new Bishop was introduced. Following that of the Holy Father, the Bishop's social teaching was as supported by Protestant leaders as it was by Catholics. I was also involved in renewal work in the diaconate, in the new Rite of Christian Initiation for Adults [rite under which adults are prepared for Baptism and reception into the Church], in training catechists, college teaching and social-justice work. I also helped in spiritual renewal, renewal of the Sacrament of Penance, the Eucharist and in many other elements of Church life. Vatican II was such a rich gift to the Church. The sixteen documents produced during Vatican II by the Bishops and published throughout the Church have only begun to influence the local congregations. Since coming to New York, I've specialized in ecumenism and since 1981 have been associated with the National Council of the Churches of Christ [NCCC].

The NCCC is a very important national expression of the ecumenical movement. It was organized in 1950 and comprises thirty-two communions—Protestant, Orthodox and Anglican church bodies—with a combined membership of 40 million Christians. They share a vision of the unity of Christian churches that includes four important elements. The first is a *common witness* [public behavior that exemplifies the word of the Gospel], both in evangelism, that is, sharing the Gospel with people who are not Christian, and in common witness to Christian values and social concerns. The second element is *action together*, common ministry and service to the community, working together to bring the Gospel to people through social service. The third element of unity is a deepened spiritual life of Christian people *together*, so that we can all pray for Church unity and for the needs of the world. Finally, ecumenism seeks to restore full, *visible* unity. In other words, this unity should be seen. What brings about the visibility? We are studying those things on which we differ in order to find ways, in Scripture and tradition, to overcome these divisions.

Since 1963 the Roman Catholic Church has been involved with the National Council of the Churches of Christ through one of NCCC's offices called the Commission on Faith and Order. The Church is a full member of Faith and Order in the United States as it is in the World Council of Churches. Because of the Church's commitment, since Vatican II, to theological dialogue and church union, this particular office with its emphasis on both aspects has an important place in its eyes. When a position opened in Faith and Order and was advertised in the Catholic press, I decided to apply and consulted Bishop Ernest Unterkoefler, who chaired the Committee on Ecumenical and Interreligious Affairs of the Conference of Catholic Bishops. He said, "Yes, it would be very helpful to us as Catholics to have you there." I applied for the job and was accepted as associate director. Now I am full director.

Faith and Order maintains a dialogue among Christians of different churches on issues that have historically divided them. For example, the Eastern and Oriental Orthodox and the Catholics share a common understanding of the Sacraments, of the Bishops, of the divine liturgy or Mass, of the Blessed Virgin, *but not of the Papacy.* You see, we have a quite prominent Pope and the Orthodox feel that their patriarchs, the Patriarchs of Constantinople, Alexandria, Jerusalem and Antioch, were at one time equal with the Patriarch of the West, our Pope. A thousand years of separation is not healed in a day. Deep differences have to be dealt with. It's the kind of issue we deal with in Faith and Order. Among the Protestants and the Catholics, we tackle the question that Luther raised about justification by grace through faith, and the question of the Sacraments relating to that, and the Church order of Bishops, and the Papacy as well. Luther claimed a primacy of God's free love (grace) and the Scripture over human effort and the structures of the Church. These are historical and theological problems that have divided us but are now being healed. Another discussion we are involved with is the racial issue. In America, we have seven major churches that rose out of racial segregation—three Black Methodist churches, three Black Baptist churches, the Pentecostal Church of God in Christ—and many small denominations. These churches did not separate from the Catholic Church but were driven out of their own parent churches because of racism. Thus, race becomes a church-dividing issue that we have to resolve theologically and in terms of the Church's teaching and life. Renewal of our racial attitudes is as important as liturgical renewal.

Over the past twenty years, the Catholic Bishops have become committed to the ecumenical movement and are trying to renew congregations, renew the clergy, renew the dioceses, promoting the ideal of ecumenism and working with them educationally. As strong supporters of theological dialogues, the Bishops are working for the full reunion of the churches as well as for the understanding of those churches that are not as active ecumenically, like the Southern Baptists. In all these endeavors, they have created a sense of real dedication on the part of many professional Catholics, whether they be priests, Brothers, Sisters or laypeople. As a result, a good number of people could do the work I'm doing here. Every non-Catholic who is working in the theological church-unity area recognizes the strong commitment of the Catholic Church. In fact, non-Catholics may be more aware of it than our own Catholic people. Priests have been so busy with the whole task of renewal in the parish that they've not had the freedom to keep up with *all* elements of renewal or to read what the Holy Father and the Bishops are saying about ecumenical work.

A real setback in our efforts is the attitude of the press. The secular press doesn't cover our progress quite, should I say, so vigorously as it takes on the conflicts within the Church. For example, *The New York Times* did not cover the papal visit to Columbia, South Carolina, in September 1987, a great ecumenical occasion when the Pope and leaders of other Christian faiths came together in celebration of the unifying progress that has been made. Deciding that that was one event they could ignore, the *Times* gave two or three days' coverage to the Pope's visit to Miami to meet with Jewish leaders. In effect, that amounts to censorship. *The New York Times* is a national newspaper with certain obligations; such selective reporting might be appropriate for a local paper where coverage is tailored to local readers. In this case, the reconciling event had to give place to conflict reporting.

Conflict sells papers more easily than reconciliation. The ecumenical work that we're about here in the NCCC doesn't get the high profile, the high visibility, in the media unless it becomes controversial. There's no way in which any of us wants to appear controversial so we try not to gear it up to be too pressworthy. It's a real irony. You can say "the first" of this and "the first" of that and the press might take it seriously. But when you're building relations on a congregational level, or on a national or international level, and things go well, then the press doesn't find it all that exciting. But outside New York, the press may be interested. In Milwaukee last summer, a big, week-long ecumenical event took place. About three hundred clergy met in theological discussion and there must have been three or four write-ups on the activities in the Milwaukee press.

On the whole, the ecumenical movement is very healthy, but it's different across the country. Over forty of the dioceses nationwide are members of the local Councils of Churches. New York is not one, but you wouldn't expect that. The Catholic Church is so large in New York and has so many pastoral priorities that you don't look for ecumenical leadership here. But go into Ohio and Indiana and Kentucky and Illinois and you'll find the dioceses working on a day-to-day basis with their ecumenical partners, developing programs for social service, for common worship, for theological education and for ministerial services such as prison, homeless, refugee and literacy work. They're part of a common community.

Certainly, the various Christian churches recognize the differences that they have, but we look toward a unity *in the Gospel* that will transcend those differences. *The full visible unity of the Christian Church* is our goal, and we recognize that Catholics have to renew themselves spiritually to long for the unity. There are still many who have not internalized or absorbed that longing. We look for the day when Orthodox and Catholic, Catholic and Protestant, will worship at the same altar table, confess the same faith, and recognize the same leadership and, indeed, be part of the same church. After all, what does it mean to be a Roman Catholic? And what does it mean to be a Southern Baptist? These designations were not found in the Bible. Despite the obvious differences, our task is to find together what it is that Christ is calling us to.

*   *   *

Anticipating certain questions, I will attempt to give some answers:

Yes, in the united Christian Church, we will still be Roman Catholic.

Yes, in the united Christian Church, there will be a place for the Pope, the Bishop of Rome. I cannot imagine being a Catholic Christian without the role of the Papacy. But I can imagine a renewed Papacy that will look quite different from anything I've experienced. Vatican II has called us to renew in *every* element of Catholic life.

Yes, in the united Church we look forward to preserving those things that are central to Roman Catholicism. But remember, there are a lot of things we cherish that are *not* central to it. We don't seek to demand of all Christians our most cherished devotions, for example. We don't even demand that of our fellow Catholics.

No, it will not be necessary for everybody to accept everything from every other Christian church. To be part of one Church, it won't be necessary for me to accept everything that Episcopalians do in their own spirituality. We have to learn what God is demanding of us in the unity of the Church. There has always been a rich Christian diversity. That is why these theological dialogues are so important.

And in answer to the question: *Will we all be called simply Christians, or will we still have our own designations?* Well, who knows the future to which the Holy Spirit is calling us?

But as we see it, we're not going to be united with the Southern Baptists as they are today, nor they with us. They don't see the Papacy as essential to the Church. On our part, we don't see that we can reject the Baptism of infants. We have to find a common ground of understanding. We've been in dialogue with the Baptists for twenty years and although we're coming to some understanding, it is very slow.

With the Lutherans, on the other hand, enormous progress has been made on the issue of the Papacy. Who would have thought, two decades ago, that we'd have a common statement on papal primacy and papal infallibility which both Catholics and Lutherans could set their names to? *Now we have that.* The Catholic Church has not officially responded to these dialogues. But they were created by theologians who were sent by the Vatican, by the Holy Father, and by the Lutheran churches. We're at an unprecedented point in our history: having these statements produced by those officially appointed by the churches. Now the churches have to find ways of making them part of their life and of seeing where we go next. I suspect that we will all be renewed in this process and we may all retain that which is essential to the Gospel in our heritage.

What about the Jews and the Muslims? Ecumenism does not apply to those who are not Christian. But in the National Council of Churches, we have a Christian-Jewish Relations Office and a Christian-Muslim Relations Office, and Faith and Order, my group, works closely with them. Faith and Order itself has a Christian-Muslim Office in Hartford, Connecticut, and in this way, we relate to the Muslim community. You see, each of the churches has related in interfaith dialogue individually, in different ways. Catholics and Presbyterians, for example, have different ways of speaking with Muslims and with Jews, and what we need as Christians is to come together and try ecumenically to relate to them. With the Hartford office, we relate to the Muslims and work together to find how Christians can understand Islam ecumenically. Together, we can then face out to the Muslim world.

From the very beginning of the United States, one can say we were on a road that contributed much to this movement—by our own understanding of equality and the ability of the Catholic Church in America to learn to live and let live. Indeed, one of the most important factors in ecumenism was the development of the Church here and its adaptation to separation of Church and State, to religious liberty and to the new social order. For decades we have lived together closely with other Christians. Way back in 1892 at the Congress of World Religions at the Chicago Exhibition, Cardinal James Gibbons of Baltimore appeared with Protestant partners, a very controversial event, but it was something we could do in the United States. People in mixed marriages (now called ecumenical marriages), serious Catholics married to serious Orthodox or Protestant Christians, became one of the great resources of the ecumenical movement. They share their faith, are loyal to their own church, nurture their children—all witness to the unity we are seeking in Christ. All of this created a groundwork in this country that made it possible when Vatican II came along to issue its decree on religious liberty, which was framed with the help of John Courtney Murray. The decree allowed the worldwide Catholic community to affirm the possibility of toleration, freedom of religion, and constitutional government. As you may know, the Roman Catholic Church had reservations about constitutional government, religious liberty and the separation of Church and State up until 1965. Although we Catholics don't tend to see ourselves as persecuting Protestants, there *are* places in the world where they suffer because of Catholic relations with the State. That's an ecumenical problem, and a vision of the separation of Church and State is a contribution that we in the United States can make.

Where we are now in the Roman Catholic Church shows a tremendous amount of ecumenical progress. If all our priests and Bishops and Roman leadership understood this progress and were sympathetic to the initiatives of Pope John XXIII, Pope Paul VI and Pope John Paul II, the ecumenical movement on the Catholic side could move forward very quickly. *But it is an educational task.* I'm convinced that the priority in the ecumenical movement for Catholics right now is *education.* Many don't know it exists. Others may know, but are held back emotionally. Although some of the documents Vatican II issued are nearly a quarter century old, *many of them are not taught in our seminaries or our Catholic schools.* There is a lot of educating to be done—on both sides. Most Christians who are not Catholic have grown up and still live with Catholics whose faith and outlook were formed *before* Vatican II. They are seeing our human, frail way of trying to internalize the reforms, and thus are witnessing a Catholicism that is not ideal. *They* need to be educated about where the Catholic Church is and where it is bound for. Non-Catholics also need to be educated *on the truth behind the headlines.* Many Protestants take their image of the Papacy from the secular press rather than from our Catholic leadership. And sometimes our Catholic press is at fault because *it* is selective.

Now, who among Catholics should educate on these ecumenical matters? I consider the Brothers and those of us who are called to the ministry of education challenged to do this. They should educate the clergy, our ecumenical partners, both Protestant and Orthodox, and our laypeople. Brothers are *doubly* suited. Those called to the ordained ministry, priests and Bishops, have a unique relationship with the Church in a way that necessitates a sense of institutional loyalty, as well as a loyalty in faith. And they may tend to be defensive about this loyalty, but theirs is a very important role. However, the educators in the Church, the Brothers and others, have more independence of the central structure and they are not seen by non-Catholics as quite so defensive. That does not mean that a priest might not do my work better than me if he were trained, but I'm an educator, and not looked upon as clergy. So in a sense I'm in a uniquely free position. And yet, I am a member of a religious community under the jurisdiction of the Church, and I am part of the institution in a public way, so that I am a public figure in the Church and carry that kind of structural relationship. My educational role is to be no less loyal to the faith than the clergy, including loyalty to Roman Catholic ecumenical commitments.

One of Luther's major points was the importance of the ministry of the baptized, the priesthood of *all* believers, and at the same time he had problems with religious life as a special state. Well, in a sense Brothers are a witness to the fact that one can be lay and, at the same time, committed to full ministry and belief in the priesthood of all believers, be loyal to the Church with its Bishops and priests, and still live a religious life under the Gospel. To my mind, Brothers are a unique witness—I don't mean to say better or worse, just different—and uniquely suited to raising some of the questions about our possible reconciliation in ecumenism. It's exciting.

Actually, since the appearance of the Vatican II document *Decree on the Apostolate of Lay People* in 1965, the Church is stressing exactly what Luther believed in—the priesthood of *all* believers. We call it *discipleship.* There is no doubt that we're all called to be disciples by our Baptism. The big challenge for Roman Catholics today is for them to realize that they *are* ministers by their very Baptism. The call has been renewed. You see, the call was not emphasized in the past because we grew up in churches where we expected the priests and the religious to be "real" Catholics and the laity was "loyal" Catholics. Laypeople would often do volunteer work that the Bishop or the priest or the Sister would ask them to do. Although discipleship has always been an understanding of our Baptism and of the Church itself, it is now a *renewed* part of that understanding.

For the parishes, the challenge is for them to become familiar with this renewed Catholic Christian discipleship and to allow parishioners to have a ministry and to call all equally to be ministers with the priest and the religious. That is the challenge that cannot be met overnight. On the other hand, many people work out their lay ministry in civil service. Numerous Catholics take their involvement in civic life as a ministry, like the governor of New York and others who are very self-consciously spiritual in their public ministry. These are great models.

It's a time of unusual bustle in the Church. There are opportunities for laypeople to get involved in social action, social justice on behalf of the poor, and work with the Black community to liberate our society from racism. They can educate people to understand the Bishops' messages on world peace, worldwide justice, and Catholic endeavor in mission work in Latin America, Africa and Asia. With the coming of the *Roe* v. *Wade* decision [the Supreme Court's approval of the right to abortion], a whole range of people came into active lay ministry on behalf of birth rights and of mothers who wanted to bring their babies into the world. Making calls throughout the country to inform women of an alternative to abortion, housewives who never saw themselves as ministers became active. And, of course, the ecumenical ministry is just one among the many.

At the personal level, ecumenism makes great strides. The Anglican Archbishop of Dublin said recently, "The cutting edge of ecumenism is the relationship *of individual Christians at a personal level."* When the Pope visited South Carolina, he met with twenty-seven United States Christians, but many of their faces were familiar to him. I would say he personally knew about one third to one half of the participants—to mention a few, Bishop Crumley of the Lutheran Church in America, Bishop Preus of the American Lutheran Church, Bishop Browning of the Episcopal Church, Archbishop Iakovos of the Greek Archdiocese, several Baptists, and Dr. George Williams from Harvard, whom he has known since his Polish days when he was Cardinal-Archbishop of Cracow (Dr. Williams visited and studied with him there).

At the St. Patrick's Cathedral service during the Week of Prayer for Christian Unity in New York this year, I witnessed Cardinal John O'Connor at his ecumenical best. The attending clergy included women from the various Protestant denominations. Before the blessing, the Cardinal said, "My sisters and brothers in the ministry, come forward and we will bless together the congregation."

Now, there are very few Bishops who welcome their sisters in the ministry to bless the congregation! Cardinal O'Connor brings his rich experience in the military, where he lived as an equal with women in ministry. It is certainly not in the experience of all our

Catholic priests and Bishops to work as equals with Protestant ministers who happen to be women. He has transformed this experience into an ecumenical gift.

Local ecumenical gatherings provide warm, unifying experiences. I remember particularly retreats devoted to the Eucharist or Communion. Christians can't share fully the Eucharist at the altar yet. But in talking with Presbyterians and Episcopalians and Lutherans about how they encounter Christ in Communion, Catholics are amazed at how deep Protestant spirituality is in terms of receiving Christ in Communion and how deep their faith is in the presence of Christ. On their part, Protestants marvel at how *personal* Communion is to the Catholic because they have been taught about our belief in transsubstantiation [the change of bread and wine into the substance of Christ's body and blood during Mass] and about the mystery with which we surround the Mass, and *not* about our personal response. The unifying and intimate reality is that it is *the same Jesus Christ* whom we receive in Communion, though we still remain divided at our altars.

Governor Cuomo as he delivered the speech at the University of
Notre Dame

Mario Cuomo

A CATHOLIC OFFICIAL RESPONDS TO THE ABORTION ISSUE

I protect my right to be a Catholic by preserving your right to believe as a Jew, a Protestant, or nonbeliever, or as anything else you choose.

The Catholic in public office faces a huge dilemma on one of the most agony-ridden issues of our time: whether to act in accordance with women's right to choose, or not choose, abortion, or to act in compliance with the dictates of a Catholic conscience that forbids it. Of our many Catholic politicians, the one who has made the most forthright and fearless statement on this is Governor Mario Cuomo of New York. In a speech delivered at the University of Notre Dame in 1984, he presented a point of view that marks a deeply felt response— one that is reasonable, pragmatic and feasible in a country of varying beliefs and non-beliefs.

The speech has created much controversy. Alexander Haig, a moderate Catholic, says in his interview, "Governor Cuomo is a dialectician of profound capability. I found it startling that he could go out to Notre Dame, my former alma mater, and espouse essentially heretical attitudes against an apparent backdrop of applause and support from the Catholic faculty!"

The seriousness with which Governor Cuomo has always accepted personal and religious responsibility adds strength to his views: he is a father of five children, a devoted family man and husband, and a practicing Catholic born and bred. Since no interview could present his arguments more cogently than the speech itself, the author asked the governor if he would allow her to use it in this book. Since he considers the speech perhaps the most important one he has made, he said, "Only if you use *all* of it." It appears here, in full.

RELIGIOUS BELIEF AND PUBLIC MORALITY: A CATHOLIC GOVERNOR'S PERSPECTIVE

(A speech delivered at the University of Notre Dame, September 1985)

I would like to begin by drawing your attention to the title of this lecture: "Religious Belief and Public Morality: A Catholic Governor's Perspective." I was not invited to speak on "Church and State" generally. Certainly not "Mondale versus Reagan." The subject assigned is difficult enough. I will try not to do more than I've been asked.

It's not easy to stay contained. Certainly, although everybody talks about a wall of separation between Church and State, I've seen religious leaders scale that wall with all the dexterity of Olympic athletes. In fact, I've seen so many candidates in churches and synagogues that I think we should change election day from Tuesdays to Saturdays and Sundays.

I am honored by this invitation, but the record shows that I am not the first governor of New York to appear at an event involving Notre Dame. One of my great predecessors, Al Smith, went to the Army–Notre Dame football game each time it was played in New York.

His fellow Catholics expected Smith to sit with Notre Dame; protocol required him to sit with Army because it was the home team. Protocol prevailed. But not without Smith noting the dual demands on his affections. "I'll take my seat with Army," he said, "but I commend my soul to Notre Dame!"

Today, I'm happy to have no such problem. Both my seat and my soul are with Notre Dame. And as long as Father McBrien doesn't invite me back to sit with him at the Notre Dame–St. John's basketball game, I'm confident my loyalties will remain undivided.

In a sense, it's a question of loyalty that Father McBrien has asked me here today to discuss. Specifically, must politics and religion in America divide our loyalties? Does the "separation between Church and State" imply separation between religion and politics? Between morality and government? Are these different propositions? Even more specifically, what is the relationship of my Catholicism to my politics? Where does the one end and the other begin? Or are the two divided at all? And if they're not, should they be?

Hard questions.

No wonder most of us in public life—at least until recently—preferred to stay away from them, heeding the Biblical advice that if "hounded and pursued in one city," we should flee to another.

Now, however, I think that it is too late to flee. The questions are all around us, and answers are coming from every quarter. Some of them have been simplistic; most of them fragmentary; and a few, spoken with a purely political intent, demagogic.

There has been confusion and compounding of confusion, a blurring of the issue, entangling it in personalities and election strategies, instead of clarifying it for Catholics as well as others.

Today, I would like to try to help correct that.

I can offer you no final truths, complete and unchallengeable. But it's possible this one effort will provoke other efforts—both in support and contradiction of my position—that will help all of us understand our differences and perhaps even discover some basic agreement.

In the end, I'm convinced we will all benefit if suspicion is replaced by discussion, innuendo by dialogue; if the emphasis in our debate turns from a search for talismanic criteria and neat but simplistic answers to an honest—more intelligent—attempt at describing the role religion has in our public affairs, and the limits placed on that role.

And if we do it right—if we're not afraid of the truth even when the truth is complex—this debate, by clarification, can bring relief to untold numbers of confused—even anguished—Catholics, as well as to many others who want only to make our already great democracy even stronger than it is.

I believe the recent discussion in my own state has already produced some clearer definition. In early summer, newspaper accounts had created the impression in some quarters that official Church spokespeople would ask Catholics to vote for or against specific candidates on the basis of their political position on the abortion issue. I was one of those given that impression. Thanks to the dialogue that ensued over the summer—only partially reported by the media—we learned that the impression was not accurate.

Confusion had presented an opportunity for clarification and we seized it. Now all of us are saying one thing—in chorus—reiterating the statement of the National Conference of Catholic Bishops that they will not "take positions for or against political candidates" and that their stand on specific issues should not be perceived "as an expression of political partisanship."

Of course, the Bishops will teach—they must—more and more vigorously and more and more extensively. But they have said they will not use the power of their position, and the great respect it receives from all Catholics, to give an imprimatur to individual politicians or parties.

Not that they couldn't if they wished to—some religious leaders do; some are doing it at this very moment.

Not that it would be a sin if they did—God doesn't insist on political neutrality. But because it is the judgment of the Bishops, and most of us Catholic laypeople, that it is not wise for prelates and politicians to be tied too closely together.

I think that getting this consensus was an extraordinarily useful achievement.

Now with some trepidation and after much prayer, I will take up your gracious invitation to continue the dialogue in the hope that it will lead to still further clarification.

Let me begin this part of the effort by underscoring the obvious. I do not speak as a theologian; I do not have that competence. I do not speak as a philosopher; to suggest that I could would be to set a new record for false pride. I don't presume to speak as a "good" person except in the ontological sense of that word. My principal credential is that I serve in a position that forces me to wrestle with the problems you've come here to study and debate.

I am by training a lawyer and by practice a politician. Both professions make me suspect in many quarters, including among some of my own co-religionists. Maybe there's no better illustration of the public perception of how politicians unite their faith and their profession than the story they tell in New York about "Fish-hooks" McCarthy, a famous Democratic leader on the Lower East Side, and right-hand man to Al Smith.

"Fishhooks," the story goes, was devout. So devout that every morning on his way to Tammany Hall to do his political work, he stopped at St. James' Church on Oliver Street in Downtown Man-hattan, fell on his knees and whispered the same simple prayer: "Oh, Lord, give me health and strength. We'll steal the rest."

"Fishhooks" notwithstanding, I speak here as a politician. And also as a Catholic, a layperson baptized and raised in the pre–Vatican II Church, educated in Catholic schools, attached to the Church first by birth, then by choice, now by love. An old-fashioned Catholic who sins, regrets, struggles, worries, gets confused and most of the time feels better after Confession.

The Catholic Church is my spiritual home. My heart is there, and my hope.

There is, of course, more to being a Catholic than a sense of spiritual and emotional resonance. Catholicism is a religion of the head as well as the heart, and to be a Catholic is to say "I believe" to the essential core of dogmas that distinguishes our faith.

The acceptance of this faith requires a lifelong struggle to un-derstand it more fully and to live it more truly, to translate truth into experience, to practice as well as to believe.

That's not easy: applying religious belief to everyday life often presents difficult challenges.

It's always been that way. It certainly is today. The America of the late twentieth century is a consumer society, filled with endless distractions, where faith is more often dismissed than challenged, where the ethnic and other loyalties that once fastened us to our religion seem to be weakening.

In addition to all the weaknesses, dilemmas and temptations that impede every pilgrim's progress, the Catholic who holds political office in a pluralistic democracy—who is elected to serve Jews and Muslims, atheists and Protestants, as well as Catholics— bears special responsibility. He or she undertakes to help create conditions under which all can live with a maximum of dignity and with a reasonable degree of freedom; where everyone who chooses may hold beliefs different from specifically Catholic ones—sometimes contradictory to them; where the laws protect people's right to divorce, to use birth control, and even to choose abortion.

In fact, Catholic public officials take an oath to preserve the Constitution that guarantees this freedom. And they do so gladly. Not because they love what others do with their freedom, but because they realize that in guaranteeing freedom for all, they guarantee our right to be Catholics: our right to pray, to use the Sacraments, to refuse birth-control devices, to reject abortion, not to divorce and remarry if we believe it to be wrong.

The Catholic public official lives the political truth most Catholics through most of American history have accepted and insisted on: the truth that to assure our freedom we must allow others the same freedom, even if occasionally it produces conduct by them which we would hold to be sinful.

I protect my right to be a Catholic by preserving your right to believe as a Jew, a Protestant, or nonbeliever, or as anything else you choose.

We know that the price of seeking to force our beliefs on others is that they might someday force theirs on us.

This freedom is the fundamental strength of our unique experiment in government. In the complex interplay of forces and considerations that go into the making of our laws and policies, its preservation must be a pervasive and dominant concern.

But insistence on freedom is easier to accept as a general proposition than in its applications to specific situations. There are other valid general principles firmly embedded in our Constitution which, operating at the same time, create interesting and occasionally troubling problems. Thus, the same amendment of the Constitution that forbids the establishment of a state church affirms my legal right to argue that my religious belief would serve well as an article of our universal public morality. I may use the prescribed processes of government—the legislative and executive and judicial processes—to convince my fellow citizens—Jews and Protestants and Buddhists and nonbelievers—that what I propose is as beneficial for them as I believe it is for me; that it is not just parochial or narrowly sectarian but fulfills a human desire for order, peace, justice, kindness, love, any of the values most of us agree are desirable even apart from their specific religious base or context.

I am free to argue for a governmental policy for a nuclear freeze not just to avoid sin but because I think my democracy should regard it as a desirable goal.

I can, if I wish, argue that the State should not fund the use of contraceptive devices not because the Pope demands it but because I think that the whole community—for the good of the whole community—should not sever sex from an openness to the creation of life.

And surely I can, if so inclined, demand some kind of law against abortion not because my Bishops say it is wrong but because I think the whole community, regardless of its religious beliefs, should agree on the importance of protecting life—including life in the womb, which is, at the very least, potentially human and should not be extinguished casually.

No law prevents us from advocating any of these things: I am free to do so.

So are the Bishops. And so is Reverend Falwell.

In fact, the Constitution guarantees my right to try. And theirs. And his.

But should I? Is it helpful? Is it essential to human dignity? Does it promote harmony and understanding? Or does it divide us so fundamentally that it threatens our ability to function as a pluralistic community?

When should I argue to make my religious value your morality? My rule of conduct your limitation?

What are the rules and policies that should influence the exercise of this right to argue and promote?

I believe I have a salvific mission as a Catholic. Does that mean I am in conscience required to do everything I can as governor to translate all my religious values into the laws and regulations of the State of New York or the United States? Or be branded a hypocrite if I don't?

As a Catholic, I respect the teaching authority of the Bishops.

But must I agree with everything in the Bishops' Pastoral Letter on Peace and fight to include it in party platforms?

And will I have to do the same for the forthcoming Pastoral on Economics even if I am an unrepentant supply-sider?

Must I, having heard the Pope renew the Church's ban on birth-control devices, veto the funding of contraceptive programs for non-Catholics or dissenting Catholics in my state? I accept the Church's teaching on abortion. Must I insist you do? By law? By denying you Medicaid funding? By a constitutional amendment? If so, which one? Would that be the best way to avoid abortions or to prevent them?

These are only some of the questions for Catholics. People with other religious beliefs face similar problems.

Let me try some answers.

Almost all Americans accept some religious values as a part of our public life. We are a religious people, many of us descended from ancestors who came here expressly to live their religious faith free from coercion or repression. But we are also a people of many religions, with no established church, who hold different beliefs on many matters.

Our public morality, then—the moral standards we maintain for everyone, not just the ones we insist on in our private lives—depends on a consensus view of right and wrong. The values derived from religious beliefs will not—and should not—be accepted as part of the public morality unless they are shared by the pluralistic community-at-large, by consensus.

That values happen to be religious values does not deny them acceptability as a part of this consensus. But it does not require their acceptability either.

The agnostics who joined the civil-rights struggle were not deterred because that crusade's values had been nurtured and sustained in Black Christian churches. Those on the political left are not perturbed today by the religious basis of the clergy and laypeople who join them in the protest against the arms race and hunger and exploitation.

The arguments start when religious values are used to support positions which would impose on other people restrictions they find unacceptable. Some people do object to Catholic demands for an end to abortion, seeing it as a violation of the separation of Church and State. And some others, while they have no compunction about invoking the authority of the Catholic Bishops in regard to birth control and abortion, might reject out of hand their teaching on war and peace and social policy.

Ultimately, therefore, the question "whether or not we admit religious values into our public affairs" is too broad to yield a single answer. "Yes," we create our public morality through consensus and in this country that consensus reflects to some extent religious values of a great majority of Americans. But "no," all religiously based values don't have an a priori place in our public morality. The community must decide if what is being proposed would be better left to private discretion than public policy; whether it restricts freedoms, and if so to what end, to whose benefit; whether it will produce a good or bad result; whether overall it will help the community or merely divide it.

The right answers to these questions can be elusive. Some of the wrong answers, on the other hand, are quite clear. For example, there are those who say there is a simple answer to *all* these questions: they say that by history and practice of our people we were intended to be—and should be—a Christian country in law.

But where would that leave the nonbelievers? And whose Christianity would be law, yours or mine?

This "Christian nation" argument should concern—even frighten —two groups: non-Christians and thinking Christians.

I believe it does.

I think it's already apparent that a good part of the nation understands—if only instinctively—that anything which seems to suggest that God favors a political party or the establishment of a state church, is wrong and dangerous.

Way down deep the American people are afraid of an entangling relationship between formal religions—or whole bodies of religious beliefs—and government. Apart from constitutional law and religious doctrine, there is a sense that tells us it's wrong to presume to speak for God or to claim God's sanction of our particular legislation and His rejection of all other positions. Most of us are offended when we see religion being trivialized by its appearance in political throwaway pamphlets.

The American people need no course in philosophy or political science or church history to know that God should not be made into a celestial party chairman.

To most of us, the manipulative invoking of religion to advance a politician or a party is frightening and divisive. The American people will tolerate religious leaders taking positions for or against candidates, although I think the Catholic Bishops are right in avoiding that position. But the American people are leery about large religious organizations, powerful churches or synagogue groups engaging in such activities—again, not as a matter of law or doctrine, but because our innate wisdom and democratic instinct teach us these things are dangerous.

Today, there are a number of issues involving life and death that raise questions of public morality. They are also questions of concern to most religions. Pick up a newspaper and you are almost certain to find a bitter controversy over any one of them: Baby Jane Doe, the right to die, artificial insemination, embryos *in vitro,* abortion, birth control . . . not to mention nuclear war and the shadow it throws across all existence.

Some of these issues touch the most intimate recesses of our lives, our roles as someone's mother or child or husband; some affect women in a unique way. But they are also public questions for all of us.

Put aside what God expects—assume if you like, there is no God—then the greatest thing still left to us is life. Even a radically secular world must struggle with the question of when life begins, under what circumstances it can be ended, when it must be protected, by what authority; it too must decide what protection to extend to the helpless and the dying, to the aged and the unborn, to life in all its phases.

As a Catholic, I have accepted certain answers as the right ones for myself and my family, and because I have, they have influenced me in special ways, as Matilda's husband, as a father of five children, as a son who stood next to his own father's deathbed trying to decide if the tubes and needles no longer served a purpose.

As a governor, however, I am involved in defining policies that determine *other* people's rights in these same areas of life and death. Abortion is one of these issues, and while it is one issue among many, it is one of the most controversial and affects me in a special way as a Catholic public official.

So let me spend some time considering it.

I should start, I believe, by noting that the Catholic Church's actions with respect to the interplay of religious values and public policy make clear that there is no inflexible moral principle which determines what our *political* conduct should be. For example, on divorce and birth control, without changing its moral teaching, the Church abides by the civil law as it now stands, thereby accepting—without making much of a point of it—that in our pluralistic society we are not required to insist that *all* our religious values be the law of the land.

Abortion is treated differently.

Of course there are differences both in degree and quality between abortion and some of the other religious positions the Church takes: abortion is a "matter of life and death," and degree counts. But the difference in approach reveals a truth, I think, that is not well enough perceived by Catholics and therefore still further complicates the process for us. That is, while we always owe our Bishops' words respectful attention and careful consideration, the question whether to engage the political system in a struggle to have it adopt certain articles of our belief as part of public morality is not a matter of doctrine: it is a matter of prudential political judgment.

Recently, Michael Novak put it succinctly: "Religious judgment and political judgment are both needed," he wrote. "But they are not identical."

My Church and my conscience require me to believe certain things about divorce, birth control and abortion. My Church does not order me—under pain of sin or expulsion—to pursue my salvific mission according to a precisely defined political plan.

As a Catholic I accept the Church's teaching authority. While in the past some Catholic theologians may appear to have disagreed on the morality of some abortions (it wasn't, I think, until 1869 that excommunication was attached to all abortions without distinction), and while some theologians still do, I accept the Bishops' position that abortion is to be avoided.

As Catholics, my wife and I were enjoined never to use abortion to destroy the life we created, and we never have. We thought Church doctrine was clear on this, and—more than that—both of us felt it in full agreement with what our hearts and our consciences told us. For me life or fetal life in the womb should be protected, even if five of nine justices of the Supreme Court and my neighbor disagree with me. A fetus is different from an appendix or a set of tonsils. At the very least, even if the argument is made by some scientists or some theologians that in the early stages of fetal development we can't discern human life, the full potential of human life is indisputably there. That—to my less subtle mind—by itself should demand respect, caution, indeed . . . reverence.

But not everyone in our society agrees with me and Matilda.

And those who don't—those who endorse legalized abortions—aren't a ruthless, callous alliance of anti-Christians determined to overthrow our moral standards. In many cases, the proponents of legal abortions are the very people who have worked with Catholics to realize the goals of social justice set out in papal encyclicals: the American Lutheran Church, the Central Conference of American Rabbis, the Presbyterian Church in the United States, B'nai B'rith Women, the Women of the Episcopal Church. These are just a few of the religious organizations that don't share the Church's position on abortion.

Certainly, we should not be forced to mold Catholic morality to conform to disagreement by non-Catholics, however sincere or severe their disagreement. Our Bishops should be teachers, not pollsters. They should not change what we Catholics believe in order to ease our consciences or please our friends or protect the Church from criticism.

But if the breadth, intensity and sincerity of opposition to Church teaching shouldn't be allowed to shape our Catholic morality, it can't help but determine our ability—our realistic, political ability—to translate our Catholic morality into civil law, a law not for the believers who don't need it but for the disbelievers who reject it.

And it is here, in our attempt to find a political answer to abortion—an answer beyond our private observance of Catholic morality—that we encounter controversy within and without the Church over how and in what degree to press the case that our morality should be everybody else's, and to what effect.

I repeat, there is no Church teaching that mandates the best political course for making our belief everyone's rule, for spreading this part of our Catholicism. There is neither an encyclical nor a catechism that spells out a political strategy for achieving legislative goals.

And so the Catholic trying to make moral and prudent judgments in the political realm must discern which, if any, of the actions one could take would be best.

This latitude of judgment is not something new in the Church, not a development that has arisen only with the abortion issue. Take, for example, the question of slavery. It has been argued that the failure to endorse a legal ban on abortions is equivalent to refusing to support the cause of abolition before the Civil War. This analogy has been advanced by the Bishops of my own state.

But the truth of the matter is, few if any Catholic Bishops spoke for abolition in the years before the Civil War. It wasn't, I believe, that the Bishops endorsed the idea of some humans owning and exploiting other humans; Pope Gregory XVI, in 1840, had condemned the slave trade. Instead, it was a practical political judgment that the Bishops made. They weren't hypocrites; they were realists. At the time, Catholics were a small minority, mostly immigrants, despised by much of the population, often vilified and the object of sporadic violence. In the face of a public controversy that aroused tremendous passions and threatened to break the country apart, the Bishops made a pragmatic decision. They believed their opinion would not change people's minds. Moreover, they knew that there were southern Catholics, even some priests, who owned slaves. They concluded that under the circumstances, arguing for a constitutional amendment against slavery would do more harm than good, so they were silent. As they have been generally in recent years on the question of birth control. And as the Church has been on even more controversial issues in the past, even ones that dealt with life and death.

What is relevant to this discussion is that the Bishops were making judgments about translating Catholic teachings into public policy, not about the moral validity of the teachings. In doing so, they grappled with the unique political complexities of their time. The decision they made to remain silent on a constitutional amendment to abolish slavery or on the repeal of the Fugitive Slave Law wasn't a mark of their moral indifference: it was a measured attempt to balance moral truths against political realities. Their decision reflected their sense of complexity, not their diffidence. As history reveals, Lincoln behaved with similar discretion.

The parallel I want to draw here is not between or among what we Catholics believe to be moral wrongs. It is in the Catholic response to those wrongs. Church teaching on slavery and abortion is clear. But in the application of those teachings— the exact way we translate them into action, the specific laws we propose, the exact legal sanctions we seek—there was and is no one, clear, absolute route that the Church says, as a matter of doctrine, we must follow.

The Bishops' Pastoral *The Challenge of Peace* speaks directly to this point. "We recognize," the Bishops wrote, "that the Church's teaching authority does not carry the same force when it deals with technical solutions involving particular means as it does when it speaks of principles or ends. People may agree in abhorring an injustice, for instance, yet sincerely disagree as to what practical approach will achieve justice. Religious groups are entitled as others to their opinion in such cases, but they should not claim that their opinions are the only ones that people of good will may hold."

With regard to abortion, the American Bishops have had to weigh Catholic moral teaching against the fact of a pluralistic country where our view is in the minority, acknowledging that what is ideally desirable isn't always feasible, that there can be different political approaches to abortion besides unyielding adherence to an absolute prohibition.

This is in the American-Catholic tradition of political realism. In supporting or opposing specific legislation, the Church in this country has never retreated into a moral fundamentalism that will settle for nothing less than total acceptance of its views.

Indeed, the Bishops have already confronted the fact that an absolute ban on abortion doesn't have the support necessary to be placed in our Constitution. In 1981, they put aside earlier efforts to describe a law they could accept and get passed, and supported the Hatch Amendment instead.

Some Catholics felt the Bishops had gone too far with that action, some not far enough. Such judgments were not a rejection of the Bishops' teaching authority: the Bishops even disagreed among themselves. Catholics are allowed to disagree on these technical political questions without having to confess.

Respectfully, and after careful consideration of the position and arguments of the Bishops, I have concluded that the approach of a constitutional amendment is not the best way for us to seek to deal with abortion.

I believe that legal interdicting of abortion by either the federal government or the individual states is not a plausible possibility and even if it could be obtained, it wouldn't work. Given present attitudes, it would be "Prohibition" revisited, legislating what couldn't be enforced and in the process creating a disrespect for law in general. And as much as I admire the Bishops' hope that a constitutional amendment against abortion would be the basis for a full, new bill of rights for mothers and children, I disagree that this would be the result.

I believe that, more likely, a constitutional prohibition would allow people to ignore the causes of many abortions instead of addressing them, much the way the death penalty is used to escape dealing more fundamentally and more rationally with the problem of violent crime.

Other legal options that have been proposed are, in my view, equally ineffective. The Hatch Amendment, by returning the question of abortion to the states, would have given us a checkerboard of permissive and restrictive jurisdictions. In some cases people might have been forced to go elsewhere to have abortions and that might have eased a few consciences but it wouldn't have done what the Church wants to do—it wouldn't have created a deep-seated respect for life. Abortions would have gone on, millions of them.

Nor would a denial of Medicaid funding for abortion achieve our objectives. Given *Roe* v. *Wade,* it would be nothing more than an attempt to do indirectly what the law says cannot be done directly; worse, it would do it in a way that would burden only the disadvantaged. Removing funding from the Medicaid program would not prevent the rich and middle classes from having abortions. It would not even assure that the disadvantaged wouldn't have them; it would only impose financial burdens on poor women who want abortions.

Apart from that unevenness, there is a more basic question. Medicaid is designed to deal with health and medical needs. But the arguments for the cutoff of Medicaid abortion funds are not related to those needs. They are moral arguments. If we assume health and medical needs exist, our personal view of morality ought not to be considered a relevant basis for discrimination.

We must keep in mind always that we are a nation of laws—when we like those laws, and when we don't.

The Supreme Court has established a woman's constitutional right to abortion. The Congress has decided the federal government should not provide federal funding in the Medicaid program for abortion. That, of course, does not bind states in the allocation of their own state funds. Under the law, the individual states need not follow the federal lead, and in New York I believe we *cannot* follow that lead. The equal-protection clause in New York's Constitution has been interpreted by the courts as a standard of fairness that would preclude us from denying only the poor—indirectly by a cutoff of funds—the practical use of the constitutional right given by *Roe* v. *Wade.*

In the end, even if after a long and divisive struggle we were able to remove all Medicaid funding for abortion and restore the law to what it was—if we could put most abortions out of our sight, return them to the back rooms where they were performed for so long—I don't believe our responsibility as Catholics would be any closer to being fulfilled than it is now, with abortion guaranteed by the law as a woman's right.

The hard truth is that abortion isn't a failure of government. No agency or department of government forces women to have abortions, but abortion goes on. Catholics, the statistics show, support the right to abortion in equal proportion to the rest of the population. Despite the teaching in our homes and schools and pulpits, despite the sermons and pleadings of parents and priests and prelates, despite all the effort at defining our opposition to the sin of abortion, collectively we Catholics apparently believe—and perhaps act—little differently from those who don't share our commitment.

Are we asking government to make criminal what we believe to be sinful because we ourselves can't stop committing the sin?

The failure here is not Caesar's. This failure is our failure, the failure of the entire people of God.

Nobody has expressed this better than a Bishop in my own state. Joseph Sullivan, a man who works with the poor in New York City, is resolutely opposed to abortion and argues, with his fellow Bishops, for change of law. "The major problem the Church has is internal," the Bishop said last month in reference to abortion. "How do we teach? As much as I think we're responsible for advocating public policy issues, our primary responsibility is to teach our own people. We haven't done that. We're asking politicians to do what we haven't done effectively ourselves."

I agree with the Bishop. I think our moral and social mission as Catholics must begin with the wisdom contained in the words "Physician, heal thyself." Unless we Catholics educate ourselves better to the values that define—and can ennoble—our lives, following those teachings better than we do now, unless we set an example that is clear and compelling, then we will never convince this society to change the civil laws to protect what we preach is precious human life.

Better than any law or rule or threat of punishment would be the moving strength of our good example, demonstrating our lack of hypocrisy, proving the beauty and worth of our instruction.

We must work to find ways to avoid abortions without otherwise violating our faith. We should provide funds and opportunity for young women to bring their child to term, knowing both of them will be taken care of if that is necessary; we should teach our young men better than we do now their responsibilities in creating and caring for human life.

It is this duty of the Church to teach through its practice of love that Pope John Paul II has proclaimed so magnificently to all people. "The Church," he wrote in *Redemptor Hominis* (1979), "which has no weapons at her disposal apart from those of the spirit, of the word and of love, cannot renounce her proclamation of 'the Word . . . in season and out of season.' For this reason she does not cease to implore . . . everybody in the name of God and in the name of man: Do not kill! Do not prepare destruction and extermination for each other! Think of your brothers and sisters who are suffering hunger and misery! Respect each one's dignity and freedom!"

The weapons of the word and of love are already available to us: we need no statute to provide them.

I am not implying that we should stand by and pretend indifference to whether a woman takes a pregnancy to its conclusion or aborts it. I believe we should in all cases try to teach a respect for life. And I believe with regard to abortion that, despite *Roe* v. *Wade,* we can, in practical ways. Here, in fact, it seems to me that all of us can agree.

Without lessening their insistence on a woman's right to an abortion, the people who call themselves "pro-choice" can support the development of government programs that present an impoverished mother with the full range of support she needs to bear and raise her children, to have a real choice. Without dropping their campaign to ban abortion, those who gather under the banner of "pro-life" can join in developing and enacting a legislative bill of rights for mothers and children, as the Bishops have already proposed.

While we argue over abortion, the United States' infant mortality rate places us sixteenth among the nations of the world. Thousands of infants die each year because of inadequate medical care. Some are born with birth defects that, with proper treatment, could be prevented. Some are stunted in their physical and mental growth because of improper nutrition.

If we want to prove our regard for life in the womb, for the helpless infant—if we care about women having real choices in their lives and not being driven to abortions by a sense of helplessness and despair about the future of their child—then there is work enough for all of us. Lifetimes of it.

In New York, we have put in place a number of programs to begin this work, assisting women in giving birth to healthy babies. This year we doubled Medicaid funding to private-care physicians for prenatal and delivery services.

The state already spends twenty million dollars a year for prenatal care in outpatient clinics and for inpatient hospital care.

One program in particular we believe holds a great deal of promise. It's called "New Avenues to Dignity," and it seeks to provide a teenage mother with the special service she needs to continue with her education, to train for a job, to become capable of standing on her own, to provide for herself and the child she is bringing into the world.

My dissent, then, from the contention that we can have effective and enforceable legal prohibitions on abortion is by no means an argument for religious quietism, for accepting the world's wrongs because that is our fate as "the poor banished children of Eve."

Let me make another point.

Abortion has a unique significance but not a preemptive significance.

Apart from the question of the efficacy of using legal weapons to make people stop having abortions, we know our Christian responsibility doesn't end with any one law or amendment. That it doesn't end with abortion. Because it involves life and death, abortion will always be a central concern of Catholics. But so will nuclear weapons. And hunger and homelessness and joblessness, all the forces diminishing human life and threatening to destroy it. The "seamless garment" that Cardinal Bernardin has spoken of is a challenge to all Catholics in public office, conservatives as well as liberals.

We cannot justify our aspiration to goodness simply on the basis of the vigor of our demand for an elusive and questionable civil law declaring what we already know, that abortion is wrong.

Approval or rejection of legal restrictions on abortion should not be the exclusive litmus test of Catholic loyalty. We should understand that whether abortion is outlawed or not, our work has barely begun: the work of creating a society where the right to life doesn't end at the moment of birth; where an infant isn't helped into a world that doesn't care if it's fed properly, housed decently, educated adequately; where the blind or retarded child isn't condemned to exist rather than empowered to live.

The Bishops stated this duty clearly in 1974, in their statement to the Senate subcommittee considering a proposed amendment to restrict abortions. They maintained such an amendment could not be seen as an end in itself. "We do not see a constitutional amendment as the final product of our commitment or of our legislative activity," they said. "It is instead the constitutional base on which to provide support and assistance to pregnant women and their unborn children. This would include nutritional, prenatal, childbirth and postnatal care for the mother, and also nutritional and pediatric care for the child through the first year of life. . . . We believe that all of these should be available as a matter of right to all pregnant women and their children."

The Bishops reaffirmed that view in 1976, in 1980, and again this year when the United States Catholic Committee asked Catholics to judge candidates on a wide range of issues—on abortion, yes; but also on food policy, the arms race, human rights, education, social justice and military expenditures.

The Bishops have been consistently "pro-life" in the full meaning of that term and I respect them for that.

The problems created by the matter of abortion are complex and confounding. Nothing is clearer to me than my inadequacy to find compelling solutions to all of their moral, legal and social implications. I—and many others like me—are eager for enlightenment, eager to learn new and better ways to manifest respect for the deep reverence for life that is our religion and our instinct. I hope that this public attempt to describe the problems as I understand them will give impetus to the dialogue in the Catholic community and beyond, a dialogue which could show me a better wisdom than I've been able to find so far.

It would be tragic if we let that dialogue become a prolonged, divisive argument that destroys or impairs our ability to practice any part of the morality given us in the Sermon on the Mount, to touch, heal and affirm the human life that surrounds us.

We Catholic citizens of the richest, most powerful nation that has ever existed are like the steward made responsible over a great household: from those to whom so much has been given, much shall be required. It is worth repeating that ours is not a faith that encourages its believers to stand apart from the world, seeking their salvation alone, separate from the salvation of those around them.

We speak of ourselves as a body. We come together in worship as companions, in the ancient sense of that word, those who break bread together, and who are obliged by the commitment we share to help out another, everywhere, in all we do, and in the process, to help the whole human family. We see our mission to be "the completion of the work of creation."

This is difficult work today. It presents us with many hard choices.

The Catholic Church has come of age in America. The ghetto walls are gone, our religion no longer a badge of irredeemable foreignness. This newfound status is both an opportunity and a temptation. If we choose, we can give in to the temptation to become more and more assimilated into a larger, blander culture, abandoning the practice of the specific values that made us different, worshiping whatever gods the marketplace has to sell while we seek to rationalize our own laxity by urging the political system to legislate on others a morality we no longer practice ourselves.

Or we can remember where we come from, the journey of two millennia, clinging to our personal faith, to its insistence on constancy and service and on hope. We can live and practice the morality Christ gave us, maintaining His truth in this world, struggling to embody His love, practicing it especially where that love is most needed, among the poor and the weak and the dispossessed. Not just by trying to make laws for others to live by, but by living the laws already written for us by God, in our hearts and in our minds.

We can be fully Catholic; proudly, totally at ease with ourselves, a people in the world, transforming it, a light to this nation. Appealing to the best in our people, not the worst. Persuading, not coercing. Leading people to truth by love. And still, all the while, respecting and enjoying our unique pluralistic democracy. And we can do it, even as politicians.

Richard Ambrose at his work desk in Birmingham

Richard Ambrose

CATHOLIC MINORITY IN ALABAMA

> *Once you separate yourself from Rome, you are no longer a Catholic. This means that you could never have a separate Catholic Church in America or anywhere. An essential ingredient of the Church is its connection with Rome.*

Walking with a firm step in parish halls throughout America is a new Catholic layman or laywoman—bright, educated, efficient and capable of assuming a leadership role in a Church that has been top-heavy with clergy for almost two thousand years. They may be insurance agents, teachers, nurses, parents who are now involving themselves in Church life as deacons, parish-council presidents, eucharistic ministers and in other areas. Andrew Greeley has characterized these men and women as "highly impressive and very durable."

Richard Ambrose, who lives in Birmingham, Alabama, is an example: he is involved, verbal and educated. A husband, and the father of two teenage daughters, he spent two years in the seminary in his youth and has developed a wide-ranging knowledge of Church history and philosophy. In addition to his trenchant comments here on such topics as Fundamentalism, the Bible, fathers, and the Catholic minority in the South, he speaks knowledgeably about anti-Catholic bias in the United States, particularly in Alabama.

Mr. Ambrose is typical of a growing segment of active Catholics in the Deep South who, perhaps because they are in a minority, have developed a dedication to their Church and an enthusiasm that is stronger here than in other parts of the country.

My family and I moved to Birmingham in 1977 when I took a position as director of adult education at St. Peter's Catholic Church. The pastor, who had been ordained in 1941, told us a lot about the history of the Catholic Church in Alabama. His first assignment had been to travel a circuit of small towns in southern Alabama, a rural area with few Catholics. He and a helper drove a truck which housed a small chapel. When they arrived in a town, they'd open the truck and stand there greeting the townspeople who had rarely, if ever, seen a Catholic priest.

Finding Catholics in rural Alabama was difficult. The scarcity of priests in the state meant that those who were Catholic when they moved here in the last century had no way to practice their faith and had gradually drifted away to other churches. Without priests or churches, they had lost contact. Our pastor described numerous occasions when he and his helper were invited into homes where they saw rosaries and statues on shelves with other family mementos. Their hosts hadn't the slightest idea what to do with them. They would often be vaguely aware that some their ancestors had been Catholic before they started going to the local churches, which were usually Baptist or Methodist.

The public exchanges between the priest and those who gathered around the truck would occasionally become heated as old prejudices and misconceptions about Catholics surfaced. Purgatory, the Pope, the role of Mary and the saints, and the use of that "secret" Latin language were frequently questioned, especially when local preachers prepared their people to challenge the traveling priest. Actually, even questions with a somewhat hostile intent helped the priest accomplish his main task, which was to begin introducing the Catholic faith into this mission territory. It was an important first step toward helping people to understand that Catholics and their priests were not strange aliens out to get them.

I'm not aware of any priests traveling around in trucks today, but at that time it was not uncommon. Of course, now that television reaches into even the smallest towns throughout the rural South, the prejudices and misunderstandings that arise when people are isolated are seen much less frequently. Much of the southern anti-Catholic bias, even in the larger cities such as Birmingham, flourished in the post–Civil War era when Catholics were grouped with Blacks, Jews and Yankees as targets of the Ku Klux Klan. That bias was very strong at the end of the last century and continued into the middle of this one.

Catholics who grew up here before the sixties remember instances when they were made to feel unwelcome even when not explicitly excluded from social and civic groups and activities. Of course, the civil-rights struggle of the sixties as well as the improved image of the Church beginning with Pope John XXIII and the second Vatican Council [1962–1965], have done much to improve the attitude of Alabamians toward Catholics.

Speaking of the civil-rights struggle, Birmingham even today continues to receive negative publicity on the national level concerning events that happened here twenty-five years ago. I guess it's sort of like the old myths about Catholics, the image sticks even though we have struggled for years to overcome the inaccuracies. It's like that for Birmingham. The events of the early sixties are etched in a generation's mind. The dramatic news clips of the dogs and fire hoses are shown over and over again. I'm sure that most people in other parts of the country are not aware of the fact that Bull Connor, the police commissioner who unleashed the dogs and fire hoses and jailed Martin Luther King, Jr., had already lost his political power base and been rejected by an electorate that recognized the need for change.

For many years, Birmingham was ruled by three city commissioners who were elected on a citywide basis. As I understand it, these commissioners divided power among themselves. It was a form of government that tended to maintain old traditions, especially racial segregation. Even before the height of the civil-rights struggles in 1963, the people had rejected the commissioner form of government in favor of a mayor and city council. Bull Connor continued to resist the new form of government even after Albert Boutwell was elected mayor. In the end, it was the refusal of Connor's police forces to follow his orders to continue the cruel treatment of Black protesters that led to the resolution of that conflict. David Vann, a prime architect of the change in government, was later elected mayor of Birmingham. His successor, Dr. Richard Arrington, a Black, is currently serving his third term as mayor.

The civil-rights situation is much better in Birmingham today, but it is still no better, or worse, than in other areas of the country. Open racial segregation has been replaced by subtler forms of economic and social discrimination that continue to deny the opportunity for full realization of the dream of true equality. In many ways, today's subtler forms of discrimination are harder to deal with.

It's certainly true in the area of anti-Catholic bias, which is rarely blatant or even publicly acknowledged. In my work as director of adult education, I would occasionally be given pieces of anti-Catholic literature, such as comic books and religious tracts, which identified the Pope as the anti-Christ and the Roman Church as the evil world power of the Apocalypse. Catechumens—adults preparing to join the Church—were the ones who received most of that material. They got it from friends who apparently were quite sincere in wanting to protect them from the dangers of becoming a Catholic.

There are many good things, however, about being a Catholic in Birmingham. Maybe we try a little harder here because we are such a small minority. Only about two percent of the people in Alabama are Catholic, even though in the USA as a whole, the percentage of Catholics is about twenty-five percent or thirty percent. In Rochester, New York, where I grew up, I think Catholics represent about half the population. As I remember it, religion wasn't discussed very much outside of home and school. In the South, it's different. When you first meet people they are just as likely to ask what church you belong to as they are to ask what you do or where you work.

In recent years, many Catholics have moved to Birmingham as a result of job transfers from other parts of the country. The influx of new people and the closeness produced by minority status seem to have helped create an enthusiasm that you don't always find in areas with a more stable population. I'm not sure; maybe it comes with being in a mission territory that gives people a *sense* of mission and a willingness to get involved in Church activities. In my own parish, parishioners are mostly middle-class professionals representing businesses and industries, as well as the medical center at the University of Alabama at Birmingham. Parishioners are well-educated and, for the most part, eager to take an active role in their Church community. I've worked with volunteers in a number of places around the country and have rarely seen people who were so willing to say yes when asked to help out around the parish. The parish has a lot of different programs and services which appeal to a broad cross-section of the Catholic population. We have special ministry programs for the elderly, engaged couples, young marrieds, singles, those who divorced or widowed, as well as the more traditional youth groups, men's club and women's club.

While I was never fully initiated into the Charismatic Renewal, my duties in adult education brought me into close contact with many of the prayer groups in the area. I was most familiar with the "God's Children" prayer group, which was started at St. Peter's in 1976 by Bob and Rita Tevebaugh. My good friend Father Paul Rohling, who is now pastor at Holy Infant of Prague Church in Trussville, has served as a spiritual adviser to the group since the time it started. One of the things that impressed me most about God's Children was their interest in studying Scripture. Scripture plays a major role in the Charismatic Renewal, a fact that is probably not as well known as the custom of praying in tongues. I'm no expert on that form of prayer, but I really believe that those who choose it are very sincere and find it to be helpful.

Alabama is in the heart of what is sometimes called the Bible Belt, and it isn't too surprising that I found Catholics here to be much more interested in knowing about the Bible than Catholics in other parts of the country where I've lived. Many times that interest is sparked by questions posed by friends and neighbors from Christian denominations that can be classified as Fundamentalist. Fundamentalists are people who take the Bible at face value, usually in the form of a particular translation, such as the King James version. Fundamentalism grew out of the Reformation traditions that tended to downplay the role of theological reflection in favor of the Bible as the sole source of knowledge about what it means to be and live as a Christian. The irony is that Fundamentalism itself appears to have become a rigid theology concerned with providing definitive explanations of how to interpret the Bible.

The favorite part of my work as a director of adult education was helping adults discover the beauty and wonder of the Scriptures that most had *not* been exposed to as they grew up. I really felt like I was spreading the Good News. Many Catholics grew up with a fear of reading the Bible. They were afraid that they might slip into inadvertent heresy by misinterpreting a Bible verse. My role was to help them see that with a few basic guidelines, they could be comfortable while discovering some of the richest parts of their faith tradition.

I'd like to say a few more words about the Scripture guidelines that Vatican II published in the document called the *Dogmatic Constitution on Revelation.* It speaks of all the ways in which God has been revealed to us and especially how the fullness of that revelation took place when God became human. The followers of Jesus passed on not only their Jewish heritage but also their faith experience of Jesus. What they passed on to us through succeeding generations is our Tradition, with a capital "T." Parts of that Tradition were written down (i.e., the Bible) and gradually came to be recognized by the Church as being God's Word. The key to properly understanding the Bible is to realize that although inspired by God, it was written by humans in human fashion using the literary forms that prevailed at the time. To understand what is written in the Bible, we have to understand what the author intended to say in his own language, in his time, within the limits of his scientific knowledge. We understand that parables are stories designed to teach a lesson. It is a little harder to recognize that when Biblical characters are quoted, the author was adhering to the standards of the day, which required that you communicate the meaning of what a person said rather than reporting word for word. This means that we don't know the precise words spoken by Jesus, but that doesn't matter because we do know the message He was trying to communicate.

Even when Catholics do learn the principles of Scripture study, however, they still find barriers between themselves and the Fundamentalists who use Scripture to try to prove certain points of faith. I'm still looking for a great one-liner that could be used to respond to challenges phrased in the form of "The Bible says thus and so. Why do Catholics . . ." So far, the best answer we have found is to say something to the effect that we don't understand it that way. The real issue here is whether the Bible is the sole source of knowledge about the realities of the Christian faith as proposed by the Fundamentalists, or whether, as the Catholic Church teaches, the Bible is an integral part of a larger Tradition. While nothing in that Tradition could contradict the true message being communicated by God in the Bible, the Bible does not exhaust the lived faith experience of Christians.

My own experiences with the Catholic Church are what I consider to be a fortunate blend of being in the right place at the right time. I grew up in what we now call the pre–Vatican II Church, going to Catholic schools and serving as an altar boy. After high school, I decided to go to the seminary to see if I had a vocation to the priesthood. I entered the seminary just as Vatican II was getting started. That meant I was able to keep up with Council developments and begin studying books covering all the divergent theological opinions that Catholic publishers were more willing to accept in the new, more open atmosphere. I spent four years in that environment. It was an exciting time for those of us who were eager to see the Church join the twentieth century.

I'm sure I had a number of reasons for leaving the seminary, but the one that stands out is that I decided that I wanted to be able to get married and have children. That would have been impossible if I stayed. At the seminary, we had a spiritual director who gave a number of talks to help us understand what celibacy means. He put it this way: The Catholic Church will ordain only men who promise to remain celibate, that is, not married. *First* you make a decision that you want to be celibate and only then can you ask the *second* question: "Do I wish to become a priest?" I'm sure that the Church might not agree with the way he expressed the choice, but I think it was very helpful. I'm sure that many of the priests who have left the active ministry over the last twenty years did so because they were not committed to celibacy as a way of life. They just accepted it as a necessary evil in their goal to the priesthood.

After leaving the seminary, I worked for a year or so and then joined the air force. After officer-training school, I married Lexi. When I left the air force, we moved to Ogdensburg, New York, where I got a job as coordinator of a religious-education program run as a cooperative venture by the two parishes in that city. In 1977, one of those long cold winters in upstate New York convinced us to seek out a warmer climate. That's how we ended up at St. Peter's here in Birmingham.

Raising children has always been an important part of our life. Peggy is twenty now and Amy is sixteen. They've had a good exposure to a wide range of religious issues which we discuss a lot at home, probably too much from their perspective. During the time I worked at St. Peter's, it was very natural to discuss religious issues connected with my job. Even after I began working for the

University of Alabama School of Medicine five years ago, we continued to discuss religious issues because we're still active volunteers. For me, the key aspect of educating a child in religion is the attitude communicated by parents at home. If religion is important to us, our children will be aware of that. If it's not important to us, they will know that. Of course, anyone who has lived with teenagers knows that they thrive on showing that they are independent thinkers. My children are no exception. The most important thing for me is that they do know that being a Catholic Christian is *very* important to Lexi and me. What they do with that information and all their religious training is something they will have to work out in their own consciences.

Both of my girls went to public schools up through eighth grade and then went to John Carroll, a Catholic high school. I have my own prejudice. I really feel that it is more important to focus on Catholic education in the formative high-school years. Children might have fond memories of their earlier training in Catholic schools, but at the same time, they seem to have managed to forget most of what they learned in those schools. In this age of scarce resources, I really wish Church leaders would put more emphasis on Catholic high schools, even if they have to let the elementary schools go. That is not a popular opinion but I wish they would at least consider it. For me, one of the good points about our local Catholic high school is that it is racially mixed and serves students from all over the metropolitan area.

I wouldn't say my daughters are "gung ho" about Catholicism. They're fairly typical adolescents in that respect. They have never been particularly active in parish activities. If Amy's friends participate, she joins in; otherwise she avoids them. Peggy is the same way. She hasn't found a group at the parish with which she can identify. I guess I'll just have to wait and see what happens as they mature. At this point neither of them is enthusiastic about parental suggestions.

I wonder about the future of the Catholic Church in this country. There has been talk about how much American Catholics resent what they consider to be rather adamant and hard-nosed attitudes in Rome, especially in the areas of sexual morality and the role of women. At the same time, more conservative Catholics still feel that the Church is much too liberal, especially in the area of social justice. Even though those tensions are real, I really doubt that we'll see a major schism or split in the Church. In Europe you have the example of Cardinal Lefèvre in France. He did not intend to start a new church, but in effect did so when he was excommunicated by the Pope for ordaining a Bishop without Rome's approval. I don't see any great surge following him into schism.

One of the nice things about being Catholic is that you have greatly divergent points of view. However, once you actually separate yourself from Rome, you are no longer a Catholic. This means that you could never have a separate Catholic Church in America or anywhere else. It would have to be called something else because an essential ingredient of the Catholic Church *is its connection with Rome.*

The fact is that there has always been discontent within the Church. It's really not a bad thing to have opposing views, as long as we continue to treat each other as Christians should. If you study the history of what happened after the Council of Trent in the sixteenth century, you'd find a great deal of turbulence in its wake, particularly since its purpose was intense reform of almost every aspect of Church life. By comparison, Vatican Council II has created much less distress. The tensions and uneasiness we've experienced should not have been unexpected.

Jeanne Simon with her husband, Senator Paul Simon of Illinois

Jeanne Simon

ECUMENICAL MARRIAGE TO A LUTHERAN

> *One way of putting my Catholic background into action is to be working as a good Democrat for the Democratic party and its principles, which I think are also the principles of the Catholic Church.*

It is not only to her work as a Democrat that Jeanne Simon brings a refreshing honesty and sense of morality but to every activity of a busy life: as an attorney, elected member of the Illinois General Assembly, lecturer, Catholic wife of a Lutheran senator, mother of two children. Her performance and the practice of her beliefs go hand in hand. For example, when she went campaigning for her husband during his bid for the presidency in 1988, she was able to combine a campaign stop in Columbia, South Carolina, with Sunday Mass at a local Black church, with particularly pleasing results.

These qualities may also have shaped her happy mixed marriage to Senator Paul Simon of Illinois. She was born into an Irish-Catholic family of Wilmette, Illinois. Paul Simon comes from a long line of Lutheran ministers in Illinois; his father and brother became ministers. After a few early crises, the marriage worked so well that when they had been husband and wife for seven years, they wrote a book called *Protestant-Catholic Marriages Can Succeed.* In this interview, Mrs. Simon recounts some of the accommodations she and her husband made to each other and how she has incorporated two separate religions into their home.

My political philosophy bears out my Catholic philosophy. In other words, one way of putting my Catholic background into action is to be working as a good Democrat for the Democratic party and its principles, which I think are also the principles of the Catholic Church. It's *faith and action* when I'm out there on the political scene.

A long time ago, before I was elected to public office, I belonged to the Catholic Interracial Council [a national organization started in 1934 to promote racial and social justice]. That was back in the middle fifties. As a layperson, I became interested in the problems of race, which were acute in Cook County, Illinois, where I lived and, of course, all over the country. That was before *Brown* v. *Board of Education*. Then, when I was elected to the Illinois General Assembly in 1956, and reelected in 1958, it seemed to me that this was one way I could work as part of the government on the things that I had been concerned about as a laywoman and member of the Catholic Interracial Council. I could work for better housing for Black people, get Black teachers a chance to actually teach, and work for employment opportunities for all Blacks. In other words, this was a positive approach to government to which I could relate my feelings as a Catholic about the injustices that I saw. That was the beginning of putting my Catholicism to work, and I think it has carried on ever since. When I see homelessness or hunger or injustice or poverty anywhere, and I can do something about it—as a politician or as the wife of a politician—I feel that's part of my background and my faith. I don't call it Catholic action. I just call it political action, but it's certainly the same darn thing, no matter what you call it.

I have never been involved with "Catholic" legislation and I would have shied away from it had it presented itself. I just didn't want to mix religion and politics. As a matter of fact, in 1958, a Protestant group in Illinois issued a questionnaire to all the candidates running for office—that was the year I was reelected—and included, among other things, the question "What is your religion?"

I wrote back and said, "My religion is none of your business."

The question was an insult. Later I found out that another state representative, Anthony Scariano, unbeknownst to me, had answered in the same way. Maybe Catholics feel a stronger urge than others not to go public on religion, but as a lawyer I truly believe in the First Amendment to the Constitution of the United States. If they intended to judge us on a religious basis, that struck me not only as wrong, but unconstitutional and illegal. There was a representative from the Catholic Archdiocese all the time in Springfield and he would offer guidance and suggestions as to how I should vote, as he did to all the members of the Assembly, Catholic or not, and he always let us know how the Bishop felt on certain issues. My response was, "That's fine," and what the Bishop thought would be taken into consideration. But it certainly was not a motivating factor in my vote.

Apart from politics, as a laywoman I have been involved with Church activities. After marriage, I became a member of the regional deanery in Troy, New York. Coming from Cook County, I had never heard of deaneries, which are Catholic women's associations. I was an officer and have spoken to many deaneries on the subject of women, particularly legislation-in-the-hopper on related issues.

Because of being so busy with Paul's presidential campaign, my work for the Church has diminished. But it's odd how just being around creates goodwill in some places. On Sunday mornings when I'm traveling, I usually can't get to Mass. But yesterday I was in Columbia, South Carolina, and I went to a little Black church there called St. Martin de Porres for ten o'clock Mass. There were only about six white people in church, including myself. It felt satisfying to see that a Catholic church was alive and well in a southern Black parish. After Mass, the priest, a Dominican, mentioned my name and said, "We have a special visitor today, Mrs. Paul Simon of Illinois. Her husband is one of the contenders for the Democratic nomination." I stood up and looked around; people nodded and smiled. Outside I shook hands. It wasn't a campaign stop, but the priest took the occasion to point out that this was a Catholic on the campaign trail coming to Sunday Mass. I felt good about that. Last month, after hearing Mass at American University in Washington, D.C., I was invited to speak on the subject of mixed marriage, religion and politics. We had a lively question-and-answer session. This makes me realize I'm still a Catholic out there and doing things in my way.

I am of Irish ancestry on both sides. I graduated from St. Giles in Oak Park, Illinois, a parochial school, and from New Trier School in Winnetka, a really fine public high school. Then on to a very traditional women's college, Barat College, in Lake Forest, Illinois, run by the Sacred Heart Order, on scholarship. I'm delighted that on May 21 I will be receiving from that college one of its most distinguished awards, the Mother Burke Award for outstanding alumnae. I loved Barat College; it was small and all-women. In those days, Catholic colleges were either for men or women. That was the norm and I never regretted it a bit. Perhaps I missed out socially, but I wasn't aware of this and seem to have made up for it, in any case. My daughter did not want to go to an all-girls school.

"Mom, I wouldn't do that for *anything!*" she said.

"Think about it, Sheila. There are a lot of benefits in not having to compete with men."

"We *have* to compete with men. That's what it's all about."

I was looking to be a judge some day on the Circuit Court of Cook County. That was my ambition—to follow the traditional path of lawyer in Cook County. After serving four years as assistant state attorney and being elected to the Illinois General Assembly and making a good record there, I felt the next step—there weren't too many women in judgeships in any case—was to have a shot at running for one of the judicial vacancies.

That was my game plan until I met Paul, who was a co-legislator in the Illinois Assembly. I quickly realized I had been waiting in vain for a Catholic Paul Simon and had found a Lutheran Paul Simon instead. Instantly we were attracted to each other. When Paul proposed, I had to rearrange my game plan. In addition to being an assemblyman, Paul was a newspaper publisher, and both his district and his papers were downstate. Our districts were three hundred miles apart. It seemed only logical for me to give up my legislative seat and move to his district, where he had a home. Giving up my seat was a big decision.

But the decision to marry a person of another faith, on both our parts, was the hardest. This was 1959. Our marriage—myself a Catholic, Paul a good Lutheran, who came from a family of Lutheran pastors—posed big problems, not so much for Paul and me but for our parents. *That's* what made it difficult. We wanted our parents to be happy about our choice. We were more concerned about them than we were about ourselves. What was very painful was that Paul's Dad, who was a Lutheran minister, could not be part of the Catholic wedding ceremony, and Paul's brother, who was also a Lutheran minister, could not take part either. I felt a resentment over this, and it stayed with me for a long time.

But things have changed. Vatican II made a difference. Our daughter Sheila was married last September *to a Lutheran in the Catholic Church*. And this time around, *no problems*. The families are happy, the ministers are happy, the priest is happy. Sheila and her husband went to the pre-Cana Conference [for spiritual guidance in preparation for marriage] and they loved it. Her Uncle Arthur, the Lutheran pastor who had not been allowed to take part in our marriage, took part in hers. In twenty-six years, what a difference! It's a real success story in its way: from our wedding, which was terrific but could have been a little happier for our parents and families, to this!

Paul and I had been married a few months and things smoothed out. Neither he nor I had any doubts about the marriage succeeding. We had faced certain important things beforehand, our values and goals were strong, and we felt we could manage just about anything. In a mixed union, couples are inclined to say, "We'll work it out later: religion, children, that sort of thing." Paul and I were sufficiently mature to realize they could be problems with us and we confronted them at the start.

For one thing, we decided our children would be brought up Catholic. Paul had worked this out in his mind. He felt, as I did, that the mother of a family has a great deal more responsibility toward seeing to the religious upbringing of the children. For us this was particularly true because we both knew that Paul would be away a good deal of the time. In our early years, he'd go to Springfield on Monday mornings and come back on Wednesday nights. When he became lieutenant governor, there were weeks when he wasn't able to be at home in Troy. I was with the children. During children's formative years, Mother is the one who sees to their prayers and takes them to Saturday or Sunday religion classes. She is the one who gets them to the church on time. That was our agreement and we carried it out.

In a mixed or ecumenical marriage like ours, the home itself presents opportunities for children to grow up in a healthy, religious atmosphere. I'm speaking of little things, details, that in the long run make up the big things. When the children were small, we subscribed to both Lutheran and Catholic magazines that lay around the house, ready to be thumbed through. There were books and newspapers. Many Christian churches have good religious art in common, which displays Christian unity—a crucifix, say, or a Rembrandt showing Christ being taken from the Cross. We had art of this nature on our walls, along with pictures of Martin Luther and Pope Pius XII. We still have a mezuzah on the door of our home in Illinois and another here in Washington. [A mezuzah is a piece of parchment that is encased and inscribed with words from the Torah stating the basic affirmation of the Jewish faith in God. The mezuzah is placed on doorposts or doors by house owners to identify themselves as Jewish.] Every Orthodox Jewish family has one. For *us* it is a reminder that a country that was half-Lutheran and half-Catholic committed the greatest crime in world history by murdering six million Jews, and it becomes a symbol in our eyes of this shameful heritage as Catholics and Lutherans. The mezuzah tells us:

NEVER, NEVER FORGET THAT LUTHERANS, CATHOLICS AND OTHER CHRISTIANS CAN COMMIT TERRIBLE CRIMES.

In our home people of all beliefs—Lutheran clergymen, Methodists, Episcopalians, Presbyterians, conservative priests, liberal monsignors, Jews, a theology professor from India, a leader from the John Birch Society, socialists—have been welcome. We have gone out of our way to bring in a diversity of viewpoints.

The fact that Paul and I were there at the cutting edge of breaking down religious prejudice gives me a good feeling *and* the fact that we wrote a book about mixed marriages. [The book, *Protestant-Catholic Marriages Can Succeed,* by Paul and Jeanne Simon, was published in 1967 by Association Press, New York.] We talked to groups, always stressing that we were committed not only to seeing our own marriage succeed but to make the path easier for others. Whenever we run into a priest or pastor who says he has read our book and used it, I think we did some good after all.

Vatican II, of course, had a great deal to do with the acceptance of ecumenical marriages. We, of course, solved our problems long before, but it has helped Sheila and thousands of families in similar situations. I am happy with the many freedoms it has brought. As a child I was happy growing up in the pre–Vatican II Church and did everything required of a Catholic and felt good about it. Yet when it came to picking out the man I wanted to spend the rest of my life with, my Church that I had really believed was with me all the way suddenly left me.

We visited Rome, Paul and I, shortly after Pope John XXIII died. We went to visit his grave and I was stirred by feelings of gratitude to this man who had opened up the windows of the Church. The windows will never be closed again. The movement is there, and it's strong. There are problems, but the direction is very, very good. As I see young priests and laymen taking a really active role in social issues, this seems the way our Church should have been going all along—recognizing the value of other religions, not looking down on Lutherans or Episcopalians or whomever, seeing people more for what they are rather than as categories of religious organization.

As politicians, Paul and I are constantly confronted with such issues as abortion, aid to parochial schools, and prayer in the public schools. Catholic groups have intimated that I'm somewhat less than Catholic for supporting Paul on abortion. But it's not a question of supporting Paul. First of all, I believe that abortion is a woman's right to choose, and as a lawyer, I supported the *Roe* v. *Wade* decision. The Church says that abortion is wrong and it has every right to say this, but *not* to impose this view on everyone in the United States of America, which, it seems to me, the Church is trying to do.

If I've contributed anything that can be of value to women, Catholic and non-Catholic alike, it's an idea that you can be a wife and mother, and strong supportive spouse, and that you can also have your own identity and your own career. Because of the circumstances of being a mother, this career may have to be dropped for a while, but it's there to come back to. Throughout married life, I believe a woman can continue to make a contribution to organizations she cares about and believes in, whether she's working for a salary or not. I've done it both ways and have enjoyed it both ways. Life as a career woman doesn't end with getting married anymore.

Father Greeley in Arizona with a young parishioner

Father Andrew Greeley

THE MANY HATS OF FATHER GREELEY

And there's Madonna, the singer . . . She is rather dramatic and wild; yet the message she is delivering to teenage young women is a message that the Church ought to be delivering, and that is that their bodies are good.

Many people know Andrew Greeley as the author of "sexy" novels that have sold millions of copies. Far fewer know him as a still-active priest, professor of sociology at the University of Arizona, and sociologist who was the first of his profession to make in-depth socioeconomic studies of American Catholics and their Church. He is also the most outspoken clergyman of his generation, as is shown on these pages. His acerbic, no-holds-barred comments on the current religious scene and the laypeople, priests and prelates within it reveal a rare comprehension.

For the first time in some detail, Father Greeley speaks of his many "other" works, especially his sociology books on Catholics, which are not generally known. Yet when he is asked where his most important contribution lies, he says quickly, "The fiction," and explains the reason. He is elated when he receives letters from readers who say they have returned to their Church because his novels introduced them to the benign and loving God they somehow had not met back in parochial school.

Although his fiction has brought him great wealth, he has given a large part of that away. He has endowed a chair in Roman Catholic studies at the University of Chicago, established a foundation for Chicago inner-city schools, and made a grant to Mundelein College in Illinois. Living a relatively simple life, he buys his own groceries and washes his own dishes.

I like being a priest. I'm not going to leave the priesthood because I write so-called "sexy" novels. Any hope that Church authorities may have had that they would get rid of me that way, I think they've long since abandoned. It is possible, however, for a Bishop to request the Vatican to expel someone from the priesthood. It is called being "laicized," or reduced to the lay state, which, of course, is pretty much of an insult to laypeople. He is not permitted to exercise his priestly functions anymore. The Vatican would have serious pause about doing that because it would make my publisher's day. Moreover, they know _I wouldn't go._ I mean, if they try to throw me out of the priesthood, I'd say, "Hey, I'm still a priest. I'm not going to stop being a priest."

In view of the fact that I write books, am I still a practicing priest? In an extended sense, yes. When Mark Harris was writing a profile on me for _The New York Times Magazine_ [January 31, 1984], he sat down for several hours and read through the mail I receive. He concluded his article with the comment: _Andrew Greeley is right. He is a parish priest. And his parish is in his mailbox._

The audience for my novels is a parish, half of whom don't go to church regularly. And I'm reaching people in those stories who are not in contact with priests. When I'm down in Tucson teaching at the University of Arizona, I work in three parishes on weekends. What I personally get from working in the parishes is feedback from breathing people. The mail is fine, but it's still nice to preach on Sunday to a congregation physically present and to talk to them in back of the church after Mass—you know, exchange conversation with them. That's something that the fiction doesn't do and it's something I've always enormously liked about being a priest. By the way, I'm not the only one who is a weekend priest. Maybe thirty percent of the priests in America teach in high schools or colleges and perform their priestly function on the weekend, so to speak.

Officially, I'm a priest in good standing in the Archdiocese of Chicago where I come from. Back in the early sixties I fell into the area of writing when Cardinal Albert Meyer, the Archbishop of Chicago, assigned me to do full-time work in writing and research, and I'm still on that assignment. In the meantime, I studied sociology at the University of Chicago and got my doctorate. My first books were not novels—they were more in the nature of sociology. Later, when I switched from writing these books to doing fiction, there was a very good reason. But before going into that, let me say a few words about my first books, since I am a sociologist, as well as a priest and novelist, and I am proud of these books which are not well known.

The first one was *Religion and Career* (1963), my doctoral dissertation. It was a study of how the young people who graduated from college in 1961 were making their career choices. It had been assumed—in the years before—that Catholics were not going to college, that they were not seeking academic careers, that there was something about Catholicism that inclined these young men and women to be anti-intellectual. Well, by 1960 and 1961, all that had changed. In their proportion to the population, Catholics were going to college, to graduate school and on to academic careers. My book marked the first time that anybody had noticed the transformation that had been going on in the Catholic population for the last decade: *that we were becoming a college-educated, upper-middle class professional population. The Hesitant Pilgrim* (1966) was a post–Vatican II book. It was an attempt to comment on the changes that were going on in the Church that were both a result of the social transformation I have just described and Vatican II. American Catholicism was caught in the intersections of two enormous social changes—the moves from the immigrant neighborhood to the suburbs and from the Counter-Reformation to the ecumenical Church. [The Counter-Reformation was a period in which the Church revitalized itself by *firmly proclaiming Catholic beliefs* in the face of dissenting Protestant groups. The ecumenical Church, on the other hand, marks the present-day desire of the Church to unite with other Christians in *one* church.]

Beginning with *Life for a Wanderer*, I did a series of ten books that were a kind of modern spiritual reading. This book was a suggestion that our life is really a pilgrimage, a trip, a time of wandering here on earth until we go home. It was a spirituality for people on pilgrimage. *The Friendship Game* was also in the genre of spirituality. *The Unsecular Man,* which I wrote about 1970, was a refutation of what certain theologians were saying about religion. A lot of people, and theologians particularly, were claiming that modern humans no longer needed religion, that because of the progress of science, religion was something that was an option but not a necessity for modern human beings. I analyzed the sociological data available and just suggested that that was a figment of the theologians' imagination. It might be true of themselves and their colleagues in the divinity schools, but it certainly wasn't true of ordinary people.

The New Agenda (1973) laid forth what the problems were with Catholics today. No longer faced with the dilemmas of immigrants, the modern Catholic had a whole new set of problems. At one time the Church devoted itself to protecting the faith of the newly arrived, but since this was no longer necessary, the Church should face up to the new problems. *Sexual Intimacy,* which came out that same year, was a book on the relationship between religion and sex. Not a sexual manual obviously, it was an attempt to deal with questions such as *What does sex mean in life? Is it just pleasure, is it just reproduction, or does it have some deep religious implications?*

In 1976 I did a book with William McCready and Kathleen McCourd called *Catholic Schools in a Declining Church,* which was one of our big sociology books. Back in 1963 we had done a survey of American Catholics and the effect of schools on them. Then in 1974, we did another survey and the nice thing about these two surveys is that we did one before Vatican II and the other after it. So we had an opportunity to measure the changes in American Catholics because of Vatican II. First of all, it turned out that the people overwhelmingly supported the Council in its changes. Although there was a decline in church attendance, this was attributable not to Vatican II but to the birth-control encyclical. One of the most astonishing findings was that the Catholic schools were, if anything, more important to the Church in a time of transition than in a time of stability.

Increasingly I'm persuaded that almost all Catholics identify with the Church but feel no constraint to keep all the rules. On the one hand, they're loyal to the Church. The poll that ABC News did when the Pope came here in September 1987 asked Catholics, "Are you currently thinking of leaving the Church?" and 94 percent of them said no. Of the six percent that said yes, only two percent said they were likely to leave. So there is this overwhelming loyalty to the Church. On the other hand, Catholics remain in the Church in their own style and on their own terms. And that is, I think, the biggest transformation in American Catholics in the years since 1960. *They are now Catholics on their own terms,* and there's nothing that their parish priest or their Bishops or the Pope can do to change that. By the way, the psychology behind their reasoning is that even if Church leaders don't approve, they think God does approve. For example, they would say about sex, one of the most poignant and powerful of the problems, that they think God understands how important sex is to married people, even if the Church doesn't understand it.

For me personally, the most important book I ever wrote was *The Mary Myth* (1977) because it helped my thinking enormously, being instrumental in my turning to novel writing and in the development of my women characters. The subject is the role of Mary in Catholic Christianity, and I argue—much of the argument is from poetry and art—that it has been Mary's role to reflect *the mother love of God.* She is a Sacrament of God loving us the way a mother loves us. The women in my novels are all created in this image. Mary is one of our most powerful resources.

I am convinced that religion begins in the imagination. It begins with experiences that renew our hope and it's encoded in our imagination in pictures and images and shared with others in stories. My book *The Religious Imagination* is a sociological analysis of the religious imagination of Catholics. Religion is experience, image and story *before* it becomes catechism and creed and theology. I'm not saying that catechism, creed and theology are unimportant, but that the origins and raw power of religion come *before* our propositions and our rational thought. Religion is, first of all, experiential. That is what I mean by the religious imagination. After reflecting on that for a long time, and understanding that the best way to pass on religion is through story, I turned to writing novels.

You've heard of the Theodore White books on the making of the American presidency? In 1976, it occurred to me that it would be interesting if someone wrote a book on the making of a pope, on the papal elections, studying as best he could the dynamics of the papal-elections office. And so I prepared to study the papal election when it next came and when it did come, there were two elections and two stories: how Pope John Paul got elected and then, immediately afterward, how Pope John Paul II got elected. From my study of these two events came the book *The Making of the Popes*.

All told, I've written about thirty nonfiction books so far, most of which are about some aspect of Catholicism in America. Of these books, I'd be inclined to single out two as particularly noteworthy: *Catholic Schools in a Declining Church* because it was the first book really to measure the effect of Vatican II on American Catholicism, and *The Mary Myth* because it lays out a new theory of the theology of religion. But if you were to ask me where my most important contribution to the Church lies, I don't think there's any doubt that it's in the fiction. Most people don't know about my sociology; they know me as a popular novelist. One of the main reasons I turned to writing fiction was to sell more books. *The Making of the Popes*, for example, sold 35,000 copies, which is not bad for a nonfiction book. *The Cardinal Sins*, the same story in fiction form, sold 3 million. Sociology books reach a limited audience and sell relatively few copies. Realizing that people like stories, I decided to try writing about God and Catholicism in fiction, in other words, writing novels *as a means of teaching religion*. It has worked; the stories have reached and affected millions. People like stories, and when you put religion in story form, you can have an enormous impact. I was just talking to someone earlier this morning who said, "You came along at the right moment. It was just at the time when a lot of Catholics were trying to figure out what their religion meant, and you appeared with your stories and told them what religion means. It has had extraordinary effect."

The scholar in me would like to argue that my sociology is a lot more important. It *is* important because my colleagues and I have really been the only ones who have been monitoring American Catholicism for the last twenty-five years. But that kind of thing is read by a limited number of people, and the stories are read by millions.

There are three big problems in the Catholic Church in America today. First of all, the preaching is very poor. There's nothing wrong with Catholicism in the United States that good Sunday homilies would not noticeably change. Every layperson I speak with agrees with me. And priests just get furious when I speak of this. The sermons—homilies, to use the right word—are terrible. Unless they're improved, nothing else can matter. The most frequent contact between the Catholic and the Church is the Sunday homily. And they're gosh-awful. Since preaching is creativity, priests have to learn to do some creative writing, and to do this, they have to do a lot of reading. And these things just aren't happening. A lot of priests are concerned about justice in the Third World, but many less are concerned about justice to the parishioners who have the right, in strict justice, to have the Gospel preached to them.

Secondly, the Church simply has to treat women better. I'm talking about their rights. [In April 1988, a few months after this interview took place, a committee of the United States Roman Catholic Bishops published a Draft Pastoral Letter on Women, with recommendations to expand the leadership roles of women at almost every level of the Church except the priesthood. The draft also condemned the "sin of sexism," and said sexist attitudes had colored the Church's teachings for centuries. The draft will now be circulated among Catholics for comment and may undergo several revisions before a final draft is presented for a vote by the National Conference of Catholic Bishops. If approved, it would effectively serve as a policy guide for the nation's Catholics.] On the one hand, through the years women have had lots of power in the Church, probably more check-signing power—I mean signing checks to make payments—than women in other institutions. But they are still second-class citizens.

Vocations—that's the third problem. We need more vocations to the priesthood and to the religious life. Again one could fault priests for not trying to recruit young men to the priesthood. The biggest obstacle, you see, is that no one asks them to be priests anymore. There are no invitations now. The morale of priests is so bad that they really don't want to recruit young men. And *that* is a terrible problem, too. Preaching, women and vocations—these are situations that could be helped without any transformation in the Papacy or even in the hierarchy.

What needs great improvement is the seminary. Today, our seminaries are terribly concerned with emotional adjustments and want to produce priests who are psychologically mature. Now, that's certainly not objectionable, I mean, it's better to have mature priests than immature ones. Whether it's being done all that successfully is something else. But the emphasis is very much on psychological principles and themes—which, by the way, are often poorly understood. In any case, there is no increase in emphasis on the two things that were missing in the seminary of our time, the first being *intellectual development.* In view of the fact that we have a well-educated laity, priests should also be well educated and by and large they are not. Their education hasn't developed the intellect nearly as much as comparable education has developed the intellect of laypeople. And, as I've already indicated, the other thing that is still being astonishingly ignored, as it was fifty years ago, is the preaching. Seminaries still don't realize *it's the most important thing we do*—it's our only contact with the people. The quality of homiletic training in the seminary, as far as I can see, hasn't changed at all.

Because of rumors and stories, Rome has investigated American seminaries in recent years. The given reason was to make sure that sound doctrine was being taught. Another reason was to find out whether some seminaries were hotbeds of homosexuality, and there were some. A report was made to Rome and I think, at least to some extent, these problems have been cleared up.

Fear and dislike of women—that is something that is instilled and disseminated in the seminaries. Sure, it has been partly an attempt to protect celibacy—an unhealthy attempt because one should be a celibate for the kingdom of God and love of people and not because one dislikes women. The celibate who dislikes women is abnormal, since the human species has been so designed that men and women are attached to one another. Furthermore, there is no fate that decrees that because a man finds a woman attractive he has to go to bed with her. Unfortunately, a lot of Church training assumed that was true and so the way to keep priests celibate was to force them to think that women were unattractive, and that was extremely unhealthy. Some of that *is* changing. But look at the Vatican policies today—they are loath to allow women to teach in the seminaries; they don't allow women to distribute Holy Communion when there are enough priests or men around to do it; they won't ask women to be altar servers. It seems to me that much of the old prejudice persists. *It has to go.* It's just intolerable.

I find it extraordinary that a very large group of Americans remain loyal to the Church despite the foolishness of the leadership and remain loyal to their parishes despite the most oppressive of pastors.

To my mind, the American laity is highly impressive and very durable. The kind of person who comes to mind immediately as typifying this, someone who is deeply religious and profoundly Catholic and, at the same time, involved in the world, is Mario Cuomo, and, *please God,* the next president of the United States. To pause on him for a moment. The conflict between Cuomo and Cardinal O'Connor seems to typify the state of the American Church. You have a layman who is not only smarter than the Cardinal, and knows more about the Catholic tradition than the Cardinal, but to all intents and purposes seems to be a more devout man than the Cardinal.

And there's Madonna, the singer. I'll get into trouble for this, but I will mention her anyway. She is rather dramatic and wild; yet the message that she is delivering to teenage young women is a message that the Church ought to be delivering to them and that is that *their bodies are good.* And it is possible to be virtuous and, at the same time, attractive, to be a "nun" and, at the same time, a vamp or a siren. This is indeed the way women's bodies and personalities are designed, both to be modest and attractive. I think that's Madonna's message. She may not fully understand this herself, though if you read the interviews with her, it seems to me that she does understand it. And certainly the young women who enjoy her music get that message. Now there may be something in her style that offends the older generation and the clergy. But the message is very, very important, and it's profoundly Catholic. I'm working on a book on religion and popular culture, and that's way I'm especially conscious of Catholics like her and Bruce Springsteen and Linda Ronstadt who have very important things to say to the Catholic population.

Today Catholicism is entering a new period, an important era in Church history that goes completely counter to the past. With Vatican II, the intellectual structures of Apologetic Catholicism collapsed almost overnight. When my generation and the generations immediate following were being educated, we were trained at Catholic colleges *to answer objections to Catholicism.* And that's why it was called Apologetic Catholicism—apologetics is an argumentative discussion *in defense* of doctrines. It was as though there was a world out there with a whole schedule of objections, and we were educated mainly to provide the answers to meet these objections. This style of Catholic teaching derived from the Council of Trent and may or may not have been appropriate. But after being ordained, I, and many others like me, *never heard any of these objections.* What I heard was questions from people looking for meaning in life. The old system of apologetics is no longer valid, if it ever was. If we're going to deal with contemporary Catholics and contemporary human beings, the style of training we need is not responses to objections that nobody expresses anymore, but responses to the needs that Catholics experience in their lives.

Index